Promoting the Emotional Well-being
of Children and Adolescents and Preventing
Their Mental Ill Health

of related interest

Meeting the Needs of Ethnic Minority Children – Including Refugee, Black and Mixed Parentage Children
A Handbook for Professionals, Second Edition
Edited by Kedar Nath Dwivedi
ISBN 1 85302 959 9

Group Work with Children and Adolescents
A Handbook
Edited by Dr Kedar Nath Dwivedi
ISBN 1 85302 157 1

A Multidisciplinary Handbook of Child and Adolescent Mental Health for Front-line Professionals
Nisha Dogra, Andrew Parkin, Fiona Gale and Clay Frake
ISBN 1 85302 929 7

Mental Health Services for Minority Ethnic Children and Adolescents
Edited by Mhemooda Malek and Carol Joughin
Child and Adolescent Mental Health Series
ISBN 1 84310 236 6

Self-Harm in Adolescence
Claudine Fox and Professor Keith Hawton
Child and Adolescent Mental Health Series
ISBN 1 84310 237 4

Students' Mental Health Needs
Problems and Responses
Edited by Nicky Stanley and Jill Manthorpe
ISBN 1 85302 983 1

The Child's World
Assessing Children in Need
Edited by Jan Horwath
ISBN 1 85302 957 2

The Developing World of the Child
Edited by Jane Aldgate, David Jones, Wendy Rose and Carole Jeffery
ISBN 1 84310 244 7

Promoting the Emotional Well-being of Children and Adolescents and Preventing Their Mental Ill Health

A Handbook

Edited by
Kedar Nath Dwivedi and Peter Brinley Harper
Foreword by Caroline Lindsey

Jessica Kingsley Publishers
London and Philadelphia

Extract on p.17 from Mental Health Foundation (MHF) (1999) *Bright Futures*. Reproduced with permisssion of the Mental Health Foundation.

First published in 2004
by Jessica Kingsley Publishers
116 Pentonville Road
London N1 9JB, UK
and
400 Market Street, Suite 400
Philadelphia, PA 19106, USA

www.jkp.com

Library of Congress Cataloging in Publication Data
Promoting emotional well-being of children and adolescents and preventing their mental ill health : a handbook / edited by Kedar Nath Dwivedi and Peter Brinley Harper ; foreword by Caroline Lindsey.
    p. cm.
    Includes bibliographical references and index.
    ISBN 1-84310-153-X (pbk.)
    1. Children--Mental health services--Handbooks, manuals, etc. 2. Teenagers--Mental health services--Handbooks, manuals, etc. 3. Child psychopathology--Prevention--Handbooks, manuals, etc. 4. Adolescent psychopathology--Prevention--Handbooks, manuals, etc. 5. Mental health promotion--Handbooks, manuals, etc. I. Dwivedi, Kedar Nath. II. Harper, Peter Brinley, 1955-
    RJ499.3.P76 2004
    618.92'89--dc22

                                2004007511

British Library Cataloguing in Publication Data
A CIP catalogue record for this book is available from the British Library

ISBN 1 84310 153 X

Printed and Bound in Great Britain by
Athenaeum Press, Gateshead, Tyne and Wear

With warm affection and esteem, this book is dedicated by the editors to their beloved families, including Radha, Amitabh, Amrita, Rajaneesh and Siddharth Dwivedi and Glynis, Katherine and Matt Harper

Contents

Foreword

This book makes a contribution to the field of child and adolescent mental health in a timely and thought-provoking way. It brings together a wide spectrum of thinking and practice in the field of mental health promotion and prevention in a readily accessible way. It is an exciting era for professionals who are seeking to contribute to the emotional well-being of children and young people in the UK. In all four countries, there is a growing recognition of the importance of good mental health for the overall health and success of individuals within their communities and for the achievement of a thriving society.

The need for a significant increase in child mental health services has not until recently been reflected in policies for investment in resources, training and workforce. However, there are now signs that the need for this is being taken seriously at last. Both in England and in Wales, there is a commitment to the development and publication of a Children's National Service Framework, based on expert advice, which will set standards for the delivery of health and social care services to children, young people and their families.

The fundamental principle which is being proposed is that 'children's mental health is everyone's business'. By this it is meant that all professionals who come into contact with children in their day-to-day work should be capable of taking action to promote their emotional well-being and to prevent mental ill health. This means understanding how to communicate with children, recognising the significance of what they are saying and knowing how to intervene or to refer on to appropriate services. It also entails whole school preventive and early intervention programmes being put in place with support from specialist services, and organising primary health care services to intervene early with mothers antenatally and postnatally, to anticipate their mental health needs and to offer parent training to promote good parenting.

Making children's mental health the concern of all professionals will potentially include those who are working in universal and primary care services, in health care, social services, early years, school and further education, youth offending and police, leisure and play services and the whole range of voluntary organisations.

Of course, this proposal has enormous training and educational implications, starting with the curriculum for children and young people themselves, and with their parents, carers and teachers. Specialist child mental health services are never going to be in a position to meet the mental health needs of a population in which one in five children has mental health difficulties and 10 per cent have diagnosable child psychiatric disorders. The implications are clear – society must strive to create environments in which the ways that children are brought up and educated take account of our evidence-based knowledge of the optimal ways to do so.

This book will help those interested in this work to consider how they might themselves contribute to this important field.

Caroline Lindsey
Co-Chair, CAMHS module, Children's National Service Framework

Preface

Over a period of more than fifteen years we have worked together in a child and adolescent mental health service (CAMHS), experiencing the highs and lows of aspirations being achieved or dashed in the ever-changing systems of the National Health Service (NHS). These experiences have seen us variously trying to influence service development at each level of service delivery. This has included contributions to the strategic direction of services, training, support and supervision of colleagues and professionals from other agencies, supporting research endeavours, to developing and delivering clinical services to children, young people and their families.

We had become increasingly concerned at the huge demand for child mental health services and at times despaired at the relative dearth of resources available to meet the demand. Of particular concern to us was the way in which the resource deficiencies had become a strong influence in the tendency of various children's agencies to medicalise children's difficulties. Editing a book which promotes emotional well-being and the prevention of child mental health difficulties represents an attempt to take seriously the need to address the multiple issues at the front end of care and to provide practitioners with information and examples of services that are seeking to provide preventive mental health services for children, young people and their families.

Editing the book was an extension of the spirit of collaboration that we have endeavoured to promote in our local services. We have been genuinely moved by the generosity and enthusiasm of the practitioners who have shared their experience, expertise, time and energy in contributing to this book. These characteristics augur well for the future of child mental health services in the United Kingdom.

Kedar Nath Dwivedi and Peter Brinley Harper

Acknowledgements

We are grateful to all our colleagues, both past and present, in the various services contributing to child mental health in Northampton. Colleagues currently working in our multidisciplinary service, whose hard work, interest and compassion make our service the unique place that it is, include Debbie Ainsworth, Dawn Bailham, Rajeev Banhatti, Seema Banta, Cazz Broxton, Sue Buckland, Dan Buys, Natalie Cook, Gina Der Kerokian, Denise Ewing, Nien Gardner, Hala Hammad, Sue Henson, Sarah Hogan, Frances Jones, Yusuf Mangera, Imran Mushtaq, Raghu Paranthaman, Jan Pawlikowski, Melanie Pearson, Sandra Roberts, Sachin Sankar, Annette Schlösser, Paul Sellwood, Miriam Silver, Vyvienne Tipler, Annie Waldsax, Katie Wheatley, Phillipa Williams-Moulton and Margaret Wysling.

The activity of secretarial and administrative staff is frequently unrecognised. Without them our services would simply grind to a halt, and we would like to pay tribute to the huge behind-the-scenes contribution they make to the shared endeavour of supporting the emotional well-being of children and young people in our area. In this regard we are particularly grateful to our respective secretaries, Naina Sadrani and Brenda Fletcher, and also to Clare Allen, Karen Amos, Brenda Baldwin, Mary Battison, Lynda Davies, Jean Gray, Avril Hart, Carol James, Sharon Mallon and Mandy Underdown.

We are also grateful for the valuable support of our colleagues from local NHS trusts and the local authority. Among others we would like to thank Fran Ackland, Jo Anthony, Sue Astrop, Lesley Austin, John Birkhead, Bob Butcher, Lalith Chandrakantha, Lesley Cockerill, Jackie Coles, Jane Coles, Sue Collier, Janet Collinson, Edward Crawford, Tracey Davis, Joy Dinnage, Ken Faisey, Ian Fernley, Charles Fox, Damian Gardner, Nick Griffin, John Hewertson, Mark Hunter, Fiona Morin, Leigh Moss, John O'Donnell, Alan Ogilvie, Sue Price, Natasa Robinson, Sheila Shribman, Anne Smith, Fiona Thompson, Andrew Williams, David Wilson and Win Zaw. Similarly from the Northamptonshire Health Care NHS Trust, we are grateful to Suheib Abu-Kmeil, Veena Acharya, Wasi Ahmad, Draha Allen, Carol Baker, David Berry, Mohan Bonthala,

Mohan Chawla, Theresa Christian, Myrna Coutts, Esme Davies, Mamdouh El-Adl, Husni El-Robb, Damian Gardner, Linda Hall, Peter Hopkinson, Jaiker Jani, Geoff Keats, Harnek Masih, Joseph Mondeh, Angela Muchatuta, Ram Mudaliar, Alex O'Neill-Kerr, James Pease, Julie Roberts, Sean Scanlon, Jonathan Shapero, Vinod Sharma, Ron Shields, Bryan Timmins, Kobus Van Rensburg and Stephen Wilson. Our thanks also go to Charlotte Gath, Andy Howard and Andrew Northall from the local Primary Care NHS Trusts, to Alison Cuthill, Derek Lucas, Martin Pratt and Jan Slater from the local authority and to Helen Beinart from Oxford.

We would also like to convey our sincere thanks to the staff in our local NHS Trusts' libraries as they have been immensely helpful, namely Sue Griffiths, Gary Meads, Ann Skinner, Kristi Smith and Anne Tales among others.

Finally our gratitude is to you, the reader. We hope that you will find that the energy you invest in reading this contribution to the field will bear fruit in the impact it has on your work.

Chapter 1

Introduction

Kedar Nath Dwivedi and Peter Brinley Harper

Many mental disorders of adulthood have their origins in childhood risk factors. In addition, mental disorders in children and adolescents are very common. A survey by the Office for National Statistics (Meltzer, Gatward and Goodman 2000) found a prevalence of mental disorders in 9.5 per cent of children in the UK. This burden of suffering is so high that effective treatment and preventive programmes are needed to reduce this burden substantially and there is no need for the two enterprises to be antagonistic, competitive or separate from each other (Offord and Bennett 2002). Some of these disorders also have a poor prognosis, thus child mental health promotion and prevention are vital and deserve high priority (Barnes 1998).

The three levels of prevention – primary, secondary and tertiary – were described by Leavell and Clark during the 1950s (Silverman 1995). However, Caplan (1964), a child psychiatrist, translated these into mental health terms. Accordingly, primary prevention seeks to decrease the number of new cases, secondary prevention lowers the rate of the disorder in the population and tertiary prevention seeks to decrease the amount of disability associated with an existing disorder. Gordon (1987) proposed another way of classifying preventive interventions, i.e. universal, selective and indicated. In 1994, the US Institute of Medicine Committee on the Prevention of Mental Disorders reviewed these classification systems and presented a framework called the Mental Health Intervention Spectrum for Mental Disorders (Mrazek and Haggerty 1994). It recognises the importance of the whole spectrum of interventions from prevention through to maintenance. It delineates the following possible interventions:

- prevention
  - universal
  - selective
  - indicated
- treatment
  - case identification
  - standard treatment for known disorders
- maintenance
  - compliance with long-term treatment (reduction in relapse)
  - after care (rehabilitation).

The committee reserved the term 'prevention' only for those interventions that occur before the initial onset of a disorder. Universal preventive interventions (such as prenatal care for all new mothers) are targeted to the general public or a whole population group. Selective preventive interventions (such as home visiting and infant day care for low birth-weight children) are targeted to individuals or a subgroup of population with a higher than average risk of developing a disorder. Indicated preventive interventions (such as parent–child interaction training programme for children with behaviour problems) are targeted to high-risk individuals with biological markers who do not meet the formal diagnostic criteria and are, therefore, sub-clinical cases. Offord *et al.* (1998) advocate an optimal mix of universal, targeted and clinical programmes for child mental health.

Mental health promotion

The Institute of Medicine report has been criticised for its unduly narrow conceptualisation of prevention to the exclusion of mental health promotion strategies (Albee 1996). When dealing with children, it appears less useful to separate promotion from prevention because the development of skills aimed at enhancing well-being can have important preventive effects, and attention to normal development can inform strategies directed at mental health problems (Barnes 1998). However, Orley and Weisen (1998) argue that mental health promotion may indeed have a place in the prevention of mental disorders but it is as effective in the prevention of a whole range of behaviour-related risks and diseases as well.

Mental health promotion aims at promoting or enhancing the capacity for mental health of individuals, families, organisations and communities. Mental health is more than merely an absence of mental disorder. It influences our capacity to form relationships, to communicate, to feel and think, to cope with loss and change and underpins our social functioning, productivity, well-being and all health.

> Mental health is the emotional and spiritual resilience which enables us to enjoy life and to survive pain, disappointment and sadness. It is a positive sense of well-being and an underlying belief in our own, and others' worth. (Health Education Authority 1998)

The concept was also applied to children by the NHS Health Advisory Service (1995) and further refined by the Mental Health Foundation (1999) as follows.

> Children who are mentally healthy will have the ability to
>
> - develop psychologically, emotionally, creatively, intellectually and spiritually
> - initiate, develop and sustain mutually satisfying personal relationships
> - use and enjoy solitude
> - become aware of others and empathise with them
> - play and learn
> - develop a sense of right and wrong
> - face problems and setbacks and learn from them, in ways appropriate for that child's age.

Mental health promotion includes strengthening individuals (such as through enhancing parenting, self-esteem, psychosocial competence and so on), communities (such as through social inclusion, anti-bullying school policies and so on) and reducing structural barriers to mental health (such as removing discrimination and inequalities in access to housing, education, employment and so on). Mental health promotion initiatives not only reduce vulnerability to mental health problems but also improve physical health, productivity and reduce sickness absence at work, behavioural and learning problems, risk-taking behaviours and child abuse (International Union for Health Promotion and Education

1999). At a wider community level, the strength of the social fabric is associated with positive health and can buffer the impact of economic deprivation or traumatic experiences. This is why the Californian mental health campaign had the slogan of 'friends can be good medicine' (Hersey and Klibanoff 1984). Promotion initiatives can include self-help, advocacy, neighbourhood and voluntary activities, as well as structures to facilitate community planning and local decision making in the provision of services. There are clear links between inequality, disintegration of the social fabric, decline in social capital, loss of emotional well-being and even mortality (Kawachi *et al.* 1997). If mental health is the key to overall health of communities, mental health promotion programmes, including that of building our social capital, deserve an urgent priority.

Rappaport (1981) makes the case for empowerment rather than prevention. He points out that prevention programmes

> aimed at so-called high risk populations, especially programs under the auspices of established social institutions, can easily become a new arena for colonialization, where people are forced to consume our goods and services, thereby providing us with jobs and money... This underlies much of what is called prevention: find so-called high risk people and save them from themselves, if they like it or not, by giving them, or even better, their children, programs which we develop, package, sell, operate, or otherwise control. (Rappaport 1981, p.13)

Empowerment aims to enhance the possibilities for people to control their own lives.

A child's likelihood of developing a mental health problem is dependent upon the interplay between the risk and resilience (or protective) factors. They can also have a cumulative effect and these factors can be within the child, within the family or within the broader environment. Child mental health problems are multifactorial in nature and if more factors are present, the risk of disorder is increased significantly. Odds ratio is a measure of the likelihood of the outcome in those exposed to a risk factor compared to those not exposed and thus indicates the increase in risk associated with a particular factor (Streiner and Norman 1996). However, risk factors lack specificity and can be common for a variety of disorders depending upon the timing or the developmental stage of the individual.

In the transactional model of organism and environmental interaction, the child's outcome at some point in time is neither the function of the initial state of the child nor the initial state of the environment but a complex result of the interactions between the child and the environment at different points in time (Sameroff 1987).

Prevention programmes may prepare children in such a way that they avoid unsatisfactory experiences and/or assist them in coping with their consequences. Thus programmes could be designed around life events and experiences, such as naturally occurring transitions, bereavement, divorce, hospitalisation, abuse, adoption, fostering and care, teenage pregnancy and so on (Cox 1993).

The new science of 'complexity' or 'chaos theory' deals with processes involved in the development of systems. It can therefore be applied to child development and thus to the heart of prevention and promotion programmes (Breton 1999). In normal development, there is a sequence of stable periods and transitions, because the changes in the environment push the child and family system to a critical moment, and transition to a more adaptive state follows. A transition is like a system tending toward near-chaos, providing a set of constructs for optimising programmes aimed at preventing mental disorders. Therefore, preventive interventions should focus on such critical moments that are followed by transitions.

Stewart-Brown (1998) highlighted the need for universal parenting programmes as an effective way of impacting on the most common mental health problem in childhood, which is an important precursor of mental health problems in adulthood. She also warns that much yet remains to be learned about the effectiveness of such programmes. Rutter (1982) also acknowledged the potential for the prevention of childhood mental disorders and similarly warned against unwarranted claims of unproven assumptions in this field. He concluded that much remains to be known concerning precisely how to intervene in order to bring about the desired results. However, prevention programmes without proven effectiveness can end up being widely disseminated (Kalter, Picker and Lesowitz 1984). Also, most programmes are designed and evaluated in the context of ideal conditions (i.e. efficacy evaluation). It remains uncertain whether the same results can be obtained in the field setting (in the absence of ideal conditions) without effectiveness evaluation (Tugwell et al. 1985).

Although there is now an accumulation of a considerable evidence base, there is still a great deal of truth in Rutter's comments, as Dryfoos (1997) observes:

> Those who have worked in the field of prevention have a difficult time accepting that high-risk behaviour continues to shape the lives of millions of adolescents. The rates seem unchangeable, no matter how hard practitioners labor to intervene. (Dryfoos 1997, p.44)

The need for such a volume

Since the late 1990s there has been a new emphasis on the importance of prevention with several publications in this field (Department of Health 1999b; Jenkins and Ustsun 1998; Lahtinen, Lehtinen and Rikonene 1999; Royal College of Psychiatrists 2002). There are some specifically related to child mental health (Carr 2002; Mental Health Europe 2000; NSW Health 2000). The *Prevention Initiatives for Child and Adolescent Mental Health* (NSW Health 2000) provides a review of evidence-based preventive programmes. Mental Health Europe (2000) has produced a directory of projects for mental health promotion for children up to 6 years in 15 EU member states and Norway. The directory has classified the projects by primary target groups, intermediary target groups and settings and provides synopses of projects and outlines the effective model projects.

Clinical intervention and support services for children and young people with mental health problems have long grappled with the challenges posed by the issue of increased demand and inadequate resources to meet the demand. It is encouraging to note that the *National Service Framework on Mental Health* (Department of Health 1999a) includes mental health promotion as its standard one. The recent increases in the financial resources made available by central government to provide more comprehensive child and adolescent mental health services has brought with it some optimism and an opportunity to consider comprehensive models for the delivery of services. However, the mental health needs of many children continue to be unmet. Key policy initiatives suggest the need to resource services at the front end of care, and as close to the community as is possible, with all agencies working together to support children's development. With the information available from a developing evidence base highlighting the efficacy of interventions, increased resources and closer working relationships between all stakeholders, there is a unique opportunity to promote emotional well-being and to put a range of programmes in place to prevent child and adolescent mental health problems.

Within child and adolescent mental health services increasing recognition is being given to the 'circular causality theory' in which 'psychologically healthy parents nurture psychologically healthy children, who in turn, become psychologically healthy parents' (NHS Health Advisory Service 1995, p.1). In addition proponents of the ecological model purport that children's lives are influenced at multiple different levels including the family, community, culture and broader society. In short, mental health outcomes are determined by factors spanning diverse contexts.

About this volume

This book draws on the experiences of a wide range of professionals working broadly and diversely in child and adolescent mental health. It provides both theoretical models and practical examples of initiatives in early intervention and prevention, giving access to a comprehensive spectrum of expertise and information that, it is hoped, will be helpful in the development of new initiatives.

This introduction has considered the case for the promotion of mental health and the prevention of mental health problems in children and adolescents, and the concept of the spectrum of interventions. It is followed by an in-depth treatment of these themes in a number of ways. Thus, Chapters 2–6 explore some of the key psychological processes (such as psychological development, attachment, emotion regulation, attention and adolescence) that directly impact on mental health and also outline the implications for promotive and preventive initiatives. Chapters 7 and 8 contain examples of promotive and preventive approaches in specific contexts (that is, through parenting and through schools). Chapters 9–11 focus on some specific mental disorders such as depression, anxiety, eating disorder and conduct disorders (and the issue of substance abuse is considered earlier, in Chapter 6). Chapters 12–14 focus on specific communities, that is, socially excluded and ethnic minorities. Chapter 15 provides a national and international dimension with its review of the best practice in a range of Greek initiatives as parts of Mental Health Europe projects.

In Chapter 2 on developmental perspective, Loh and Wragg describe important developmental contexts and considerations that underpin psychological theories of emotion and emotional responses. They highlight the importance of the primary psychosocial processes like reinforcement, modelling and the labelling of emotion by significant others, at each stage of development. These are important considerations to be taken into account in the development of new initiatives.

Bailham and Harper, in Chapter 3 entitled 'Attachment theory and mental health', outline the origins of attachment theory and its application to infant development, with particular emphasis on the work of Daniel Stern and his focus on attunement in early parent–child relationships. The application of theory to clinical practice and disorders of attachment are considered before providing a unique perspective on the interaction between developmental difficulties and the development of attachment relationships in children and adolescents. The framework implicit in attachment theory provides guiding principles for mental health professionals and wider services to use in practice and in the development of services aimed at the improvement of the mental health of children and young people. The provision of interventions that are sensitive, consistent and containing are crucial in the promotion of mental health and the ability of children to regulate their emotions and develop a healthy, well-integrated sense of self.

Various aspects such as emotional differentiation, self-regulation, desomatisation and utilisation in the development of emotional management skills are discussed in Chapter 4 by Dwivedi on 'Emotion regulation and mental health'. Vulnerability and protective factors have a significant impact on the trajectory of development and directly influence emotion regulation or dysregulation, which in turn impacts on mental health. Dwivedi outlines these complex processes and provides information on public health programmes facilitating the development of emotional competence.

The process of attention and its impact on mental health is addressed in Chapter 5 on 'Attention and mental health' by Banhatti. He considers the definition, development and importance of attention in cognitive processing and problem solving. The factors affecting attention (and thereby, mental health) are identified and the complex, interrelated neurodevelopmental processes involved in the child's developing capacity for attention is simplified and made easily accessible. A consideration of possible preventive interventions and the management of attention problems at primary, secondary and tertiary levels are outlined.

The process of adolescence is discussed from a psychoanalytic perspective by Guggenbühl from Switzerland in Chapter 6 on 'Addiction as a mark of adulthood: the enduring fascination of drugs and alcohol among adolescents'. It also provides a European perspective on promotion and prevention in child mental health. This engaging account of the challenges and rites of passage to be negotiated by young people in their transition to adulthood provides a perspective within which an understanding of the implicit dynamic issues is made explicit.

Drawing on her experience as a psychotherapist, Waldsax's Chapter 7 on parenting highlights the importance of parenting in the promotion of positive mental health and in the prevention of the escalation of mental health issues. The Northampton Model that she has been instrumental in developing places a particular emphasis on the relational aspects in the delivery of parenting interventions. Consideration is given to the role of self-awareness, self-esteem, self-reflection and the provision of a 'good enough' holding environment in promoting and empowering parents in meeting both their own and their children's developmental needs. Professionals are challenged to use supervision creatively to support themselves and the work they undertake in this often complex and demanding area.

Just like the family and parenting environment, schools are also a potentially very fertile environment within which to promote mental health. Chapter 8 by Coley and Dwivedi entitled 'Life Skills Education through schools' considers the tensions between the current drive for excellence and achievement in numeracy and literacy, and the development of emotional literacy and life skills in children. The Life Skills Education initiative has been promoted by the World Health Organization (1997) and the chapter shares the experience of its implementation in Northamptonshire.

Chapter 9 on 'Prevention of depression and anxiety in children and adolescents' by Hayes uses as its rationale for prevention the serious (often lifelong) effects of depression and anxiety. The prevalence of anxiety and depression in children and adolescents is increasing. Research evidence shows that a cognitive behavioural framework can be clinically effective, and encouraging results are emerging from a psychoeducational approach using a cognitive behavioural framework. Hayes's account demonstrates the key psychoeducational prevention principles using case material, and draws together the implications for using such an approach by any professional.

There has been a growing interest in eating disorder prevention programmes since the early 1990s. Stewart's Chapter 10 on 'Prevention of eating disorders' introduces the main form of eating disorders, their prevalence, the known risk factors and their wide-ranging consequences. She contends that the high morbidity and mortality of eating disorders highlights the need for the development of programmes for young people that help to prevent eating disorders as well as identifying and intervening at an early stage. The evidence suggests that the more successful programmes are based on cognitive behavioural strategies, the development of a positive body image and the promotion of self-esteem, using interactive methods. The challenge of designing and conducting prevention programmes is discussed, and the literature on evaluation of prevention programmes is reviewed.

Dwivedi and Sankar in Chapter 11 start their account of 'Promotion of prosocial development and prevention of conduct disorders' by outlining the pathogenesis and epidemiological features of conduct disorders in children and adolescents, and provide an outline of the associated vulnerability and protective factors. There are some key mediators in the development of conduct disorders and the chapter focuses on a number of mediators through which preventive interventions can be targeted. The aetiology of conduct disorders is multifaceted and accordingly the authors of this chapter contend that to be successful the interventions need, by definition, to be multidimensional. The evidence base and the practical aspects of the spectrum of interventions for the prevention of conduct disorders in children and adolescents are also described.

The prevention of social exclusion is a primary target, central to many government policies in the UK. Callaghan and Vostanis address ways of preventing mental health problems in 'children looked-after' by local authorities, young offenders and homeless children and families in Chapter 12 on 'Prevention of mental health problems in socially excluded children and young people: a model for mental health service provision'. Evidence on the complex mental health needs of these children is presented and the need for a multi-agency approach in managing existing problems and preventing mental health problems in later life is then proposed. For all children vulnerable to social exclusion the promotion of endeavours supporting their reintegration to education and community activities predicates outcome. Support and training of frontline staff, particularly through the role of the primary mental health worker, and using a consultation model are presented as ways in which early detection of mental health problems can be undertaken. Access to specialist mental health services in a timely and direct way also has a significant impact on outcomes, and service models and an evaluation of findings on the interventions used in such services is presented. Finally, the chapter emphasises the importance of ongoing training for all staff involved in the delivery of care and services to children and adolescents who are socially excluded.

In Chapter 13, entitled 'Developing culturally sensitive services to meet the mental health needs of ethnic minority children', Harper and Dwivedi address many of the issues associated with the development and delivery of services to ethnic minority children and their families. The nature of child mental health issues is described at both the social/systemic level and at the individual/child level. Service development challenges involved in establishing a service implemented through a community outreach worker in Northampton are outlined, and this is followed by a case example which typifies the nature of the work undertaken in this context. Following this account is Chapter 14, entitled 'Ethnic minority children and families and mental health: preventive approaches', in which Messant explores the reasons for the low uptake of child mental health services by ethnic minority families and also provides an informative description of two preventive services developed in Tower Hamlets (an inner-city London borough). Together these chapters provide an outline of service issues, challenges and some ways in which local services have developed responses to meet some of the mental health needs of ethnic minority children and their families.

The book ends with a European dimension through Chapter 15 on 'The Mental Health Europe projects and the Greek perspective' by Kolaitis and Tsiantis. In the context of an initiative to promote (throughout the European Union) best practice in the promotion of mental health and the prevention of mental disorders in children and adolescents, the Association for the Psychosocial Health of Children and Adolescents (APHCA) was selected to act as the Greek representative in two projects. Best practice in a range of Greek initiatives was reviewed. The research that is reported highlights the considerable scope for promotion and preventive initiatives. However, the lack of a clear strategic government direction and associated mental health policies is given as a key underlying factor in the relatively limited role of mental health professionals in promotion and prevention in the mental health field. The need for training and support of professionals, the development of systematic databases and the exchange of information are outlined as possible ways in which promotion and prevention can be progressed.

Thus, the volume has attempted to provide a tapestry of chapters around the theme of emotional well-being of children and adolescents and prevention of their mental disorders. Included in these are chapters on some key psychological processes, public health approaches, environmental contexts, psychiatric conditions, vulnerable communities and intervention initiatives. Facilitating an exchange of information has been a primary motivation underlying the preparation of this book. However, it also includes the theoretical and conceptual underpinnings, sharing of practical and experiential evidence, advice and good practice. We are sure that the volume will not only be helpful for academics, researchers, planners and practitioners, but also serve as a springboard for further initiatives and literature in the field.

References

Albee, G.W. (1996) 'Revolutions and Counter-revolutions in Prevention.' *American Psychologist 51*, 11, 1130–1133.

Barnes, J. (1998) 'Mental Health Promotion: A Developmental Perspective.' *Psychology, Health and Medicine 3*, 1, 55–69.

Breton, J.J. (1999) 'Complementary Development of Prevention and Mental Health Promotion Programs for Canadian Children Based on Contemporary Scientific Paradigms.' *Canadian Journal of Psychiatry 44*, 3, 227–233.

Caplan, G. (1964) *Principles of Preventive Psychiatry.* New York: Basic Books.

Carr, A. (2002) *Prevention: What Works with Children and Adolescents?* Hove: BrunnerRoutledge.

Cox, A. (1993) 'Preventive Aspects of Child Psychiatry.' *Archives of Disease in Childhood 68*, 5, 691–701.

Department of Health (DoH) (1999a) *National Service Framework for Mental Health: Modern Standards and Service Models.* London: DoH.

Department of Health (DoH) (1999b) *Our Healthier Nation.* London: DoH.

Dryfoos, J.G. (1997) 'The Prevalence of Problem Behaviours: Implications for Programs.' In R.P. Wessberg, T.P. Gullotta, R.L. Hampton, B.A. Ryan and G.R. Adams (eds) *Enhancing Children's Wellness*, 8, London: Sage.

Gordon, R. (1987) 'An Operational Classification of Disease Prevention.' In A. Steinberg and M.M. Silverman (eds) *Preventing Mental Disorders.* Rockville, MD: Department of Health and Human Services.

Health Education Authority (HEA) (1998) *Community Action for Mental Health.* London: HEA.

Hersey, J.C. and Klibanoff, L.S. (1984) 'Promoting Social Support: The Impact of California's "Friends can be Good Medicine" campaign.' *Health Education Quarterly 11*, 3, 293–311.

International Union for Health Promotion and Education (1999) *The Evidence of Health Promotion Effectiveness: Shaping Public Health in a New Europe.* Brussels and Luxembourg: International Union for Health Promotion and Education.

Jenkins, R. and Ustsun, T.B. (eds) (1998) *Preventing Mental Illness: Mental Health Promotion in Primary Care.* New York: Wiley.

Kalter, N., Picker, J. and Lesowitz, M. (1984) 'School Based Developmental Facilitation Groups for Children of Divorce: A Preventive Intervention.' *American Journal of Orthopsychiatry 54*, 613–623.

Kawachi, I., Kennedy, B.P., Lochner, K. and Prothrow-Stith, D. (1997) 'Social Capital, Income Inequality and Mortality.' *American Journal of Public Health 87*, 9, 1491–1498.

Lahtinen, E., Lehtinen, V. and Rikonene, E. (eds) (1999) *Framework for Promoting Mental Health in Europe.* Helsinki: Stakes.

Meltzer, H., Gatward, R. and Goodman, R. (2000) *Development and Wellbeing of Children and Adolescents in Great Britain.* London: Stationery Office.

Mental Health Europe (MHE) (2000) *Mental Health Promotion for Children up to 6 Years: Directory of Projects in the European Union.* Brussels: MHE.

Mental Health Foundation (MHF) (1999) *Bright Futures.* London: MHF.

Mrazek, P.J. and Haggerty, R.J. (eds) (1994) *Reducing Risks for Mental Disorders: Frontiers for Preventive Intervention Research.* Washington, DC: National Academy Press.

NHS Health Advisory Service (1995) *Together We Stand.* London: HMSO.

NSW Health (2000) *Prevention Initiatives for Child and Adolescent Mental Health.* Sydney: NSW Health Department.

Offord, D.R. and Bennett, K.J. (2002) 'Prevention.' In M. Rutter and E. Taylor (eds) *Child and Adolescent Psychiatry*, 4th edn. Oxford: Blackwell.

Offord, D.R., Kraemer, H.C., Kazdin, A.E., Jensen, P.S. and Harrington, R. (1998) 'Lowering the Burden of Suffering from Child Psychiatric Disorder: Trade-offs Among Clinical, Targeted and Universal Interventions.' *Journal of the American Academy of Child and Adolescent Psychiatry 37*, 686–694.

Orley, J. and Weisen, R.B. (1998) 'Mental Health Promotion: What It is and What It is Not.' *International Journal of Mental Health Promotion 1*, 1, 41–44.

Rappaport, J. (1981) 'In Praise of Paradox: A Social Policy of Empowerment over Prevention.' *American Journal of Community Psychology 9*, 1–25.

Royal College of Psychiatrists (RCP) (2002) *Prevention in Psychiatry, CR104.* London: RCP.

Rutter, M. (1982) 'Prevention of Children's Psychosocial Disorders: Myths and Substance.' *Pediatrics 70*, 6, 883–894.

Sameroff, A.J. (1987) 'Transactional Risk Factors and Prevention.' In J.A. Steinberg and M.M. Silverman (eds) *Preventing Mental Disorders: A Research Perspective.* Rockville, MD: NIMH, US Department of Health and Human Services.

Silverman, M.M. (1995) 'Preventing Psychiatric Disorder.' In B. Raphael and G.D. Burrows (eds) *Handbook of Studies in Preventive Psychiatry.* Amsterdam: Elsevier.

Stewart-Brown, S. (1998) 'Evidence Based Child Mental Health Promotion: The Role of Parenting Programmes.' In K.N. Dwivedi (ed) *Evidence Based Child Mental Health Care.* Northampton: Child and Adolescent Mental Health Service.

Streiner, D.L. and Norman, M. (1996) *PDQ Epidemiology,* 2nd edn. Toronto: Mosby.

Tugwell, P., Bennett, K.J., Haynes, R.B. and Sackett, D.L. (1985) 'The Measurement Iterative Loop: A Framework for the Critical Appraisal of Needs, Benefits and Costs of Health Interventions.' *Journal of Chronic Disease 38,* 339–351.

World Health Organization (1997) *Programme on Mental Health: Life Skills Education in Schools.* Switzerland: WHO.

Chapter 2

Developmental Perspective

Ezra Loh and Jillian Wragg

Introduction

In today's frenetic and somewhat stressful world, the struggle to manage emotions is very obvious. We are often bombarded with stories of people who fail to contain themselves and cause serious harm to themselves or others. Now more than ever it is important to focus upon normal development and maintenance of good emotional health.

The technological revolution, especially in the field of information technology, has led to more information being made available and accessible to the layperson. Self-diagnosis has also become more common in recent years. Information is recognised by the government as necessary not just in empowering the user but also in facilitating a more collaborative approach between professionals and clients. This has been shown to improve the effectiveness of interventions (Department of Health 2002). In the light of the British government's initiatives and policy which emphasise clinical governance, effectiveness and accountability, mental health professionals should be moving towards evidence-based practice which would assist in the process of providing accurate and up-to-date information to everyone.

In order to complete a book which would focus upon the promotion of emotional well-being for children and adolescents, it is vital to build a secure foundation using the theoretical underpinnings which have already been established. This would provide a solid basis upon which interventions (which will be discussed later in the book) could be built. It seems that there are critical stages in a young person's development where such interventions could be targeted. During these transitional times children and young people may be more vulnerable to environmental adversity, which accentuates the need to target these children for health promotion to prevent mental ill health. However, it is very important to understand these developmental aspects before further interventions can be developed. Dwivedi further elaborates the theme of emotional regulation in Chapter 4 in this volume.

The chapter will begin with a discussion around the theoretical aspects and the issues affecting emotional development according to the following stages:

- infancy (birth until 2 years)
- early childhood (2–5 years of age)
- middle childhood (6–11 years of age)
- adolescence (12–18 years of age).

Though constrained by physical and cognitive abilities, primary psychosocial processes like reinforcement, modelling and labelling of emotions by others (e.g. parents) are also of crucial importance at each stage. Current concepts derived from contemporary research will also be reviewed and finally the future directions will be explored.

Infancy (birth until 2 years)

During infancy, rapid growth and development occurs, especially in the socio-emotional aspect. There is much truth in suggestions that the early emotional attributes (including the basic infantile temperaments), socialisation skills and trends that emerge in infancy serve as the basis for all social-emotional development for the rest of the lifespan.

Temperament
Behavioural styles

Differences among children's behaviour can be seen even in infancy as they are born with a tendency toward certain moods and styles of reacting to people and events in their lives in specific ways. Infants are also noticeably more proactive rather than passively reactive to stimulation. This preferred style of responding is called temperament. They reach out to affect their environment to the extent that individual differences in temperament and styles of behaving affect parents and influence the direction of development in significant ways.

Researchers have delineated three broad styles of temperament: these are 'easy', 'difficult' and 'slow-to-warm-up' types of infants (Thomas and Chess 1977). A more recent study described most young infants according to these three basic types of temperaments: about 40 per cent being 'easy', about 10 per cent being 'difficult' and about 15 per cent 'slow to warm up' (Berger 2000).

Obviously, neither parents nor children fit neatly into these categories. Most parents use a combination of styles, and most children have elements of different temperamental styles.

In both cases, however, one style usually predominates. However, since family and other life experiences can make a difference, temperament by itself is not destiny. Parents will find life more harmonious if they attune to their child's temperament as in so doing they recognise their child's particular strengths. In a new situation, unlike the easy child who needs little help in adapting, the slow-to-warm-up child does best if not hurried and allowed time to think about the situation, while the difficult child may need advance warning and practice of the appropriate behaviour. Thinking about one's own temperamental style and whether it meshes with one's child's temperamental style often helps. For example, an active on-the-go parent may have to learn patience in dealing with a slow-to-warm-up child.

Goodness of fit

We see parents developing various styles of interacting with their children; apparently some styles seem to work better than others and one tends to wonder what works best for whom and in what situations and settings. Nonetheless, parenting is not a one-sided activity; it is a dynamic, reciprocally interactive situation, and children also have styles or temperaments that in turn affect their parents' styles and which can elicit different responses. Apparently, mismatch of mother's (or any regular caregiver's) and infant's temperaments can result in an extended series of mutually unrewarding interactions.

No matter what the child's temperament, it is the harmony, more specifically known as the goodness of fit, between mother or caregiver and child which is important. In a circular fashion, the behaviour of one frequently influences the responses of the other, or the infant's characteristics interact with parental attributes. A growing body of evidence (Baumrind 1989; Bell 1971; Darling and Steinberg 1993) suggests that the behavioural styles or temperaments of infants (and young children for that matter) have a 'releasing' effect and initiating role on their parents (or regular caregivers). Thus parents may be confronted with difficult infant characteristics like 'pathological' crying, disturbed sucking patterns, unusual sleep–wake cycles, and distractibility. They may be confused and react inappropriately, especially when such infantile demands and distressed condition present as signals, which are difficult for any carer to interpret in the first place.

Sleep patterns

Many parents have found much difficulty understanding their infants' sleep patterns. It may be useful to know that the 'sleep cycle' of infants is biologically determined and is regulated by a system of neurones situated in the core of the brain (Herbert 1998). It is thus not surprising that an infant's pattern of sleeping is said to be as individual a matter as the uniqueness of the young child's developing personality (Anders, Goodlin-Jones and Sadeh 1999; Ficca, Fagioli and Salzarulo 2000; Goodlin-Jones *et al.* 2001; McGraw *et al.* 1999). Since this basic sleep cycle is endowed and therefore not learned, parents cannot actually alter it. Furthermore brief periods of night waking are quite common in infancy. On the other hand, babies wake for a variety of emotional besides physical reasons. Being at the beginning of their lives, babies can be viewed as extremely emotionally dependent on those who care for them and as they grow, they learn from experience that their primary carers are there when they need them. If these babies receive this confidence from the carer, they can be helped to begin to settle themselves or to entertain themselves for a bit when they are awake (Shuttleworth 2001).

Feeding habits and mother–infant interaction

Differences in infants' temperaments can also explain the differing feeding patterns of newborns and infants. Starting from the first few hours of birth, the newborn baby is very alert and oriented to faces, often making full eye contact with his or her parents or carers.

Consequently, these critical moments could be regarded as the best times to nurse and bond, which are believed to be key events in the child's development of attachment experiences. After these first few hours, the infants become very sleepy, as if they were recovering from the physical stresses of labour and birth, sometimes much to new mothers' concern. After the first 24 hours, most babies resume their alertness and become even more interested in feeding and interacting with their mothers or carers. The social and emotional context in which the infant or young child feeds should be attended to. There is usually no difference between daytime and night-time sleep habits in the first few months while the time between feeding is variable from one infant to another. Thus, it may be sensible for the parent to adapt the feeding times according to the cycles of hunger and satisfaction expressed by the infant or young child.

Furthermore, during sessions of feeding (e.g. breast feeding), maternal sensitivity is required to respond appropriately to the intervening pauses from feeding and the occasional eye contacts during feeding.

In subsequent weeks and months, mothers and babies somehow work out their own 'optimal' feeding patterns, mainly on a subconscious or unintentional level, based on how they interact with each other. However, in order that the mother can adapt her parenting style to her new baby's needs, it is crucial for her to have enough physical and emotional security herself.

Expression of emotions

Before infants acquire speech, emotion is the first 'language' that parents and infants use to communicate with each other. Often this is facilitated by an optimal interactive relationship with their primary caregiver. Infants however differ from each other in the onset of expressing emotion, though one has to be reminded that crying is the most important and universal mechanism newborns have for communicating with their world. In fact, it is useful for mothers to identify babies' three types of cries: the basic cry, the anger cry and the pain cry. Similarly, smiling, another important communicative affective behaviour of the infant, presents in two different types. The infant retains the reflexive smile (which is a primitive reflex response with a survival value) and the social smile (this normally begins when the infant is 4–6 weeks old in response to a face).

By 3 or 4 months, the infant experiences anger, surprise and sadness. Thus when the infant reaches 5 to 7 months old, a wide variety of 'normal' fears will be expressed in different situations and settings (King, Hamilton and Ollendick 1988; Morris and Kratochwill 1983). For instance, young infants are easily alarmed and frightened by loud noises, loss of support and strangers as well as sudden, unexpected and looming objects. Shame and shyness set in by the age of 6–8 months. Then as they grow older they manifest a range of emotions including separation anxiety from parents and a fear of strangers (by 8–9 months), contempt and guilt (by 2 years). Anxiety is a fundamental and universal response to a wide range of life events and is in fact a normal adaptation to particular environmental circumstances. It has positive survival and reward value preparing (or driving) the individual to maximum efficiency in the event of extreme threat. Anxiety has in fact been called 'fear spread thin' (Herbert 1998).

Maternal attachment or bonding

The infant's transactions with the early socio-emotional environment, especially in the context of the one-to-one relationship between the infant and the primary caregiver, significantly influence the biological development of brain structures. The caregiver, usually the mother, enters into an ongoing communicative relationship with the infant, which in optimal circumstances enables the infant to access various affect-regulating functions. In response to the mother's warm, responsive, sensitive and non-intrusive behaviour, the infant participates in these intimate face-to-face interactive experiences that generate and sustain adequate levels of positive affect to stimulate the growth of new synaptic (neurological connections) links in the developing brain (Schore 1994). On the other hand, Schore reported that an infant's mistuned dyadic affective interactions, which often happen with a non-empathic caregiver, could lead to long-term neurobiological and socio-emotional consequences e.g. insecure attachments. Apparently, the infant's cognitive perceptions of the social environment, manifested as insecure attachment behaviour, are stored in neuronal templates in the limbic system, which is connected to the management of emotion. Unfortunately there are indications that these early behaviours may be associated with later vulnerability to some psychiatric and psychosomatic disorders (Carlson 1998).

Infant attachment

Definition

Attachment can be defined as an intense emotional relationship that is often specific to two persons, which endures over time, and in the event of prolonged separation from the partner is accompanied by stress and sorrow. While this definition applies to attachment formation at any point in the life cycle, our first attachment experience is crucial for healthy socio-emotional development as it acts as a template for all subsequent relationships (Gross and McIlveen 1998).

Development of attachment in infants

Attachment in infants happens over several phases (Gross and McIlveen 1998)

1. *Pre-attachment phase:* this lasts for about three months. Babies at the age of 6 weeks begin to be attracted to other humans in preference to inanimate features in the environment. Besides smiling to just anyone (i.e. social smiling), babies at this age will also engage in behaviours like nestling and gurgling.

2. *Indiscriminate attachment phase:* infants begin to develop the ability to distinguish between people at about 3 months. They make attempts to discriminate between familiar and unfamiliar people. Thus these infants will seem to be at ease with strangers and even allow them to handle and look after them without becoming noticeably distressed, unless the stranger does not provide adequate care. This phase ends when the infant is about 7 months old.

3. *Discriminate attachment phase:* this phase begins when the infant has developed specific attachments (or a strong innate tendency to become attached to one particular person, or monotropy) and can reliably distinguish the mother from other people, i.e. they will have developed object permanence. Infants who have developed object permanence will actively seek the proximity of their mother or some other person and will become distressed when separated, i.e. develop separation anxiety. Then when they are about 8 months old they will avoid proximity with unfamiliar people, causing at lease some infants to cry or move away.

4. *Multiple attachments phase:* additional attachment figures e.g. the father, siblings, grandparents or even other infants begin to form from about 9 months onwards. At this age, the infant appears to be increasingly independent of the primary caregiver.

The types of attachments that infants form with their caregivers

Although attachment to the mother is qualitatively different from any subsequent attachments, there is little difference in how children form attachments to mothers and fathers. Despite the infant's attachments being variable in strength, multiple attachments appear to be the norm, and the mother is not always or necessarily the main attachment figure (Gross and McIlveen 1998).

Ainsworth *et al.* (1978) discovered that infants form one of three basic attachments to the caregiver: anxious-avoidant (15%), securely attached (70%) and anxious-resistant (15%). It was also found that the caregiver's sensitivity, or the quality of response to the baby's needs, is the crucial feature determining the quality of attachment. The sensitive caregiver perceives things from the infant's perspective, correctly interprets the child's signals, responds to his or her needs, and is accepting, cooperative and accessible. By contrast, the insensitive caregivers interact almost exclusively in terms of their own wishes, moods and activities. Furthermore, Ainsworth's research indicated that infants of sensitive caregivers develop secure attachments, whereas infants of insensitive caregivers develop insecure attachments (either anxious-avoidant or anxious-resistant). (Please see also Chapter 3 by Bailham and Harper in this volume.)

The role of play in an infant's socio-emotional development

The contemporary perspectives on play place emphasis on both the social and cognitive aspects of play, i.e. sensorimotor and pretence or symbolic play behaviour. Infants can derive pleasure from exercising their existing sensorimotor schemas. Thus, initially, infants engage in exploratory and playful visual and motor transactions by about 3 or 4 months of age. Around the age of 9 months, infants begin to explore and play with novel objects, especially toys that make noise or bounce. These infants also begin increasing the use of objects in symbolic play, transforming and substituting objects and even acting toward them as if they themselves were these other objects. Infants of around 12 months of age prefer toys that perform when they act on them and enjoy making things work and exploring cause and effect. By 18 months, infants engage in dramatic or 'make-believe' play which reaches a peak at about 4 or 5 years of age, before subsiding and gradually being replaced by more reality-based interests. Play, in general, facilitates an infant in developing an integrated sense of self and 'separateness' from other objects and persons. Through play infants also have the opportunity to express their emotions (e.g. fears, aggression and fantasies) in a safe environment besides acquiring social skills useful for their next stage of development (Herbert 1998).

Early childhood (2 to 5 years)

Expression of emotions

The tasks of emotional development

During toddlerhood, children develop a more reliable understanding of increasingly complex emotions. The development of emotions at this stage can be best understood in terms of the tasks that need to be accomplished (Herbert 1998). These are

- to differentiate between emotion states in self and others (the significance of emotions)
- to learn to contain emotions and the socially appropriate or acceptable expression of emotions (the regulation of emotions)
- to distinguish between expressed and felt emotions in self and others
- to understand the impact of emotions on behaviour and relationships (the regulatory capacity of emotions).

Since each emotional state has a biological significance (i.e. in terms of survival or learning), differentiating between emotions is important. Thus, the four basic emotions of happiness, sadness, anger and fear begin to be distinguished with increasing clarity. For instance, fears of the dark, being left alone, small animals and insects are common in preschool children. It is good to remember that in addition to the functional usefulness of fears, parents can also make use of the child's fear to avoid danger and anxiety about the loss of love or approval (which is vital for ensuring compliance and internalisation of rules and values) in the task of socialisation (Wright 1971). The recognition, in self and others, of emotions such as guilt, disgust, jealousy, relief and shame (which is common across cultures) becomes more reliably measurable in later childhood and adolescence.

Regulating one's own emotions is a lifelong process. Even from an early age, learning to contain and appropriately express emotions is learnt from the caregiver and peers both by direct intervention (e.g. parental management of tantrums) and vicariously (e.g. observation of adults' and peers' emotional responses to situations). Most preschoolers will gradually develop the understanding that they can hide some of their feelings from other people under certain circumstances and vice versa which is dependent in part on the development of the theory of mind, quite similar to the understanding of cognitive deception. It is useful to know that emotions can be regulated as well as being regulatory. The regulatory function of emotions is seen when it is acknowledged that emotions may influence the interpretations of events, potential responses to events or situations, and the behaviour of the individual and others.

An outline of emotional development

Just as the child has mastered the art of using specific cries and vocalisations to distinguish different needs between birth and 18 months, the expression of emotional words develops between 18 and 24 months. This, in some ways, paves the way for the increased use of pretend play to express feelings, especially the expression of anger (temper tantrums), which begins to become more established at the age of 2 years old. With the development of the use of language, talking with carers, siblings or peers about their own feelings (in play or humour) begins to enrich both the imaginative as well as the cognitive aspects of emotional development. This may have a broad variation across the population but an increased sharing of emotion generally leads to increased interpersonal cooperation.

Communication of emotions

As a means of understanding the meaning of emotions, emotional communication with others is important from toddlerhood onwards. In toddlerhood, this may be through play, gesture and facial expression. Furthermore, it is an important component in social development. Small beginnings of shared emotional experiences and memories – increasingly with same-sex friends (or small groups of friends playing dolls together), brings relief from being 'understood' and enhances friendship. The exposure to emotional communication that facilitates the expression and resolution of difficult emotions increases the likelihood of the development of skills and abilities in emotional communication, understanding and regulation. This phenomenon is most rapid in toddlerhood or early childhood and continues throughout adolescence and adulthood. These qualities are important in that they facilitate the development of constructive responses to conflict.

The role of play in a toddler's socio-emotional development

Play can be described as an exciting and pleasurable activity, which can satisfy the curiosity and desire for new information and something un-usual (Berlyne 1960). Children can thus encounter novelty, complexity, uncertainty, surprise and incongruity (Santrock 1999) in play, which are all useful elements in nurturing the toddler's socio-emotional develop-ment. In this respect, Santrock (1999) also referred to Mildred Parten's six identifiable stages, as follows:

- unoccupied play (child not engaging in play but just looking around)
- solitary play (child plays alone)
- onlooker play (child watches other children play)
- parallel play (child plays separate from or alongside others, may mimic others' play)
- associative play (child plays with others with routine, but without an organised structure; more interested in others than tasks at hand)
- cooperative play (child plays with others with routine, in a group with a sense of group identity and organised activity, acceptance of rules and 'productivity').

While Parten's categories are oriented towards social play (i.e. that in-volves social interactions with peers), constructive play combines sensorimotor or practice repetitive play with symbolic representation of ideas. Children engaging in self-regulated creation or construction of a product or a problem solution are said to be involved in constructive play. Play is essential to the young child's emotional health since it is a pleasurable activity that is engaged in for its own sake. Play also in-creases affiliation with peers, releases tension (which according to both Freud and Erikson (1965) will help the child master anxieties and con-flicts, and is thus an essential useful form of human adjustment which trains children to cope with life's problems), advances cognitive develop-ment (children can practise their competencies and acquired skills in a relaxed, pleasurable way as proposed by Piaget (1950)), increases explo-ration (especially the symbolic and make-believe aspects of play, as when a child substitutes a stick for a horse and rides the stick as if it were a horse, as suggested by Vygotsky (1978)) and provides a safe haven in which to engage in potentially dangerous behaviour.

Middle childhood (6 to 11 years)

Cognitive development

Emotional development in older children is strongly linked to a progression in their cognitive abilities. Piagetian theory (1950) suggests that children in this age group span the pre-operational and the concrete-operational phases of cognitive development. Essentially, children still use concrete thinking, i.e. their thinking is still quite rigid and related to what they can see and touch. However, their thoughts gradually become more logical and organised. When children reach the age of 5 to 11 years they begin to develop a greater understanding of the complexity of emotion (although there is quite a difference between a 5-year-old and an 11-year-old). It is apparent that individuals can experience more than one emotion at a time and that emotion can be motivated by internal and/or external factors (Harter and Whitesell 1989).

A further skill which is mastered by children of this age group is the ability to regulate their own emotions, e.g. thinking positively might improve a sad mood. Therefore, school-aged children have the ability to use specific cognitive strategies such as distraction or reconceptualisation of a situation in order to manage their feelings. Children of this age can also see that emotions can fade if one refrains from focusing upon them (Harris, Lipian-Mark and Man-Shu 1985). Younger children, however, see the changing of emotion as being due to a situational change. The ability to negotiate their own emotions and regulate the way they feel is a vital skill in emotional development and has a strong impact, not only upon an individual's social relationships but also his or her mental health. The way in which children manage their emotions is highly correlated with the way in which this is modelled to them by their parents and the opportunities they are afforded to manage their feelings (e.g. when parents encourage the expression of emotions by talking about them).

The ability to mask an emotional state also appears later in childhood and is linked to the skills of emotional regulation already mentioned. By this age, most children have a good understanding of cultural norms and socially acceptable behaviour. Leading on from the latter understanding is the development of empathy. With increasing age, sensitivity to the emotions of others is usually accompanied by prosocial behaviour, i.e. an attempt to assist someone else who is experiencing emotional distress.

Pride, shame and guilt

As young people's ability to understand themselves develops, self-conscious emotions such as pride, shame and guilt begin to emerge. Erikson's (1965) Eight Stages of Man model described the socio-emotional development of individuals. During the stage relating to middle childhood, the task is to conquer feelings of failure. The struggle is between 'industry versus inferiority'. If children do not achieve in the important areas of their lives, such as sport, schoolwork and social relationships, they may develop feelings of inadequacy, or conversely pride, if they are successful.

Theorists seem to have experienced difficulty in defining embarrassment, guilt and shame. Keltner and Buswell (1997, p.20) argued that: 'the antecedents, experience, and display of embarrassment, and to a limited extent its autonomic physiology, are distinct from shame, guilt, and amusement'. The consensus appears to be that embarrassment is less negative and less invasive than guilt or shame. Guilt seems to be a cognitive and an emotional experience, which usually occurs when individuals believe that they have not acted in accordance with their 'ideal self'. This is also related to the understanding that they are responsible for contravening a moral standard. As children develop an understanding of others' inner states, they are able to experience guilt about causing harm to others or not acting upon their behalf. Ferguson and Stegge (1998, p.20) described guilt as 'an agitation-based emotion or painful feeling of regret that is aroused when the actor actually causes, anticipates causing, or is associated with an aversive event'.

The term 'shame' has often been used interchangeably with guilt. However, many researchers now see the concepts as separate. Ferguson and Stegge (1998) defined shame as

> a dejection-based, passive, or helpless emotion aroused by self related aversive events. The ashamed person focuses more on devaluing or condemning the entire self, experiences the self as fundamentally flawed, feels self-conscious about the visibility of one's actions, fears scorn and thus hides from others. (Ferguson and Stegge 1998, p.20)

In summary, middle childhood heralds the development of more sophisticated cognitive abilities that allow children to self-monitor, manipulate emotions and reason more efficiently. The range and complexity of emotions also develop during this time period.

Adolescence (12 to 18 years)

Adolescence is traditionally viewed as a period of great change and transition. This includes biological factors, such as reaching puberty; psychological factors, such as further cognitive, intellectual and moral development; and finally social factors, such as societal expectations. The stereotypical view of adolescence is that it is a time of great confusion and turmoil. However, this may not be the case as some of the literature is now indicating that most individuals manage to navigate adolescence without developing any significant social, emotional or behavioural difficulties (Steinberg 1999). In fact some studies (Brooks-Gunn and Reiter 1990; Peterson 1985) have indicated that 'puberty is not characterized by "raging" hormones and the turmoil once associated with puberty was exaggerated' (Steinberg and Morris 2001, p.91). Steinberg (1999) also noted that typical adolescent problems, such as substance abuse, unemployment and delinquency, are often short-lived and have usually settled by adulthood. It is also important to note that the idea of adolescence and the expectations of young people are culture specific and there are vast differences in how adolescents are viewed around the world.

From an emotional perspective adolescents have refined their ability to regulate their emotions, particularly in relation to how they expect others to respond to their expression of emotion. They also have a greater emotional literacy and have more skill in interpreting social situations. Given the importance of peer approval it is also a period of time when adolescents are acutely aware of the evaluation of others. Therefore, this is a time of great self-consciousness, which can lead to distress and anxiety. Interestingly girls are much more likely to express their concerns and seek social support than boys. This may explain the fact that more boys than girls commit suicide (Gould *et al.* 2003).

Self-identity

Research into identity has generally supported Erikson's (1968) model apart from his ideas around the timing of identity work. Later research indicates that most young people begin to explore their identities during late adolescence or even early adulthood. Harter (1999) found that teenagers begin to move away from comparing themselves to their peers to more stable self-concepts. They also begin to assess themselves along a number of dimensions such as the academic, social, moral, physical, etc. At this time in their lives, adolescents seem to be most influenced by their appearance and this is a crucial factor in the development of overall self-esteem (Usmiani and Daniluk 1997). Self-esteem appears to fluctuate a great deal initially but stabilises with age (Alasker and Olweus 1992). There also appear to be variations in self-esteem in relation to gender and ethnicity. For example males have been found to have greater self-esteem than females (Deihl, Vicary and Deike 1997) and black adolescents were also found to have a higher level of self-esteem than white adolescents (Gray-Little and Hafdahl 2000).

Puberty

Not only are adolescents at a stage when they are making transitions, such as moving from junior to senior school, but also they are undergoing major physical changes which have a big impact upon emotion. The psychoanalytic school refers to this phase as the genital stage. Alongside the physical growth, it is certainly a time of increased interest in the opposite sex. This is an area which has received little research (Steinberg and Morris 2001) but the effect of romantic involvement, at this stage of development, has the potential to create a significant impact upon adolescents' feelings and ultimately their mental health.

Self-esteem

Along with the biological changes associated with puberty come a variety of cognitive changes, which impact upon self-esteem and self-image. Such cognitive advances may mean that adolescents think more about themselves and their futures. Peterson (1985) discussed the difference between girls and boys in terms of their level of maturity. It seems that boys who mature late feel less competent and have low self-esteem. In contrast, early maturing boys are more confident and positive about themselves. However, they are more likely to become involved in antisocial behaviours (Williams and Dunlop 1999). Early maturing girls, on the other hand, seem more predisposed to developing emotional difficulties. In addition to low self-esteem they are also more likely to experience higher rates of anxiety, depression and eating disorders (Ge, Conger and Elder 1996). It is likely that the changes in body shape play a significant role in the development of such difficulties during adolescence.

Group identity

Conflict with parents can arise as a result of the struggle for autonomy, which is the main aim of this stage. It is during this phase that adolescents begin to withdraw emotional connections to their parents and begin to develop greater attachments to their peers. However, the importance of appropriate parenting is very clear. Children whose parents were deemed to be 'authoritative' were psychologically healthier than children whose parents were 'permissive, authoritarian or indifferent' (Baumrind 1978). Not only do young adults understand the concept of identity, but also they have the ability to experience guilt about more general issues such as poverty, persecution, war, famine, etc. It is also the case that when guilt is reduced, individuals can act without remorse, for example if they believe that they have no control over the events of life (i.e. they have an external locus of control) and therefore they believe that they are not responsible for a particular outcome. Additionally individuals can believe that their action was not a transgression of the law or societal rules.

Depression

Most stereotypical teenagers are viewed as experiencing extreme moodiness. However, the evidence for this has been quite weak. In fact one study found that boys felt more positive as puberty progressed and girls showed little mood variability during this developmental stage (Richards and Larson 1993). However, for some this can be a painful process, which leads to mental health problems such as depression. Ge *et al.* (1994) indicated that around 35 per cent of adolescents experience low mood and 7 per cent reached the criteria for clinical depression. Studies have also shown that girls experience higher rates of depression than boys (Peterson, Sarigani and Kennedy 1991).

Although the causes of depression are not fully understood, researchers are convinced of a genetic link to depression (Goodyer 2001). There also appear to be a variety of psychological and social factors involved. For example, those with parents who have poor parenting skills show less warmth and those who witness domestic violence are more at risk of developing depression (Graham and Hughes 1995). This does not mean to say that children in stable environments do not develop depression. One of the major difficulties appears to be in detecting the problem. Brown University (2002) suggested that even parents with good relationships with their children do not seem to realise when their child is depressed. It is likely that this lack of understanding is due to the myth that all adolescents are temperamental. It is important that further research is carried out in this area and that families are educated about mental health issues. Chapter 9 by Claire Hayes in this volume deals further with this theme.

Overall, adolescent development is focused on refining the personality, establishing a belief system, belonging to a peer group and independence. All of these factors can have a significant impact upon emotional development and can be a time when mental health difficulties are more likely to emerge but it is also important to bear in mind that the majority of young people, given facilitative environments, personalities and levels of support, successfully navigate their way through adolescence.

Future directions

In the past much of the research on mental health has been focused towards pathology and identifying abnormalities. It has also been very biased towards adults. It is only in recent times that more thought has been given to the mental health of children and young people. It is particularly heartening to see the government targeting this area and putting money into the development of many new projects to support families and promote emotional well-being.

Further research into how positive emotions such as happiness are developed and maintained would be useful in order to shift the balance from merely identifying those who are viewed as abnormal in terms of their thoughts, feelings and behaviour. In fact 'positive psychology' (Seligman 2003, p.126), where 'happiness and well-being are the desired outcomes of positive psychology', is a developing area. It is hoped that this research will extend to the development and maintenance of positive emotions from childhood, which could provide greater insight and lead to the development of early interventions constructively to alter the emotional trajectory.

New research into emotional development has begun to focus upon temperament, sex differences, cross-cultural differences, how psychotherapy affects brain structure and neurotransmitters, autistic spectrum disorders and emotional intelligence/literacy. Emotional development is indeed a crucial area, which deserves a great deal more research. It is hoped that with greater understanding of how emotions develop future interventions can be created which will help professionals and parents to encourage emotional well-being in increasing numbers of young people.

References

Ainsworth, M., Behar, M.C., Walters, E. and Wall, S. (1978) *Patterns of Attachment: A Psychological Study of the Strange Situation.* Hillsdale, NJ: Erlbaum.

Alasker, F. and Olweus, D. (1992) 'Stability of Global Self-evaluations in Early Adolescence: A Cohort Longitudinal Study.' *Journal of Research on Adolescents 1,* 123–145.

Anders, T., Goodlin-Jones, B. and Sadeh, A. (1999) 'Sleep Disorders.' In C. Zeanah (ed) *Handbook of Infant Mental Health.* New York: Guilford.

Baumrind, D. (1978) 'Parental Disciplinary Patterns and Social Competence in Children.' *Youth and Society 9,* 239–276.

Baumrind, D. (1989) 'Rearing Competent Children.' In W. Damon (ed) *Child Development Today and Tomorrow.* San Francisco, CA: Jossey-Bass.

Bell, R.A. (1971) 'Stimulus Control of Parent or Caretaker Behaviour by Offspring.' *Developmental Psychology 4,* 63–72.

Berger, K.S. (2000) *The Developing Person through Childhood and Adolescence.* New York: Worth.

Berlyne, D.E. (1960) *Conflict, Arousal, and Curiosity.* New York: McGraw-Hill.

Brooks-Gunn, J. and Reiter, E.O. (1990) 'The Role of Pubertal Processes.' In S.S. Feldman and G.R. Elliott (eds) *At the Threshold: The Developing Adolescent.* Cambridge, MA: Harvard University Press.

Brown University (2002) *Child and Adolescent Behaviour Letter 18,* 4.

Carlson, E. (1998) 'A Prospective Longitudinal Study of Attachment Disorganization/Disorientation.' *Child Development 69,* 1107–1128.

Darling, N. and Steinberg, L. (1993) 'Parenting Style as Context: An Integrative Model.' *Psychological Bulletin 113,* 3, 487–496.

Deihl, L.M., Vicary, J.R. and Deike, R.C. (1997) 'Longitudinal Trajectories of Self-esteem from Early to Middle Adolescence and Related Psychosocial Variables among Rural Adolescents.' *Journal of Research on Adolescence 7,* 393–411.

Department of Health (2002) *Keys to Partnership: Working Together to Make a Difference in People's Lives.* Summary Version. London: DoH.

Erikson, E. (1965) *Childhood and Society.* Harmondsworth: Penguin.

Erikson, E. (1968) *Identity, Youth, and Crisis.* New York: Norton.

Ferguson, T.J. and Stegge, H. (1998) 'Measuring Guilt in Children: A Rose by Any Other Name Still has Thorns.' In J. Bybee (ed) *Guilt and Children.* San Diego, CA: Academic Press.

Ficca, G., Fagioli, I. and Salzarulo, P. (2000) 'Sleep Organization in the First Year of Life: Developmental Trends in the Quiet Sleep-Paradoxical Sleep Cycle.' *Journal of Sleep Research 9*, 1–4.

Ge, X., Lorenz, F.O., Conger, R.D., Elder, G.H. and Simons, R.L. (1994) 'Trajectories of Stressful Life Events and Depressive Symptoms During Adolescence.' *Developmental Psychology 31*, 467–483.

Ge, X., Conger, R.D. and Elder, G.H. (1996) 'Coming of Age Too Early: Pubertal Influences on Girls' Vulnerability to Psychological Distress.' *Child Development 67*, 386–400.

Goodlin-Jones, B., Burnham, M.M., Gaylor, E.E. and Anders, T. (2001) 'Night Waking, Sleep-Wake Organization, and Self-soothing in the First Year of Life.' *Developmental and Behavioral Pediatrics 22*, 4, 226–233.

Goodyer, I.M. (2001) 'Life Events: Their Nature and Effects.' In I.M. Goodyer (ed) *The Depressed Child and Adolescent*, 2nd edn. Cambridge: Cambridge University Press.

Gould, M.S., Greenberg, T., Velting, D.M. and Shaffer, D. (2003) 'Youth Suicide Risk and Preventive Interventions: A Review of the Past 10 Years.' *Journal of American Academic Child and Adolescent Psychiatry 42*, 4, 386–405.

Graham, P. and Hughes, C. (1995) *So Young, So Sad, So Listen.* London: Gaskell and RCP.

Gray-Little, B. and Hafdahl, A.R. (2000) 'Factors Influencing Racial Comparisons of Self-esteem: A Quantitative Review.' *Psychological Bulletin 126*, 26–54.

Gross, M. and McIlveen, R. (1998) *Psychology: A New Introduction.* London: Hodder and Stoughton.

Harris, P.L., Lipian-Mark, S. and Man-Shu, Z. (1985) 'Insight into the Time Course of Emotion among Western and Chinese Children.' *Child Development 56*, 4, 972–988.

Harter, S. (1999) *The Construction of the Self: A Developmental Perspective.* New York: Guilford.

Harter, S. and Whitesell, N. (1989) 'Developmental Changes in Children's Emotion Concepts.' In C. Saarni and P.L. Harris (eds) *Children's Understanding of Emotion.* New York: University of Cambridge Press.

Herbert, M. (1998) *Clinical Child Psychology: Social Learning, Development and Behaviour.* Chichester: Wiley.

Keltner, D. and Buswell, B. (1997) 'Embarrassment: Its Distinct Form and Appeasement Functions.' *Psychological Bulletin 122*, 250–270.

King, N.J., Hamilton, D.I. and Ollendick, T.H. (1988) *Children's Phobias: A Behavioural Perspective.* London: Academic Press.

McGraw, K., Hoffman, R., Harker, C. and Herman, J. H. (1999) 'The Development of Circadian Rhythms in a Human Infant.' *Sleep 22*, 3, 303–310.

Morris, R.J. and Kratochwill, T.R. (1983) *Treating Children's Fears and Phobias: A Behavioural Approach.* New York: Pergamon.

Peterson, A.C. (1985) 'Pubertal Development as a Cause of Disturbance: Myths, Realities, and Unanswered Questions.' *Genetic, Social and General Psychology Monographs 111*, 205–232.

Peterson, A.C., Sarigani, P.A. and Kennedy, R.E. (1991) 'Adolescent Depression: Why More Girls?' *Journal of Youth and Adolescence 20*, 247–271.

Piaget, J. (1950) *The Psychology of Intelligence*. London: Routledge and Kegan Paul.

Richards, M.H. and Larson, R. (1993) 'Pubertal Development and the Daily Subjective States of Young Adolescents.' *Journal of Research on Adolescents 3*, 145–169.

Santrock, J.W. (1999) *Lifespan Development*. New York: McGraw-Hill College.

Schore, A. (1994) *Affect Regulation and the Origin of the Self: The Neurobiology of Emotional Development*. Hillsdale, NJ: Erlbaum.

Seligman, M.E.P. (2003) 'Positive Psychology: Fundamental Assumptions.' *The Psychologist 16*, 3, 126–127.

Shuttleworth, J. (2001) 'Crying and Sleeping in the First Months of Life.' *Understanding Childhood series*. London: Child Psychotherapy Trust.

Steinberg, L. (1999) *Adolescence*, 5th edn. Boston, MA: McGraw-Hill.

Steinberg, L. and Morris, A.S. (2001) 'Adolescent Development.' *Annual Review of Psychology 52*, 82–101.

Thomas, A. and Chess, S. (1977) *Temperament and Development*. New York: Brunner/Mazel.

Usmiani, S. and Daniluk, J. (1997) 'Mothers and their Adolescent Daughters: Relationship between Self-esteem, Gender Role Identity and Body Image.' *Journal of Youth and Adolescence 26*, 45–62.

Vygotsky, L.S. (1978) *Mind in Society: The Development of Higher Psychological Processes*. Cambridge, MA: Harvard University Press.

Williams, J.M. and Dunlop, L.C. (1999) 'Pubertal Timing and Self-reported Delinquency among Male Adolescents.' *Journal of Adolescence 22*, 157–171.

Wright, D. (1971) *The Psychology of Moral Behaviour*. Harmondsworth: Penguin.

Chapter 3

Attachment Theory and Mental Health

Dawn Bailham and Peter Brinley Harper

Attachment theory describes the development of emotional bonds in early infancy, highlighting the importance of the quality of early parent–child relationships on child mental health. The theory advocates how interactions between the young child and the primary caregiver over the first two years of life provide the building blocks for their relationship, as well as the child's overall emotional development. The quality of this early relationship also has important implications for the child's neurological, physical, emotional, behavioural, cognitive and social development.

Attachment theory provides a framework for preventive and treatment programmes for children at different developmental ages. Early preventive programmes focus on minimising stress in caregivers, addressing factors such as parental psychopathology that could compromise parenting ability, and assisting parents in developing skills to provide consistent and responsive parenting. In older children attachment interventions focus on providing the child with an environment that is conducive with the emotional and interpersonal factors associated with a secure attachment.

The basis of attachment theory is the early relationship between the child and the parent. According to attachment theory, how a parent responds to the child's signals of distress can foster a secure attachment relationship between caregiver and child. A young child is biologically predisposed to signal distress by displaying 'attachment behaviours' such as crying to gain contact with the parent. If the parent responds to the child's distress the child will then feel safe and secure, and the child's anxiety is alleviated. The quality of the parent–child relationship is dependent on the parent's response to the child's needs over time. Parents who are responsive, empathic and consistent in their responses to the child will provide the secure base that the child needs.

The origins of attachment theory

John Bowlby, the founding father of attachment theory, was born in London in 1907. Bowlby's background was in medicine, psychology and psychoanalysis. His experience of working with maladjusted children led him to believe that interference in the development of or failure to form attachment relationships with a caregiver in early infancy predisposed an individual to serious psychological problems in adulthood. The aim of Bowlby's theory of attachment was to view psychopathology or mental health within a developmental context, with emotional bonds being pivotal in early child development.

Bowlby was also influenced by ethology. He was particularly interested in animal studies of parenting. Lorenz (1952) observed newly hatched goslings following their mother, and exhibiting behaviour that could be described as 'anxiety', in the form of cheeping and searching when separated from the mother. Harlow (1958) conducted studies with infant monkeys separated from their mothers at birth. The infant monkeys were raised with either a wire surrogate that provided a feeding bottle only, or a furry surrogate covered in terry nappy material that provided comfort without a feeding bottle. The infant monkeys demonstrated a clear preference for the furry surrogate, spending up to 18 hours a day with it. Harlow argued that this finding disproved a purely physiological drive theory of bonding. Bowlby was dissatisfied with the lack of scientific evidence in the prevailing theories of child development of his time and he looked to ethology to bridge that gap.

Mary Ainsworth took attachment theory a stage further with the development of the observational assessment technique of the 'strange situation' (Ainsworth *et al.* 1978). She was interested in the relationship between attachment and exploratory behaviour in infants, and how infants interact with their caregiver when separated and reunited.

With the strange situation technique Ainsworth found a way of classifying early mother–child attachment status, and assessing the quality of the attachment relationship between mother and child. The strange situation technique has now been used in well over 30 different studies, and has been found to be a reliable and valid measure of early attachment status (Van Ijzendoorn and Kroonenberg 1988). Ainsworth identified three initial classification types:

- *Secure:* the infant is distressed by separation but on reunion is quickly comforted.

- *Insecure-avoidant:* the child shows few overt signs of distress on separation and ignores or avoids the mother on reunion.

- *Insecure-ambivalent:* the infant becomes highly distressed by separation and cannot easily be pacified on reunion. The child seeks contact but then resists, alternating between anger and clinging behaviour.

At a later stage a fourth category was added, *insecure-disorganised/disorientated:* these children show unusual stereotyped behaviours on reunion with the parent (Main and Solomon 1990). Disorganised/disorientated attachment behaviour in children in more recent years has been found to be associated with unresolved experiences and trauma in the parents (Main and Solomon 1990; Van Ijzendoorn 1995).

Bowlby's theory has been applied to psychotherapy, a developmental perspective of mental health, and as a basis for early intervention work with parents and their children. Likewise Ainsworth's strange situation technique has promoted the clinical utility of attachment theory. Attachment theory has had a major influence on the cultural understanding of children's early relationships and has been instrumental in reforming the way children are now hospitalised. Bowlby and James Robertson conducted direct observations of children in hospital separated from their parents, illustrating the extent of emotional distress the children experienced (Robertson and Bowlby 1952). The children became tearful, crying and calling for their parents, but would then become indifferent, apathetic and withdrawn. These children would then distance themselves from other children, staring into space, showing a lack of interest in food or playing. The children would then appear to recover until their parents re-emerged. However, on the parents' return the children would show behaviours indicative of protest, such as displays of anger or clinging behaviour.

Since the mid-1990s, attachment has become more of a theoretical construct used primarily for research and intervention in adult relationships (Feeney and Noller 1996), as opposed to a framework for understanding deviations in the early dyadic relationship. There has been an absence of research extending the theory further, for instance, considering how early relationships become the scaffolding for future relationships between the child and significant others, such as teachers and peers. Attachment theory is an interpersonal process model that demonstrates how early relationships shape a child's perception of security, trust in self and others, and self-belief in the form of working models. The theory also explains the concept of affect regulation, that is, with consistent responsive parenting a child learns to identify, label and cope with emotional expression in an age-appropriate adaptive fashion. The latter of course has important implications for the development of emotional well-being in children and how disruptions, or an absence of strong attachment bonds in infancy, can lead to childhood psychopathology. Attachment theory is therefore well placed to be the framework within which preventive child mental health programmes and interventions can be developed.

Both Bowlby and Ainsworth advocated the mother as the primary caregiver. However, they recognised that the primary caregiver did not necessarily have to be the child's biological mother. Although Bowlby did not mention fathers, he would not have excluded fathers as primary caregivers. Instead he preferred to focus on the mother as the pivotal person.

Early attachment relationships and the development of internal working models

During the first 24 months of life the infant's brain undergoes extensive neuronal development. It is during this period that the infant's attachment behaviours are activated and finely tuned by interactions in the child's environment. Through these early interactions between the child and the primary caregiver, the child develops an attachment behavioural system that becomes a model of the world in which the self and significant others are represented. This model provides a scaffold that forms the basis of later interpersonal relationships and encodes a particular pattern of attachment relationships. For instance an individual with an ambivalent attachment (insecure-ambivalent attachment style) may have developed a working model of others as 'unobtainable' and of themselves as 'unworthy of love'.

It can take several months for the attachment behavioural system to develop and only by the age of 6 months are babies able to seek proximity to their caregivers, feel secure in their presence, and protest at signs of separation. If infants' neurodevelopment is following the expected trajectory, they will begin to show signs of emotional expression by smiling at approximately 4 weeks of age. Meltzoff and Moore (1989, 1994) cite evidence that shortly after birth, infants are aware of the disparity between their behaviour and the behaviour of others, and that infants have a tendency to show greater interest in behaviour that mirrors their own (Meltzoff 1990). At about 3 months infants change and are more likely to be attentive to the behaviour of others that reflects their behaviour but that is slightly imperfect (Watson 1994). This coincides with the time that infants begin to smile in response to faces. This early smiling behaviour is a signal to their caregivers and is likely to produce a response from them. When the caregiver smiles at the infant, the infant sees a reflection of its own emotional responses. This dyadic relationship between emotional expression in the infant and recognition and responsiveness in caregiver has been described as 'affective attunement' (Stern 1985). An episode of affective attunement may last for only a few seconds, but in the first two years of life the caregiver and infant will experience many of these episodes. These episodes of affective attunement will influence the developing brain of the child, and have considerable impact on neurological, physical, emotional, behavioural, cognitive and social development. Bowlby also spoke of the lively interactions between caregiver and child, that contained animated facial expressions and vocalisations followed by periods of disengagement. The affective responses to the infant are in most cases imperfect to the temporal, spatial and sensory parameters of the infant, but evidence suggests that the infant's developmental trajectories may be particularly sensitive in detecting these imperfect matches. These interactions appear to be particularly relevant to the infant's development of the sense of self and emotional self-regulation (Gergeley and Watson 1999). It has been proposed that infants are sensitive to the contingencies between their emotional expression and their caregivers' attempts to attune to these displays, whether perfect or imperfect. The caregivers' reflective responses to their infants at times of distress, in an attempt to soothe and comfort their children, restore a state of emotional regulation. Repeated experiences, in which infants' levels of distress are reduced resulting in emotional regulation, will aid children in the development of a self-regulating mechanism. Stern *et al.* (1985) suggest that in the first four to five months of life, infants' main achievement is to form 'the sense of a core self and core others'. Before the first year of life infants do not fully understand that they are separate beings from their caregivers, but gradually they become more self-directed. The affective interchanges in the form of affective attunement between caregiver and child are important for the child to develop emotional regulation, as well as for the development of the origin of the self (Schore 1996). The focus of early intervention programmes therefore is to alleviate caregiver stress and help the caregiver to develop the skills that will promote affective attunement between caregiver and child. Research studies that have a focus on attachment-based interventions have advocated the importance of videotaping parent–child interactions (Marvin *et al.* 2002). The aim of the videotape is to provide parents with the opportunity to reflect on their own behaviour, thoughts and feelings regarding the child's behaviour, as well as advice on how they can improve their interactions with their child.

During the second half of the first six months of life, the foundations of the attachment relationship become stronger. Children become more discriminating in their response to their caregiver's voice, as opposed to the voices of other family members. Caregivers in turn respond to the strengthening of their relationship with their baby. It is important to emphasise that this is *not* a one-way process with the baby becoming more attached to the caregiver, but rather that it is a dyadic and reciprocal process involving both the caregiver and the child. Brazelton and Cramer (1991) provide evidence that caregivers who return to work within a year of giving birth to their babies have a higher incidence of physiological disturbance than caregivers who stay at home with their babies. The study also showed a corresponding higher occurrence of infection in the babies of caregivers who return to work. The study highlights the dyadic links between caregiver and child, which not only is confined to emotional processing, but also has corresponding effects on physiological processes, and carries important implications for social policy and its impact on infant mental and physical health.

This is an intricate process between caregiver and child and developmental difficulties in the child or maternal mental illness, such as over-anxiety or depression, can have a significant impact on the quality of the relationship. This process therefore influences the child's development of internal working models of self and other. It is an *affective* model, and forms the blueprint of the child's responses to subsequent relationships into adulthood.

Internal working models of self and other

An internal working model develops through early interactive experiences between the caregiver and the child, and over time generalises to a schema or representational model that enables the child and later the adult to predict and interact in their interpersonal relationships. For example an individual who is securely attached will hold a representational model of 'others' as responsive and reliable, and the self as being worthy of love and attention. Likewise a child with an insecure attachment will view others as untrustworthy, unpredictable and possibly even dangerous, and themselves as unworthy of love. The notion of internal working models has explanatory power, as children are thinking and feeling beings that actively process past experiences. However, because of their ambiguity these are difficult concepts to measure and substantiate (Rutter 1995).

Working models of self and other play a role in the development of affective responses or emotional regulation as well as the formation of cognitive representations of beliefs about the self and others. Bowlby (1978, 1979) and Tomkins (1991, 1993) both advocate the importance of attentional processes and cognitive strategies in interpreting the impact of sensory-affective stimulation. Frequently experienced emotions are thought to become ingrained within the child's evolving personality, and are described by Tomkins (1993) as 'ideoaffective organisations'.

These ideoaffective organisations fulfil the role of modulating incoming sensory information, and are linked to rules and strategies for the interpretation, evaluation and control of emotionally loaded scenes or events. Early interactive experiences between caregiver and child can therefore shape the child's attentional processes to negative affect, for example 'deactivation or minimising' negative emotions and 'hypervigilance' are found in children with avoidant and ambivalent attachment styles respectively. Bowlby (1978) and Tomkins (1993) are explicit that early parental responses to the child's expression of both negative and positive emotions are important in the development of emotional regulation. There is evidence that caregivers respond to emotional expressions and gestures they interpret as the most vigorous. Some caregivers respond more perceptively to their infants' expressions of positive affect, while others respond more sensitively to signs of distressed affect in their children (Stern et al. 1985). Tomkins suggests that caregivers influence their children's emotional development by expressing their own biases or patterns of emotional responding, as well their beliefs about the expression of emotion. Importantly they can shape children's 'ideoaffective organisation' by their responses to their children's displays of emotion. According to Bowlby (1981) the dyadic relationship is crucial to the development of emotional regulation as it is to the formation of cognitive structures such as internal working models. These factors stress the importance of parenting groups and interventions that encourage parents to adjust their responses to their children according to children's behaviour, for example, providing firm and consistent boundaries for inappropriate behaviours such as temper tantrums, but also being flexible to respond positively to their children's attempts to behave and display emotions appropriately.

Disorders of attachment

We have discussed how difficulties in attachment relationships manifest themselves, but what are the implications of these difficulties for child mental health?

Diagnostic manuals such as the *International Classification of Disorders* (ICD-10: WHO 1992) and *Diagnostic and Statistical Manual of Mental Disorders* (DSM-IV: American Psychiatric Association 1994) contain diagnostic criteria for attachment disorders. They explicitly state that no single diagnostic classification can cover the various types and severity of attachment disorders seen in clinical practice. ICD-10 outlines two diagnostic disorders of attachment. They are reactive attachment disorder (F94.1) and disinhibited attachment disorder (F94.2) and both have an effect on children's interpersonal and social functioning. The manifestation of a reactive attachment disorder is most noticeable in children's difficulty in developing appropriate social relationships. These children usually also demonstrate some degree of emotional disturbance with strong resistance to changes in their environment. In addition the children may show other behaviours such as fearfulness or hypervigilance, and may not be easily comforted. Some children often interact poorly with peers, and can be aggressive to others, or engage in self-harming behaviours. In some extreme cases there may also be growth retardation. The disorder is likely to occur because of parental neglect or serious mishandling. In clinical practice there is little doubt that reactive attachment disorder exists, but the boundaries of the disorder are unclear, as the behaviours tend to overlap with other disorders such as pervasive developmental disorder. Children with disinhibited attachment disorder at the age of about 2 years display a pattern of attachment that is non-selective. The main manifestation of the disorder is clinging behaviour directed towards certain attachment figures. It is a disorder most commonly found in children raised in institutions, but can occur in other environments where a child has had frequent changes in caregivers.

Attachment disorders in preschool and school-age children

These disorders can take many forms, but in preschool children behaviours such as a lack of attachment behaviour are not uncommon. These children appear at times to be in a world of their own and have difficulty forming peer relationships. Some children demonstrate social promiscuity by being over familiar with strangers and precocious in their behaviour, which also puts them at considerable risk.

Young children with reactive attachment disorder show an ambivalent pattern of social responses and this is most evident during partings and reunions with caregivers. These youngsters will show an unusual pattern of response to caregivers when being comforted, such as looking away from their caregivers. The children's reaction to their caregivers will often be ambivalent, a mixture of wanting to approach the caregivers or avoiding them, as if they are unsure how to respond. They may also show a disturbance in emotional responsiveness, such as withdrawing or aggression either directed towards themselves or others. These factors often impede peer relationships despite the child wanting to interact with other children. Children with disinhibited attachment disorder by the age of 4 years often present with attention-seeking behaviour, and on occasions they can be socially promiscuous with strangers.

A common manifestation in preschool and some school-age children is separation anxiety. This can present as a reluctance to separate from caregivers for even short periods, for instance when attending nursery or going to bed at night. In extreme cases some children will not even play a distance away from a caregiver, preferring to sit on the caregiver's lap. Other manifestations include excessive aggression with peers, psychosomatic disorders such as tummy ache and eating disorders. However, these behaviours can be seen in 'normal' children at times when they feel insecure and should not be confused with reactive attachment disorder, which is an abnormal type of insecurity. Clinical intervention for these children would involve determining the underlying reason for their insecurity, which could be wide-ranging such as parental illness, bullying,

parental divorce and bereavement. When the underlying cause is identified and treated, the child's behaviour usually improves. Children with
reactive attachment disorder show an abnormal pattern of insecurity
across differing social contexts, fail to respond to comforting, and usually show emotional disturbance in the form of apathy, misery or fearfulness.

Symptoms of attachment disorder change with developmental age,
and children with attachment disorders in middle and later childhood
frequently have difficulty forming appropriate attachment relationships.
They may show attention-seeking behaviour with difficulty in sustaining peer relationships. These children may also present with emotional
or behavioural disturbance. Some school-age children may present with
phobias, particularly in relation to school. In addition, these children
may present with underachievement in schoolwork and aggressive
behaviour.

Although children with attachment disorders start life with shaky
foundations, many of the difficult behaviours they experience can be
minimised by changes in their environment and by the responses of significant others. Children with reactive attachment disorder have the
capacity for social reciprocity, unlike children with pervasive developmental disorders. In extreme circumstances if children are removed from
harsh adverse parental environments and accommodated in good quality
foster care, many of the secondary emotional and behavioural difficulties that impair the children's mental health can be reduced. Preventive
work should involve effective multi-agency communication between
health, social services and education, and a common understanding of
the child's history and presenting problems. Schools can be instrumental
in providing a secure consistent environment for young people with
these difficulties by preventing labelling of the children, and working
closely with other agencies in attempting to ameliorate school phobia
and aggressive behaviours presenting in the children.

The interaction between developmental difficulties and the formation of attachment relationships

Proponents of attachment theory have recognised that factors within the
child could interfere with the development of a secure attachment relationship. Evidence is now emerging that negative emotionality in a child
is associated with an insecure attachment (Thompson, Connell and
Bridges 1988; Vaughn et al. 1992). Previously the source of disturbance

in attachment relationships was felt to result primarily from the caregiver's lack of consistency and responsiveness to the child's needs.

Premature infants are a group of children at particular risk. This is due to a number of factors in addition to the physical separation between caregiver and child following birth. The premature infant is nursed in an artificial environment, alien in comparison to the mother's womb. The neonate is often subjected to painful procedures. Until a few years ago it was believed that because of the immaturity of the neonate's sense receptors, poor myelination of nervous fibres and absence of subcortical reflex responses, the neonate would have a low perception of painful stimuli. Findings in the areas of neonatology and anaesthesia are now disproving these assumptions (Gasparoni *et al.* 1990). There is evidence of an increase in phobias, fears and early warning symptoms of a psychopathological nature in children who have a history of being hospitalised on neonatal units (Negri 1980).

Romana Negri is a consultant infant neuropsychiatrist who works with caregivers and infants in a neonatal unit in Italy; she aims to facilitate improvements in the mental health of neonates. Her work involves improving the relationship between infant and caregiver by minimising parental anxiety, because anxiety can seriously impede the development of a secure attachment relationship between caregiver and child. There is some limited evidence to suggest that caregivers of pre-term infants who engage in baby massage while their child is on the neonatal unit can develop a more fulfilling relationship with their infants, with both caregiver and baby enjoying the physical contact (Blakemore-Brown 2002).

This has implications for service delivery because the priority of neonatal units is to save the child's life and establish physiological homeostasis to promote normal healthy physical development. Romana Negri's work indicates that services should also consider therapeutic interventions such as baby massage on the units to foster secure attachment relationships between parent and child to facilitate the child's emotional development and minimise later mental health difficulties.

The dyadic relationship between caregiver and child is dependent on consistent responsive parenting, but it is equally dependent on the child's displays of attachment behaviour, such as crying and signals of contentment and reassurance, when comforted by the caregiver. A caregiver is more likely to respond positively to a child who smiles and coos when comforted or played with. The process of affective attunement relies on the caregiver's ability and willingness to respond to the child's displays of emotion, the child's ability to enjoy contact with the parent and express positive emotions, as well as recognise the caregiver's attempts to mirror the child's emotion. Therefore children with developmental difficulties that interfere with the development of social communication skills are likely to be compromised in attachment relationships. In these circumstances caregivers have to use all their resources to engage and form a rewarding relationship with their child.

There is limited literature investigating the incidence of insecure attachment in caregivers of children with autism. Children with autism characteristically have an inability to engage appropriately with others because of faulty interwoven patterns of sensory, communication and attentional skills. In early development, caregivers of an autistic child often notice a difference in the child's ability to interact when they compare them to their non-autistic children. This includes a lack of eye contact, and a lack of responsiveness to attempts at reciprocal touch, talk or gaze (Blakemore-Brown 2002).

Howlin (1998) conducted a controlled observational study with autistic and non-autistic children and their caregivers. It was evident during the study that when the caregivers of the non-autistic children played with the autistic children, their communication style became odd and stilted. However, when the caregivers of the autistic children were observed playing with the non-autistic children, their communication style reverted to a normal mode. This is an important study because it highlights the complexities involved in parenting a child with an autistic spectrum disorder. Health professionals should be as cautious in applying labels such as attachment disorder, as they are to applying labels of autistic spectrum disorder. Applying labels without extensive assessment, observation and multi-agency liaison should be avoided, because the consequence of misdiagnosis can seriously undermine the confidence of caregivers and could be even more detrimental to the relationship between caregiver and child.

Many children display behaviours evident of an autistic spectrum disorder, but the degree of their behavioural disturbance does not fulfil the criteria consistent with diagnostic classification. A number of children display subtle behaviours that are indicative but not diagnostic of a developmental disorder (e.g. mild autistic features). Nonetheless these behaviours may interfere with the development of a secure attachment relationship.

A good synonym to describe this complex interaction is the 'chicken or egg' scenario. What in fact comes first, the child's developmental difficulties, or the disturbed attachment relationship between the caregiver and child? Green *et al.* (2001) highlight the difficulty in differentiating between developmental vulnerability and relational factors underlying disorganised behaviour in children. Willensen-Swinkels *et al.* (2000) found that children with pervasive developmental delay demonstrated different attachment styles, but there was an increased incidence of disorganised attachment and this was most noticeable in children with learning disabilities. Likewise higher levels of infant disorganisation have been found in children with cognitive developmental delay in infancy and Down syndrome (Atkinson *et al.* 1999; Lyons-Ruth, Easterbrooks and Cibelli 1997). Evidence from animal studies indicates that stressful parenting can increase a child's tendency to show disorganising stress responses; low-contact parents can cause alterations in hypothalamopituitary axis functioning in their pups, resulting in the pups having heightened stress reactions in response to stressors. Spangler and Grossman (1999) cite evidence from longitudinal studies that disorganised behaviour is linked to higher levels of autonomic arousal and the adrenocortical response to stress associated with separations. An interactional model has been proposed that children with developmental disorders are more vulnerable and hence susceptible to disorganisations because of their lower resilience to low contact parenting (Barnett, Butler and Vondra 1999). The reality is that the child's behaviour difficulties represent an expression of the complex interaction between both these and many other factors.

Attention deficit hyperactivity disorder (ADHD) is a controversial diagnosis, and as yet there is no consistent theory of the origins of the disorder. A number of explanations have been proposed. These include genetic transmission, neurological anomalies, a disturbance in neurochemistry, viral infections, etc. The most popular theory to date is that the disorder is genetically inherited and this causes early neurological impairment of the developing brain. (Please see Chapter 5 by Banhatti in this volume for further details on ADHD.) Negri (1994), from her work with neonatal infants, believes that early attachment difficulties in infants lead to an increased incidence of autism and ADHD in children born prematurely and nursed on neonatal units. Ladnier and Massanari (2000) propose that many cases of ADHD have common features of an early history of childhood trauma and attachment difficulties. Ladnier and Massanari (2000) state that the early environment is as important in influencing the development of the child's brain as genetic inheritance, hence the child's early experiences will determine the quality and quantity of the development of neuronal circuits within the child's brain. They emphasise that the quality of the interactions between caregiver and child in the first three years of life will be the greatest influence in determining the course of the child's emotional development, and ability to learn and function as a psychologically healthy adult.

The work of the aforementioned authors has led to the development of an etiological model of ADHD based on developmental trauma (Ladnier and Massanari 2000). The model proposes that many children who present with ADHD have experienced some sort of disruption in attachment before the age of 2 years, which has resulted in developmental deficits in the child. The family system in which the child grows up is often dysfunctional and not able to provide a protective support system for the child. These influences are likely to be greater for children who already have some form of developmental difficulty arising from either the prenatal period, birth injury, premature birth or genetic transmission. This model highlights the importance of identifying the complex interaction of factors underlying the presentation of ADHD; as yet no single causative factor has been identified. Clinical interventions should therefore not just focus on pharmacological intervention but also relational factors impinging on the child.

Internal working models and attachment behaviour in adolescents

Bowlby (1969) stressed the importance of the strength of child and caregiver attachment relationships from the period of pre-adolescence to adulthood, suggesting that healthy self-reliance and individuation arise from a secure attachment (Grotevant and Cooper 1986; Steinberg 1990). Bowlby did not feel that adolescent rebellion was necessarily a sign of healthy individuation.

Freeman (1997) found that adolescents from secure dyads tended to cite caregivers as their primary attachment figure into early adulthood, to be eventually replaced by intimate partners. Secure adolescents also reported being able to communicate with parents about relationships and stressful situations. Adolescents classified as 'dismissing' or 'avoidant' had a tendency to name themselves as the primary attachment figure, while preoccupied or ambivalent adolescents were more likely to choose a sibling or a peer as an attachment figure.

Zimmerman and Grossman (1996) followed up adolescents whose attachment classifications had been previously made before the age of 6 years. They found that maternal attachment classifications predicted adolescent attachment style. However, this was found only in families where risk factors such as divorce, separation and life-threatening illness had not occurred. The longitudinal study found that children at 10 years of age who were found to have a dismissing or avoidant attachment style rated their mothers as being less available and they themselves tended to avoid problems in school.

The evidence indicates that there is some consistency in internal working models from early childhood to adolescence. However, stressful life events or trauma in the post-infancy period may disrupt the development and course of a secure attachment style. The implications of these findings stress the importance of identifying children that may be particularly vulnerable following stressful life events such as divorce and parental ill health, and providing them with supportive interventions.

Disorders of attachment in adolescence

Adolescence is a critical period for the development of self-reliance, and the negotiation between adolescent and caregiver of age-appropriate autonomy. Difficulties in attachment relationships can cause difficulties for adolescents with the process of individuation. Other problem behaviours noted in adolescents with attachment disorders include addictive symptoms, antisocial behaviour, delinquency, eating disorders, psychosomatic illness and self-harm.

An important cognitive ability that becomes most evident in adolescents is 'reflective function', an ability to evaluate oneself and the environment and construct a meaningful account of social interactions and life events (Fonagy 2000). Reflective function enables adolescents to develop the ability to interpret their own actions and the actions of others in a comprehensible and purposeful way thus facilitating social reciprocity. The development of this ability is dependent on the quality and quantity of early interactions between caregiver and child in early infancy as well as later childhood. Fonagy, Steele and Steele (1991) suggest that a secure attachment relationship offers the child conditions to learn about others' minds by exploring the mind of the caregiver during early interactions. By being exposed to the mental state of a sensitive and responsive caregiver the child finds an image of him- or herself in the caregiver's mind as a worthy human being motivated by beliefs, feelings and intentions. Hence a secure attachment is the core condition for the development of self-agency and reflective functioning in adolescence. Longitudinal research highlights the association between secure attachment, frustration tolerance, ego control, self-recognition, social cognition and emotional regulation (Fonagy *et al.* 1991, 1994; Meins *et al.* 1998). In some circumstances where there is a history of severe dysfunction in the parent–child relationship some adolescents never acquire the ability to develop a 'reflective function', and this results in an inability to develop a psychologically stable sense of self and trust in others. These adolescents tend to focus on their own distress and aspects of the environment that they feel they can manipulate and control. They will have difficulty with the development of the reflective process, and hence the ability to think flexibly and understand the mental states and intentions of others. Adolescents who have experienced severe maltreatment internalise a sense of badness; this will interfere with their sense of control, sense of self, and ability to regulate emotional distress. The adolescents may also have developed dysfunctional beliefs about the self and others that could lead to distorted relationship patterns and sense of agency (Pynoos, Steinberg and Wraith 1995), and could render them vulnerable to the development of personality difficulties in adulthood.

Therefore it is crucial for staff working with vulnerable adolescents to apply attachment principles in their work by encouraging openness (open communication unless the information is detrimental to the young person's well-being), the provision of choices, sensitivity and responsiveness. It is essential that health professionals provide adolescent clients with consistency, for example, following through an agreed plan of action, as well as being honest about difficulties that may be encountered. By providing these parameters consistently over time, health professionals may help to reduce the impact of children's pre-existing distorted beliefs about themselves and others, and their subsequent affects on social, emotional and interpersonal functioning.

Summary

Attachment theory provides a framework through which to understand the emotional development of children from birth to adolescence and into adulthood. The theory emphasises how environmental factors such as early interactions between caregiver and child in the first three years of life shape the development of the child's brain. Attachment theory provides an understanding of the development of mental health problems such as separation anxiety, school phobias, aggression and addictions in children and adolescence. It also provides a psychotherapeutic framework for working with children and adolescents as well as the systems within which they live.

Attachment theory can provide a framework to guide health professionals. It can also provide the tools and principles for health professionals and wider services to improve the mental health of children and young people. The basis of the theory is relatively simple and mirrors the ingredients of an early secure parent–child relationship, providing the child with sensitivity, consistency, recognition and containment of his or her emotional distress. By providing these ingredients children or adolescents should develop a more integrated sense of self, with an associated ability to regulate their emotions, and adopt a more adaptive view of themselves and others.

References

Ainsworth, M., Blehar, M., Waters, E. and Wall, S. (1978) *Patterns of Attachment: Assessed in the Strange Situation and at Home.* Hillsdale, NJ: Erlbaum.

American Psychiatric Association (APA) (1994) *Diagnostic and Statistical Manual of Mental Disorders,* 4th edn. Washington, DC: APA.

Atkinson, L., Chisholm, V.C., Scott, B., Goldberg, S., Vaughn, B.E., Blackwell, J., Dickens, S. and Tam, F. (1999) 'Maternal Sensitivity, Child Functional Level, and Attachment in Down Syndrome.' In J.I. Vondra and D. Barnett (eds) *Atypical Attachment in Infancy and Early Childhood among Children at Developmental Risk.* Monographs of the Society for Research in Child Development 64 (3, serial no. 258), Oxford: Blackwell.

Barnett, D., Butler, C.M. and Vondra, J.I (1999) 'Atypical Patterns of Early Attachment: Discussion and Future Directions.' In J.I. Vondra and D. Barnett (eds) *Atypical Attachment in Infancy and Early Childhood among Children at Developmental Risk.* Monographs of the Society for Research in Child Development, 64 (3, serial no. 258), Oxford: Blackwell.

Blakemore-Brown, L. (2002) *Reweaving the Autistic Tapestry: Autism, Asperger Syndrome and ADHD.* London: Jessica Kingsley Publishers.

Bowlby, J. (1969) *Attachment and Loss, Vol. 1, Attachment.* London: Hogarth Press; New York: Basic Books; Harmondsworth: Penguin Books, 1971, 2nd edn., 1982

Bowlby, J. (1978) 'Attachment Theory and its Therapeutic Implications.' In S.C. Feinstein and P.L. Giovacchini (eds) *Developmental and Clinical Studies.* New York: Jason Aronson.

Bowlby, J. (1979) *The Making and Breaking of Affectional Bonds.* London: Routledge.

Bowlby, J. (1981) 'Psychoanalysis as a Natural Science.' *International Review of Psychoanalysis 8,* 3, 243–256.

Brazelton, T.B. and Cramer, B. (1991) *The Earliest Relationship*. London: Karnac.

Feeney, J. and Noller, P. (1996) *Adult Attachment.* London: Sage.

Fonagy, P. (2000) 'The Development of Psychopathology from Infancy to Adulthood: The Mysterious Unfolding of Disturbance in Time.' Paper presented at the World Association of Infant Mental Health Congress, Montreal, Canada, January.

Fonagy, P., Steele, H. and Steele, M. (1991) 'Maternal Representations of Attachment during Pregnancy Predict the Organization of Infant–Mother Attachment at One Year of Age.' *Child Development 52*, 891–905.

Fonagy, P., Steele, M., Steele, H., Higgitt, A. and Target, M. (1994) 'The Emanuel Miller Memorial Lecture 1992: The Theory and Practice of Resilience.' *Journal of Child Psychology and Psychiatry and Allied Disciplines 35*, 231–257.

Freeman, H. (1997) 'Who Do You Turn To? Individual Differences in Late Adolescent Perceptions of Parents and Peers as Attachment Figures.' Unpublished doctoral dissertation, University of Wisconsin, Madison.

Gasparoni, M.C., Auriemma, A., Poggiani, G., Polito, E., Serafina, G. and Colombo, A. (1990) '11 dolore nel neonato. Atti del convegno – relazione 111.' Convegno di neonatologia della societa Italiana di pediatria Zingonia, January.

Gergeley, G. and Watson, J.S. (1999) 'Early Socio-emotional Development: Contingency Perception and Social-biofeedback Model.' In P. Rochet (ed) *Early Social Cognition: Understanding Others in the First Months of Life*. Hillsdale, NJ: Erlbaum.

Green, J.M., Goldwyn, R., Peters, S. and Stanley, C. (2001) 'Subtypes of Attachment Disorganisation in Young School Age Children.' Paper presented at the biennial meeting of the Society for Research on Child Development, Minneapolis, April.

Grotevant, H.D. and Cooper, C.R. (1986) 'Individuation in Family Relationships.' *Human Development 29*, 82–100.

Harlow, H. (1958) 'The Nature of Love.' *American Psychologist 13*, 673–685.

Howlin, P. (1998) *Children with Autism and Asperger Syndrome: A Guide for Practitioners and Carers*. Chichester: Wiley.

Ladnier, R.D. and Massanari, A.E. (2000) 'Treating ADHD as Attachment Deficit Hyperactivity Disorder.' In T.M. Levy (ed) *Attachment Interventions*. San Diego, CA: Academic Press.

Lorenz, K. (1952) *King Solomon's Ring*. London: Methuen.

Lyons-Ruth, K., Easterbrooks, A. and Cibelli, C. (1997) 'Infant Attachment Strategies, Infant Mental Health Lag and Maternal Depressive Symptoms: Predictor of Internalising and Externalising Problems at Age 7.' *Developmental Psychology 33*, 681–692.

Main, M. and Solomon, J. (1990) 'Procedures for Identifying Infants as Disorganised/Disorientated during Ainsworth's Strange Situation.' In M.T. Greenberg, D. Cichetti and E.M. Cummings (eds) *Attachment in the Pre-School Years: Theory Research and Prevention*. Chicago: University of Chicago Press.

Marvin, R., Cooper, G., Hoffman, K. and Powell, B. (2002) 'The Circle of Security Project: Attachment-based Intervention with Caregiver Pre-school Child Dyads.' *Attachment and Human Development 14*, 1, 107–124.

Meins, E., Fernyhough, C., Russell, J. and Clark-Carter, D. (1998) 'Security of Attachment as a Predictor of Symbolic and Mentalising Abilities: A Longitudinal Study.' *Social Development 7*, 1–24.

Meltzoff, A.N. (1990) 'Foundations for Developing a Concept of Self: The Role of Imitation in Relating Self to Other and the Value of Social Mirroring, Social Modelling and Self Practice in Infancy.' In D. Cicchetti and M. Beeghley (eds) *The Self in Transition: Infancy to Childhood.* Chicago: University of Chicago Press.

Meltzoff, A.N. and Moore, M.K. (1989) 'Imitation in Newborn Infants: Exploring the Range of Gestures Imitated and the Underlying Mechanisms.' *Developmental Psychology 25*, 954–962.

Meltzoff, A.N. and Moore, M.K. (1994) 'Imitation, Memory and the Representation of Persons.' *Infant Behaviour and Development 17*, 83–99.

Negri, R. (1980) 'Problemi metodologici della prevenzione del neonato a rischio.' *Neuropsichiatria Infantile 230–231*, 859–878.

Negri, R. (1994) *The Newborn in the Intensive Care Unit: A Neuropsychoanalytic Prevention Model.* London: Clunie Press (Karnac).

Pynoos, R.S., Steinberg, A.M. and Wraith, R. (1995) 'A Developmental Model of Childhood Traumatic Stress.' In D. Cicchetti and D.J. Cohen (eds) *Developmental Psychopathology, Volume 2. Risk and Disorder and Adaptation.* New York: Wiley.

Robertson, J. and Bowlby, J. (1952) 'A Two-year-old Goes to Hospital: A Scientific Film.' *Proceedings of the Royal Society of Medicine 46*, 425–427.

Rutter, M. (1995) 'Clinical Implications of Attachment Concepts: Retrospect and Prospect.' *Journal of Child Psychology and Psychiatry 36*, 4, 549–571.

Schore, A.N. (1996) 'The Experience-dependent Maturation of a Regulatory System in the Orbital Prefrontal Cortex and the Origin of Developmental Psychopathology.' *Development and Psychopathology 8*, 59–88.

Spangler, G. and Grossman, K. (1999) 'Individual and Psychological Correlates of Attachment Disorganisation in Infancy.' In J. Solomon and C. George (eds) *Attachment Disorganisation.* New York: Guilford.

Steinberg, L. (1990) 'Autonomy, Conflict and Harmony in the Family Relationship.' In S.S. Feldman and G.R. Elliott (eds) *At the Threshold: The Developing Adolescent.* Cambridge, MA: Harvard University Press.

Stern, D. (1985) *The Interpersonal World of the Infant.* New York: Basic Books

Stern, D.N., Hofer, L., Haft, W. and Dore, J. (1985) 'Affect Attunement: The Sharing of Feeling States between Mother and Infant by Means of Inter-modal Fluency.' In T.M. Fields and N.A. Fox (eds) *Social Perception in Infants.* Norwood, NJ: Ablex.

Thompson, R.A., Connell, J.P. and Bridges, L.J. (1988) 'Temperament, Emotions and Social Interactive Behaviour in the Strange Situation: An Analysis of Attachment System Functioning.' *Child Development 59*, 1102–1110.

Tomkins, S.S. (1993) *Affect, Imagery, Consciousness, Volume 3, Anger and Fear*. New York: Springer.

Van Ijzendoorn, M.H. (1995) 'Adult Attachment Representations, Parental Responsiveness and Infant Attachment: A Meta-analysis on the Predictive Validity of the Adult Attachment Interview.' *Psychological Bulletin 117*, 387–403.

Van Ijzendoorn, M.H. and Kroonenberg, P.M. (1988) 'Cross Cultural Patterns of Attachment: A Meta-analysis of the Strange Situation.' *Child Development 59*, 147–156.

Vaughn, B.E., Stevenson-Hinde, J., Waters, E., Kotsaflis, A., Lefever, G.B., Shouldice, A., Trudel, M. and Belsky, J. (1992) 'Attachment Security and Temperament in Infancy and Early Childhood: Some Conceptual Clarifications.' *Developmental Psychology 28*, 463–473.

Watson, J.S. (1994) 'Detection of Self: The Perfect Algorithm.' In S.T. Parker, R.W. Mitchell and M.L. Boccia (eds) *Self-Awareness in Animals and Humans Developmental Perspectives*. New York: Cambridge University Press.

World Health Organization (1992) *The International Statistical Classification of Diseases and Related Health Problems, Tenth Revision*. Geneva: WHO.

Willensen-Swinkels, S.H.N., Bakermans-Kroneburg, M.J., Buitelaar, M.H. and Van Ijzendoorn, M.H. (2000) 'Insecure and Disorganised Attachment in Children with a Pervasive Developmental Disorder: Relationship with Social Interaction and Heart Rate.' *Journal of Child Psychology and Psychiatry 41*, 759–769.

Zimmerman, P. and Grossman, K. (1996) 'Transgenerational Aspects of Stability in Attachment Quality between Parents and their Adolescent Children.' Paper presented at the biennial meeting of the International Society for the Study of Behavioural Development, Quebec City, Canada, December.

Chapter 4

Emotion Regulation and Mental Health

Kedar Nath Dwivedi

Emotional competence includes how emotions are acknowledged, expressed and regulated or managed. Emotions involve at least three components (Rutter 1980):

- physiological changes in both the central and the autonomic nervous system
- a feeling state which has immediate meaning and significance for the individual
- a bodily expression in terms of vocalisation, facial activity and patterning, together with bodily posture and movement.

Even in newborn babies it is possible to discern the precursors of emotional responding. There appear to be three basic patterns: a state of contentment, a state of distress, and a state of cataleptic immobility. Cataleptic immobility occurs in infants of all species and consists of sudden motionlessness with sleep-like respiration and staring non-convergent eyes. Such a response is usually triggered by a dangerous situation. In human infants these cataleptic immobility responses disappear usually after two months. However, many of their features may reappear in the form of catatonic and hypnotic phenomena in life.

A whole range of factors influences the development of emotional competence. Just as the growth of a plant depends upon the quality of its seed, manure, water, air, sunshine and so on, similarly emotional development depends not only upon the genetic and biological potentials, but also upon the extent of concurrent cognitive and motor development, cultural context and the quality of parenting, training and so on. Just as the ability to walk and talk and to become dry and clean (i.e. urinary and faecal continence) depends upon the training one receives, similarly the development of emotional competence is also dependent on the quality of the training that the child receives. The process of emotional development has several aspects, such as differentiation, self-regulation, desomatisation and utilisation.

Emotional differentiation and acknowledgement

One of the important aspects of development of emotional competence is emotional differentiation. Out of the two basic emotional states of contentment and distress a huge variety of specific emotions emerge, such as anger, jealousy, guilt, joy, pride, delight, love, anxiety, shame, humiliation, disgust and so on. A study in Amsterdam, Oxford and a remote village in eastern Nepal revealed a similar developmental pattern of emotional understanding in children (Harris *et al.* 1987).

It is suggested that there are several steps in the development of 'theory of mind' or mind-reading ability in normal children (Baron-Cohen 1997; Happe 1994). These are as follows:

- joint attention, i.e. looking where another is looking (by 1 year)
- inferring goal from gaze, i.e. understanding that behaviour is goal directed and that goals or intention can be deduced from behaviour e.g. gaze (by 2 years)
- mentally labelling objects, i.e. first evidence of meta-representation (from 2½ years as evidenced in pretend play)
- talking about mental states, i.e. growing awareness that you can think about your own thoughts (by 30 months): 'You know what? Mummy thought I was asleep but I was just pretending!'
- understanding that seeing leads to knowing, i.e. an awareness of the unique and personal nature of knowledge derived from perception (by 3 years)
- understanding the mental–physical distinction, i.e. distinguishing mental entities from physical ones, showing a greater understanding of the ethereal nature of mental

constructs, e.g. Jane has a biscuit, Harry is thinking about a biscuit, who can eat their biscuit? (from 3 years)

- understanding true belief: e.g. John believes his dog is in his bedroom, Rob believes the dog is in the kitchen, where will John/Rob look for the dog? (from 3 years)

- understanding false belief which includes understanding that people will act on their beliefs even if these conflict with reality, e.g. if John believes his dog is in the bedroom he will look there even if the dog is in fact in the garden (from 3 years)

- understanding the appearance–reality distinction, i.e. when shown an ambiguous object such as a stone egg, children with a mental age of 3 or over can normally say what it looks like and what it is

- deception emerges in normal children at around 4 years of age; by 5 years most children show deliberate manipulation of others' intentional states and comprehend the nature of deception as deliberately manipulating another's knowledge by giving them a false belief.

In some children, the process of emotional differentiation may be poor. It is not rare to meet children who are emotionally illiterate, who cannot identify more than a limited number of feelings such as boredom, anger, etc. This may be due to poor training. Conditions conducive of attachment disorder can increase the vulnerability for this. Problems of emotional differentiation are also seen in autistic spectrum disorder and alexithymia. Alexithymia is a construct with cognitive and affective characteristics that have been found in many patients with psychosomatic illness, substance abuse, post-traumatic stress disorder and eating disorders. The features include difficulty identifying and describing subjective feelings, difficulty distinguishing between feelings and bodily sensations of emotional arousal, constricted imaginal capacity (paucity of fantasies) and externally oriented cognitive style.

In a study by Denham et al. (2002) children's deficits in emotional knowledge assessed at age 3 and 4 predicted subsequent aggression. This has particular importance as preschool disruptive behaviour can be associated with later psychopathology including delinquency, school failure and substance abuse. It has also been found that aggressive children are more likely to have impulsive and hostile attributions of others in social interactions with peers.

Thus, the extent of cognitive development has an influence on the nature and comprehension of emotional experiences. For example, mixed feelings are not understood during pre-operational phase (Piaget 1970). Similarly young children have difficulty in realising that one can hide one's true feelings or can put one's feelings out of their awareness. The fact that feelings can also be preconscious begins to be appreciated by adolescence. During the phase of egocentric thinking (2–4 years), children tend to understand the causes of others' feelings in terms of their own.

The context always has a very powerful influence on the constructions placed on emotion. Cultural factors determine which emotions are sanctioned and those which are discouraged. Descriptions and analysis of emotions are fundamentally culturally constructed and constituted. These are appraisals that guide people in what they feel and experience. Furthermore, just like individuals, cultures can also be young or mature. For example, in the Indian cultural context, as early as in the sixth century BC, a detailed, coherent and systematised theory of consciousness became available, something that began to happen in Western science only in the nineteenth century AD (Reat 1990).

Culture influences the process of emotional maturation and development of perspectives and skills for their constructive management (Dwivedi 1996, 1997a; Lokare 1997). Not only the emotional concepts but also their location and meaning may be different in various cultures. For example, in the Indian theory of *Rasa*, emotions are grounded not only in mind and body but also in food, nature, music, play, seasons and scent. The theory of *Rasa* was established several millennia ago, as evident in Bharat's (200 BC) *Treatise on Dramatology* (*Natyashastra*) concerning the enjoyment and purpose of play, poetry, dance, ritual and so on (de Barry *et al*. 1958). The main purpose of these aesthetic forms has been to activate and refine the emotions already present and also to help their transformation into divine bliss inherent in all humans.

Self-regulation, tolerance and management of emotions

The second aspect of emotional maturation involves self-regulation (Fisher *et al*. 1992) and the development of an increasing capacity to tolerate emotions. In order to facilitate the development of tolerance, parents allow their infants to experience emotions but intervene to protect them from being overwhelmed by excessively intense or prolonged emotions (Dwivedi 1993a). Such interventions have a dual function. On the one hand, children are protected from being traumatised by overwhelming, unbearable and shattering emotional experiences while on the other hand, this protection enables children to learn themselves to use some soothing, comforting or distracting strategies. This helps the development of an increasing capacity to tolerate emotions through self-regulation of affect. We all know that some babies when they wake up at night cannot settle again unless they are fed. Others can manage their feelings with the help of breast substitutes such as their thumb or dummies. Still others can easily satisfy themselves through hallucinating a breast and sucking it (Krystal 1988).

The acquisition of a capacity for emotional tolerance through self-regulation of affect develops through identifying with parental interventions and in the context of parental encouragement. As the babies grow, they can identify with their caregivers and can initiate self-soothing or comforting interventions themselves, as soon as their emotions begin to exceed their capacity to tolerate. Good enough parents enable their children to exercise such measures for self-regulation of their emotional states. However, self-regulation and tolerance of emotions can be affected in many ways. If a parent has general aversion to physical contact or feels jealous of any other soothing object, children may be discouraged or even punished for any self-soothing activity. These children are unable to develop a sense of accessibility to the automatically controlled parts of themselves or to their affect regulatory functions. Such a developmental incapacity can lead to a variety of mental health problems such as psychosomatic illnesses, substance abuse, total dependence on one's partner for sexual arousal and so on (Krystal 1988).

There are a number of developmental games that promote the child's confidence and trust that the primary object is still there with whom reunion will occur (despite separation from the object). Therefore, in order to master the distressing feelings of separation anxiety children are helped to participate in a normal developmental line with a sequence of certain interactive play proceeding from 'peekaboo' to object tossing, being chased, hide and seek, bye-bye and so on (Kleeman 1967, 1973). Those who have not been enabled to master their distressing separation anxiety feelings in this way tend to continue creating situations whereby they might be chased and held, as if needing to play such developmental games in a disguised form. This manifests as disorders of conduct, running away, violence, joy riding and so on in order to engage others in disguised developmental play (Willock 1990).

Attachment is another aspect of the developmental process. It may begin as a stimulation-seeking behaviour. Even babies exhibit stimulation-seeking behaviours. In the beginning these behaviours are non-specific, but soon the baby begins to approach particularly stimulating objects. This is described as attachment (and bonding by the parent). In times of distress there is a heightened need for proximity (such as soothing body contact) with the attachment figures. So tiredness, illness or strange environment can lead to such a proximity-seeking behaviour. Under stress, there is a need to seek proximity with the familiar person or environment, even though that very person or the environment may be the cause of the stress. Adults too may feel the same need as evidenced in the prolongation of marital disharmony.

Some individuals may have a much stronger predisposition to stimulation-seeking behaviour. If the stress is too severe, intense, chronic or prolonged or the attachment figures rejecting, physically or emotionally unavailable, then the stimulation-seeking behaviour can become rather generic, indiscriminate and disorganised, appearing even hostile and violent. Even in adults, the desire to reach out and touch some one can become so intense that it can become disguised, confused, hurtful, even fatal (Mawson 1987).

The concept of disorganised attachment (Green and Goldwyn 2002) i.e. exhibiting a variety of contradictory or bizarre responses (Main, Kaplan and Cassidy 1985) appears to be more predictive of psychopathology. The base rate of disorganisation in low-risk families has been found to be 15 per cent, and in high-risk families the rate is about 80 per cent (Van Ijzendoorn, Marcoen and Schoefs 1996). Parenting factors such as severe and/or chronic maternal depression, disrupted affective communication, hostile/intrusive parental behaviours, dissociative states, unresolved loss and trauma seem to be associated with disorganised attachment. The sequelae of disorganised attachment include bizarre fantasy, poor self-esteem, disorganised cognitions, poor social perception, contradictory ambivalent responses, emotional disturbance, hypervigilance and arousal, aggressiveness and controlling interactions with others. Children with disorganised attachment are highly vulnerable to attachment disorders.

The living environment for a toddler is like a jungle. As the toddler becomes mobile, he or she begins to explore the environment by climbing, running, pushing, pulling, biting, poking and so on. The parents need to keep a close enough eye on such an adventurer, because these exciting objects can also attack, cut, hurt, bite, shout, poison, burn or electrocute and they can be experienced as very frightening 'beasts'. If the parents are neglectful or hurtful themselves, the child may go on engaging in risky behaviours to elicit parental concern and may have no other option than to employ the primitive aggressive defences of the jungle to cope. These behaviours can then become habitual, increasing the vulnerability for the development of mental and personality disorders.

Children can be exposed to emotional experiences that may be excessive. If the caregiver is unable to protect the child from overwhelming emotions, a state of psychic trauma can threaten to destroy all psychic functioning. For the child, such trauma means shattering of psychic or ego functions, a state of disorganisation, timeless horror, an unbearable hell, an utter helplessness. Subsequently such emotions are perceived as particularly dangerous and the child will grow up dreading such dangerous feelings (e.g. of abandonment, rejection, etc.). At the slightest possibility of such a feeling arising into consciousness, the child panics at the prospect of being flooded by it. Therefore, various strategies may be evoked to defend against being overwhelmed. These strategies often include induction of altered states of consciousness either psychologically (through anger, dissociation), physically (through soothing or distracting rituals, overbreathing, violent or destructive outbursts) or chemically (through substance abuse) thus increasing the vulnerability for mental and personality disorders.

The mental mechanism of dissociation can be induced as a protective device when a child is faced with intolerable assault, hurt, torture, torment or abuse and is helpless or unable to avoid or escape from it. In such a state of inescapable suffering the child's natural defence mechanisms enable them to detach emotionally and dissociate from the otherwise unavoidable pain. This may manifest as experience of floating near the ceiling and looking at what is happening, becoming part of the wall, taking imaginary walks, becoming the long hand of the clock, holding the breath to stop crying, and other means of inducing self-hypnotic trance, dissociation and anaesthesia. It can also lead to identification with the aggressor. When the child grows up and has violent outbursts, these are triggered by the subtle reminders of the hurtful past experience.

The process of identification can be so subtle that the child even sounds, talks and appears like the aggressor, as if 'bewitched' or 'possessed' by the mental state belonging to the aggressor (Dwivedi 1993b, 1993c). The child may not remember the incidents or the feeling of hurt, but acts it out as a substitute for memory. The traumatic experiences from the preverbal periods can perhaps be communicated only through action. Thus, within a violent individual is a screaming child feeling hurt. Without help, the individual is unable to make contact with the feelings of hurt in the screaming child within and to comfort it. If this could happen, the need for dissociation or for the identification with the aggressor would diminish.

Emotional processing occurs spontaneously throughout life and involves modification of memory structures that underlie emotions (Foa and Kozak 1986). Thus emotional responses increase or decrease with experience. Once one has perceived one's life from a certain point of view, for example, serious depression, the process of sensitisation makes it much easier to take on that perspective in the future. Also, an experience of major emotional dysregulation through the process of 'kindling' places the person at risk for subsequent mood dysregulation (Munoz 1998). Kindling was discerned in animals in relation to seizure. Accordingly, once a stimulus of high intensity has triggered seizure response in an animal, the process of kindling enables the animal subsequently to respond to low-intensity stimulus with seizure as well. In the past, before kindling, the low-intensity stimulus would not have been able to trigger the seizure response. This concept of kindling has also been applied to human affective disorders as well.

Desomatisation and expression

The third developmental aspect of emotional competence is desomatisation. In the beginning, all emotional expression or its communication is through somatic or massive bodily responses. However, with maturation, motor control, cognitive development and learning one begins to use various symbolic gestures (such as for initiating comforting, expressing affection, separation, loss, anger and so on) and words. Such a development is heavily influenced by caregivers helping the child acquire various verbal and nonverbal communication skills and to identify and articulate their feelings and needs. An integral part of good parenting is the great pleasure that the caregivers take in the slightest difference in baby's vocalisations and their encouragement of the growing child to recognise and put their feelings into words rather than just act these out. However, in certain families, communication of emotions may be discouraged leading to an increased emphasis on internal responses to stress and to psychosomatic illnesses. Similarly, some parents may respond only to intensely emotionally charged communications. The child, therefore, has to continue to use emotions to communicate or control others and develops a histrionic style of relating.

Utilisation

The fourth aspect of emotional maturation is utilisation. Growing self-awareness enables children to begin to treat their emotions as signals to themselves so that emotional energy can be utilised for problem solving, planning and implementing of constructive strategies. As children mature they also learn how to get in touch with their almost hidden feelings and how to explore an apparent complexity of feelings. They appreciate the role of these feelings in a whole range of mental and physical activities and begin to learn to utilise this important channel of influence.

The psyche is a complex hierarchical structure of systems or programmes involving feeling, thinking and behaviour. Emotions endow these programmes with a specific qualitative value such as motivation. They also connect cognitive elements and contribute to their storage and mobilisation according to context. Thus, emotions play a central role not only in organising and integrating cognition but also in a variety of mental functions, such as motivation, information processing, memory, behaviour and so on (Ciompi 1991).

However, most of the time, the emotional aspects of these mental operations may remain preconscious. The Freudian view of emotion was influenced by hydraulics. For example, temper builds up, and then it is discharged. Or lust keeps growing until consumed and starts again. In the East, for example, in India, as early as the sixth century BC, there was already a coherent theory of emotions. Accordingly, there was no state of emotionlessness, just as there is no state of weatherlessness, as there is always weather. By expanding or intensifying one's consciousness through meditation, it is possible to become aware of emotions that would have otherwise been preconscious. In the Eastern cultures, this fact has been utilised for many millennia for mental cultivation through meditation (Dwivedi 1994a, 1994b, 2002). If we can create a space of awareness, reflection and metaperspective around our experiences, processes, interactions, etc., this is supposed to lead to happiness, otherwise to misery, as apparent from the epistemology of the Sanskrit words *Sukha* and *Dukha*. *Sukha* means happiness and *Dukha* means misery or suffering. In their epistemology, *Kha* means space, *Su* means good and *Du* means bad. Therefore, *Sukha* is good space and *Dukha* is bad space. Here space is in the sense of clearance between the hub and the axle of a wheel, in other words, space of awareness and reflection around experiences, processes, interactions, etc.

If a child does not learn how to utilise the emotional experience as a signal for initiating constructive action and use its energy for implementing such an action, this may lead to an experience of panic, crippling the individual. When emotions become intense, not only do they break into conscious awareness, but also their excessive intensity can even trigger a chain of disastrous consequences such as violent or destructive acting out, alcohol and drug abuse, psychosomatic illness and even psychogenic death. The Eastern approaches have further developed the utilisation aspect of emotional maturation for the purposes of dealing with overwhelming feelings and in fact, as a means of achieving enlightenment. Otherwise, faced with an intense feeling, we usually feel as if an emotional state is everlasting and forget the fact that all emotions are only transient and if we do not fight, indulge or actively avoid, they will just run their course. The meditative practices often involve harnessing their energy for creative and constructive purposes, analogous to taming a tiger (Dwivedi 1990; Rinpoche 1987).

Emotional responding

We all know that our minds are very skilled in mixing the real with the unreal, so that it is difficult to take them apart; it is just like milk mixed with water. For example, if some one becomes insulting, hurtful or nasty, it would be natural to feel hurt or angry. Immediately, within split seconds the breathing, heart rate, blood pressure, skin conductance, etc. can change dramatically. These changes may take place even without our knowledge and certainly without our permission, as if someone has pushed a button. Nowadays technology has advanced so much that we have touch-screens, remote control and all sorts of timing devices. Human machinery is equally sophisticated. There is a variety of ways in which it can get turned on and off. And once it is turned on, it can stay on for some time.

So, we remain in such a state of mind even after the person has stopped being hurtful. The mind keeps going over and over the said phrases, the demeanour, the tone, the look, the accent and so on. It gets glued to these mental objects (which are just memories in this instance). This keeps stirring up the feelings of hurt, anger, etc. Even if someone else may be nice to us, we might not notice this because the mind is too busy with the other (hurtful) mental object. Eventually, maybe after an hour or so, we might feel not so churned up; those feelings might go out of our consciousness and become latent or dormant.

However, later in the day, even if we are in a pleasant situation, we might suddenly remember the event and once again the heart rate, breathing, etc. changes dramatically. No one is insulting us then, it is purely a memory but the mind treats it as if it is real. Even the next day, the day after and so on, the same thing may happen again and again. People who have had very traumatic experiences know how distressing these flashbacks can be.

Mental objects (memories) that stir up feelings don't have to be only memories involving ourselves. Even imagination or fantasy about third parties can have a similar effect. For example, if we watch a horror film at night, most of us would feel scared, although there is no real creature or blood, but only a glass screen, light, shade and electronics. The windows and curtains that felt so warm during the day may appear infested with ghostly beings. An erotic film can in a similar way produce arousal in the viewer, although no one is doing anything in reality to him or her. Thus, our minds are very skilled in mixing the real with the unreal.

It is also possible that when we feel angry, we may feel so angry that we may even lash out and attack. So, it seems as if there are three layers of emotional responding. When the particular feeling is dormant or latent, it is as if in the first layer. When it has been stirred up by the mental object, it is in the second layer, and when it spills over into physical or verbal action, it is in the third layer. Between the second and third layer, there is a kind of gear box. Thus the relationship between the amount of feelings and the amount of action depends upon the gear we are in. Sometimes we can put our car into neutral gear and rev the engine but the car doesn't move. This is similar to what happens in dreams: a lot of feelings, but no bodily movements. On a slope the car can keep running down in the neutral gear without the accelerator being pressed; similarly, in a group situation, one can get easily carried away with certain actions without much feeling. It is not uncommon to see fewer feelings leading to more actions or more feelings leading to less action depending upon which gear one is in. Many readers will also have come across the reverse gear, where people feel one thing but behave in an opposite way.

Enhancing emotion regulation

From the Buddhist point of view, meditation helps with emotion regulation in several ways, for example, by:

- developing wisdom and cutting through the deep-rooted sense of 'self' as a product of illusory processes and not taking things personally
- expanding our consciousness, becoming aware of subtle emotions and thus, better managing various mental operations
- early detection of emotional processes to initiate interventions or coping strategies
- harnessing the energy inherent in emotions to use for constructive and creative purposes.

Some of the meditative practices e.g. from Buddhist teachings can thus be of enormous help in improving emotion regulation in a variety of ways. By learning to expand one's consciousness, one can become aware of even subtler (otherwise preconscious) emotions and thus, better manage various mental operations (such as information processing, learning, memory, decision making, creativity, motivation and so on). By early detection of emotional processes, one can promptly initiate coping strategies or interventions before the emotions grow to produce a crippling effect.

Public health programmes

Programmes facilitating the development of emotional competence can feed the roots of a variety of initiatives for mental health. An urgent need for several prevention initiatives for child mental health, such as for disaffected children, disruptive, antisocial, bullying and violent behaviours, teenage pregnancy, post-traumatic stress, deliberate self-harm, depression, anxiety disorder, eating disorder, school refusal and effect of bereavement, separation, divorce and parental mental disorder and so on, has already been identified (Dwivedi 2000a; Dwivedi and Varma 1997a, 1997b; Royal College of Psychiatrists 2002).

Child mental health is everyone's business. For example, emotional development needs to be an integral part of the school curriculum, school ethos and school life, just as it needs to be an integral part of parenting, family life, work life and the health services (Orbach 1998). Schools have a critical role to play in creating emotionally competent children (Mental Health Foundation 1999). This can include extra-curricular (such as a mental health promotion initiative), integrated (as part of the school curriculum such as PSHE, i.e. personal, social and health education) or infused (as part of academic subjects such as emotional communication skill as part of language class) activities (please also see Chapter 8 by Coley and Dwivedi in this volume). PATHS (Promoting Alternative Thinking Strategies) is a school-based intervention designed to improve children's ability to discuss and understand emotions (Greenberg *et al.* 1995). The possibilities are countless and each school can be unique in the way its creativity manifests in this matter beyond the recipe books (Dwivedi 2004). For example, children already exhibiting problems of emotional development in the form of conduct disorders or emotional disturbance and therefore vulnerable to further mental and personality disorders may be offered training in emotional management skills. Skilfully conducted group work can offer a valuable opportunity for children to catch up with various aspects of their emotional development (Dwivedi 1993d).

Effective group work can enhance self-esteem, prosocial skills, emotion regulation, self-control and ability for reality testing. To be effective, it has to be gradual, systemic and experiential, in the sense that different aspects of emotional and cognitive processes are not only intellectualised but also experienced in a safe and contained manner and their maturational milestones are gradually mastered in a supportive atmosphere. Group work can utilise the psychotherapeutic principles of positive mirroring and merging. Positive mirroring and merging are the processes that are also involved in the development of central ego or the 'feel good factor'. Through mirroring the baby feels delighted in the delight of the parent, who is delighted in the delight of the baby. As a baby has limited abilities, it is unable to handle the world adequately but can do so through the parents, who appear to become omnipotent and almighty for the baby. A sense of belonging or merging with such an omnipotent being makes one feel equally omnipotent oneself. Group work can recreate opportunities for such mirroring and merging. Group work also provides opportunities for using stories, enactment and play, etc., which have powerful therapeutic impact on human development, insight, emotional management and behaviour (Dwivedi 1997b, 1997c, 2000b).

Inadequate or inappropriate parenting can lead to poor or defective emotional development. For example, emotional differentiation depends upon learning about different emotions. If children do not get enough guidance, they may not be able to learn to differentiate between different emotions. Desomatisation involves a shift from using only bodily or somatic expressions to also using symbolic and linguistic ones. However, adequate parenting is essential for not only developing such communication skills but also for discerning and articulating one's emotional states and needs. The ways in which the significant others cope with their own feelings and facilitate, encourage, direct or control others' handling of feelings have an important impact on children's emotional development.

Therefore, enhancing parenting skills is one of the most important contributory factors in the development of emotional competence in children (Dwivedi 1997d, 2002). Various developmental aspects of emotional skills, just like the development of speech, walking and sphincter control, require appropriate help and training from caregivers (Dwivedi 1993a). Some parents are unable to facilitate adequate emotional development of their children. This may be either because of their lack of awareness, their own emotional immaturity or because of their preoccupation with their own emotional needs due to marital, alcohol, financial, housing and employment problems. Such parents do need help with their parenting skills.

In conclusion, emotion regulation is the most essential component of mental health and requires full attention of any society interested in it. Emotion dysregulation can lead to a variety of mental and personality disorders. Similarly, the development of emotion regulation is influenced by parenting, schooling, psychoeducational and socialising opportunities.

References

Baron-Cohen, S. (1997) *Mind Blindness: An Essay on Autism and Theory of Mind: Learning, Development and Conceptual Change.* Cambridge, MA: The MIT Press.

Ciompi, L. (1991) 'Affect as Central Organising and Integrating Factors: A New Psychosocial/Biological Model of the Psyche.' *British Journal of Psychiatry 159*, 97–105.

de Barry, W.T., Hay, S., Weiler, R. and Yarrow, A. (1958) *Sources of Indian Tradition.* New York: Columbia University Press.

Denham, S.A., Caverly, S., Schmidt, M., Blair, K., Demulder, E., Caal, S., Hamada, H. and Mason, T. (2002) 'Preschool Understanding of Emotions: Contributions to Classroom Anger and Aggression.' *Journal of Child Psychology and Psychiatry 43*, 7, 901–916.

Dwivedi, K.N. (1990) 'Purification of Mind by Vipassana Meditation.' In J. Crook and D. Fontana (eds) *Space in Mind.* Shaftesbury: Elements.

Dwivedi, K.N. (1993a) 'Emotional Development.' In K.N. Dwivedi (ed) *Group Work with Children and Adolescents*. London: Jessica Kingsley Publishers.

Dwivedi, K.N. (1993b) 'Child Abuse and Hatred.' In V.P. Varma (ed) *How and Why Children Hate*. London: Jessica Kingsley Publishers.

Dwivedi, K.N. (1993c) 'Confusion and Underfunctioning in Children.' In V.P. Varma (ed) *How and Why Children Fail*. London: Jessica Kingsley Publishers.

Dwivedi, K.N. (1993d) 'Group Work in Child Mental Health Services.' In K.N. Dwivedi (ed) *Group Work with Children and Adolescents*. London: Jessica Kingsley Publishers.

Dwivedi, K.N. (1994a) 'Social Structures that Support or Undermine Families from Ethnic Minority Groups: Eastern Value Systems.' *Context 20*, 11–12.

Dwivedi, K.N. (1994b) 'Mental Cultivation (Meditation) in Buddhism.' *Psychiatric Bulletin 18*, 503–504.

Dwivedi, K.N. (1996) 'Meeting the Needs of Ethnic Minority Children.' *Psychiatry On-Line: An International Journal of Psychiatry* (Transcultural Mental Health On Line) 1.0 www.priory.com/journals/chneeds.htm

Dwivedi, K.N. (1997a) 'Introduction.' In K.N. Dwivedi and V.P. Varma (eds) *Depression in Children and Adolescents*. London: Whurr.

Dwivedi, K.N. (ed) (1997b) *Therapeutic Use of Stories*. London: Routledge.

Dwivedi, K.N. (1997c) 'Management of Anger and some Eastern Stories.' In K.N. Dwivedi (ed) *Therapeutic Use of Stories*. London: Routledge.

Dwivedi, K.N. (ed) (1997d) *Enhancing Parenting Skills*. Chichester: Wiley.

Dwivedi, K.N. (ed) (2000a) *Post-traumatic Stress Disorder in Children and Adolescents*. London: Whurr.

Dwivedi, K.N. (2000b) 'Therapeutic Powers of Narratives and Stories.' *Context 47*, 11–12.

Dwivedi, K.N. (2002) 'Culture and Personality.' In K.N. Dwivedi (ed) *Meeting the Needs of Ethnic Minority Children*. London: Jessica Kingsley Publishers.

Dwivedi, K.N. (2004) 'Addressing Emotional and Behavioural Issues in Schools through Self-management Training: Theory and Practice.' In J. Wearmouth (ed) *Approaches to Understanding Student Behaviour*. Milton Keynes: Open University.

Dwivedi, K.N. and Varma, V.P. (eds) (1997a) *Depression in Children and Adolescents*. London: Whurr.

Dwivedi, K.N. and Varma, V.P. (eds) (1997b) *A Handbook of Childhood Anxiety Management*. Aldershot: Arena.

Fisher, L., Nakell, L.C., Terry, H.E. and Ransom, D.C. (1992) *Family Process 31*, 269–287.

Foa, E.B. and Kozak, M.J. (1986) 'Emotional Processing and Fear: Exposure to Corrective Information.' *Psychological Bulletin 99*, 1, 20–35.

Green, J. and Goldwyn, R. (2002) 'Annotation: Attachment Disorganisation and Psychopathology: New Findings in Attachment Research and their Potential Implications for Developmental Psychopathology in Childhood.' *Journal of Child Psychology and Psychiatry 43*, 7, 835–846.

Greenberg, M.T., Kusche, C.A., Cook, E.T. and Quamma, J.P. (1995) 'Promoting Emotional Competence in School-aged Children: The Effects of the PATHS Curriculum.' *Development and Psychopathology 7*, 117–136.

Happe, F.G.E. (1994) 'An Advanced Test of Theory of Mind: Understanding of Story Characters, Thoughts and Feelings by Able Autistic, Mentally Handicapped and Normal Children and Adults.' *Journal of Autism and Developmental Disorders 24*, 1–24.

Harris, P., Olthof, T., Terwogt, M.M. and Hardman, C.E. (1987) 'Children's Knowledge of the Situations that Provoke Emotion.' *International Journal of Behavioural Development 10*, 3, 319–334.

Kleeman, J.A. (1967) 'The Peek-a-boo Game. Part I: Its Origins, Meanings and Related Phenomena in the First Year.' *Psycho-analytic Study of the Child 22*, 239–273.

Kleeman, J.A. (1973) 'The Peek-a-boo Game. Part II: Its Evolution and Associated Behaviours especially Bye-bye and Shame Expression during the Second Year.' *Journal of American Academy of Child Psychiatrists 12*, 1–23.

Krystal, H. (1988) *Integration and Self-healing*. Hillsdale, NJ: Analytic Press.

Lokare, V. (1997) 'Cultural Aspects of Anxiety in Children.' In K.N. Dwivedi and V.P. Varma (eds) *A Handbook of Childhood Anxiety Mangagement*. Aldershot: Arena.

Main, M., Kaplan, N. and Cassidy, J. (1985) 'Security in Infancy, Childhood and Adulthood: A Move to the Level of Representation.' In I. Bretherton and E. Waters (eds) *Growing Points of Attachment*, Monographs for the Society for Research in Child Development, Oxford: Blackwell.

Mawson, A.R. (1987) *Transient Criminality: A Model of Stress Induced Crime*. New York: Praeger.

Mental Health Foundation (MHF) (1999) *The Big Picture: Promoting Children and Young People's Mental Health*. London: MHF.

Munoz, R.F. (1998) 'Preventing Major Depression by Promoting Emotion Regulation: A Conceptual Framework and some Practical Tools.' *International Journal of Mental Health Promotion 1*, 1, 23–33.

Orbach, S. (1998) 'Emotional Literacy.' *Young Minds Magazine 33*, 12–13.

Piaget, J. (1970) 'Piaget's Theory.' In P.H. Mussen (ed) *Carmichael's Manual of Child Psychology*, vol. I. New York: Wiley.

Reat, N.R. (1990) *Origins of Indian Psychology*. Berkeley, CA: Asian Humanities Press.

Rinpoche, D.A. (1987) *Taming the Tiger*. Eskadelmuir: Dzalendra.

Royal College of Psychiatrists (2002) *Prevention in Psychiatry. CR 104*. London: RCP.

Rutter, M. (1980) 'Emotional Development.' In M. Rutter (ed) *Scientific Foundations of Developmental Psychiatry*. London: Heinemann Medical.

Sayadaw, L. (1981) *Manuals of Buddhism*. Rangoon: Department of Religious Affairs.

Van Ijzendoorn, K., Marcoen, A. and Schoefs, V. (1996) 'The Internal Working Model of the Self, Attachment and Competence in 5-Year-Olds.' *Child Development 67*, 2493–2511.

Willock, B. (1990) 'From Acting Out to Interactive Play.' *International Journal of Psychoanalysis 71*, 321–324.

Chapter 5

Attention and Mental Health

Rajeev Banhatti

For the mind is restless, turbulent, obstinate and very strong, O
Krishna, and to subdue it, I think, is more difficult than controlling
the wind.

> Arjuna to Lord Krishna in the
> *Bhagavadgita* (Prabhupada 1986, Chapter 6, verse 34, p.344)

Arjuna is a famous character from *Mahabharata*, an epic poem from Indian mythology. He was a great archer and a story from his childhood
goes something like this: one day Drona (the teacher) called all the
princes (his disciples) to look at a tree. 'Can you see the bird sitting on the
tree?' he asked. 'Yes,' they replied. 'Can you see anything else?' he asked.
They described various things like the sky, the leaves, the clouds, etc.
'No, no,' cried Drona. Then it was Arjuna's turn to answer the same questions. 'I can see only the bird,' said Arjuna in reply to all his questions.
'Which part of the bird?' asked Drona. 'Its head,' replied Arjuna. 'Well
done!' cried Drona. 'You are a true archer. The archer must not see anything except his target. Only then will he be able to shoot it perfectly.'

Introduction

In writing this chapter the intention has been for it to not become yet another piece about attention deficit hyperactivity disorder (ADHD) as already many excellent (Barkley 2002; Hill and Taylor 2001) and some
not so excellent articles and books are easily available. In reading about
attention it soon became apparent that very little has been written about
the development of attention as a normal mental process and also that
the concept itself is used in many different ways. Even the *Concise Oxford*

Dictionary gives four distinct meanings of the term. 'Attention!' shouted by a military sergeant is very different from 'Will you kindly pay some attention to what I am saying', though the former is almost guaranteed a response from the listener! The following definition is preferable as it is precise enough to have a fairly specific meaning, but at the same time broad enough to accommodate the range of meanings associated with the term. Attention is the ability or application of that ability to select a salient object or idea. It usually works in tandem with other cognitive processes. This definition allows us to include the process of paying attention to the external world, which is full of objects, or the internal world, which is full of ideas.

Types of attention

Attention is best studied as a process closely linked to at least two other processes, namely, perception and memory. Perception refers to the immediate awareness or recognition of a sensory impression. Attention is not a part of perception, but it modifies and even makes it possible. Perception is further processed in the brain and a meaningful interpretation (apperception) leads to either storage to memory or relegation out of awareness. In day-to-day life, attention is like a link between the external world presenting living organisms with multiple sensory stimuli and internal processes of ascribing meaning, comparing them with previous stimuli or meanings, leading to either a volitional or involuntary influence on the organisms' pre-existing cognitive content or structure.

Western psychologists and psychiatrists have usually focused more on attention to external stimuli as these are more amenable to observation and research. Eastern thinkers have, on the other hand, focused on attention to an increased awareness of the internal world.

Attention can be focused actively, and this is also called concentration. Active focused attention can be for very short events like hitting a snooker ball with a cue or throwing a dart, or it can be for long sustained periods like planning the next move in chess. On the other hand, attention can also be divided between many stimuli in the external and internal world. Divided attention (Taylor 1980) is very similar to being aware of various things simultaneously. This can vary from listening to two auditory stimuli simultaneously (dichotic listening) to watching something on a screen while listening and talking to someone else on the phone and jotting down something else (intersensory integration). In a social context, this can be seen when a good host is able to attend to many guests almost simultaneously without appearing too hurried.

In many children with so-called ADD or ADHD, focused attention on various tests is normal, but inhibition of distracting stimuli and lack of motivation to attend, rather than lack of ability to attend, is more of a problem. Van der Meere (1996) has suggested an interesting state/process distinction of attention. Processes are defined as discrete and short-term events that mediate between stimulus and response. State fluctuations modulate the processes but are not in themselves part of them. So, when measuring attention span in children (or any experimental subjects), state factors could be the time given to do the task or the incentives, the feedback given to the subject and the presence or absence of the experimenter. Children with ADHD appear to have normal attentional processes but have a deficit in regulating state fluctuations. Hence, Van der Meere's suggestion of the name 'state regulation deficit' instead of 'attention deficit'.

Developmental considerations

In general attention appears to develop from a simple process (which is dependent on external factors associated with a stimulus) into a complex web of cognitive processes, which are more dependent on internal processes of selecting what stimulus is most important to respond to in comparison with many other stimuli in the environment. Contrary to Piaget's (1954, 1970) belief, modern experiments indicate that babies as young as 12 hours old are capable of integrating information across the senses of sight, sound and touch and also of transferring learning from one sense to another (Rose and Ruff 1987). The neonate prefers stimuli which are moving and have a lot of contrast in colours as opposed to those which are still and homogenous. One can see the process of selection very early on during development, but it is more dependent on external factors. Infants aged 2–4 months select novel stimuli over stimuli which are already familiar in their memory store.

This way one can see that even at this early an age, the child has started storing data which are usually completely inaccessible to conscious awareness in later life. At 2 months the infant appears to focus and sustain attention more on a stimulus which is moderately discrepant from a previous stimulus rather than the same or a very discrepant stimulus. Kagan's (1970) experiments more than 30 years ago are still important in understanding how attention develops in children. By the time a child is 12 months old, 'activation of hypothesis' becomes more influential than just the discrepancy or other factors associated with a stimulus. A child will start listening and ascribing meaning to various aspects of the context and the stimulus to generate a hypothesis to decide whether to attend to it or not. The more extensive the child's memory store, and the better the ability to interpret the stimulus and the context, the longer the child can attend to any task. More recently, following the same line of experiments, various tests of attention have been developed. These are mentioned later in the chapter. During infancy and early childhood the process of self-regulation is intimately linked to attention and Chapter 4 by Dwivedi in this volume also looks at the process of self-regulation.

During the first few months infants develop more control over their sense organs (eyes, ears) and also their motor processes (body movements). During the next few months, they develop a more sophisticated capacity to be selective about their attention. At toddler and later pre-school stage, they start exploring their environment more and attend to anything that is interesting, exciting, rewarding and novel. Even normal children can appear very hungry for a diet of stimuli to attend to, making them look quite fidgety, hyperactive and distractible. Various authors have suggested models of studying attentional processes and have demonstrated how attention progresses through various levels of maturation during the first ten years of life (Blondis *et al.* 1991; Wright and Vliestra 1975). By 5 years of age children begin to perceive and process stimuli quite systematically (Abravanel 1968). Interestingly, this coincides with the practice of children starting school.

As mentioned earlier, attention is not a unitary process. It is dependent on other cognitive processes and also influences them in return. Sohlberg and Mateer (1992) describe a model of attention based on their work with traumatic brain-injured population. They describe problems in sustained attention relating to duration and consistency, selective and divided attention. They also describe a clinical model of attention which includes processes of focusing, sustaining, selecting, alternating and dividing attention. Now it appears that this model is not going to be of great help to remedy the problems of large numbers of people with ADHD, as in many children with ADHD attentional ability appears normal, but motivation, responding to reinforcements and poor impulse control can appear to be the core problems and more relevant to management (Barkley 2002). It is very likely that different anatomical circuits are involved in different aspects of attention as described later on in this chapter. Development of executive functions like planning and organisation of tasks, as well as the development of working memory are important developmental processes which are linked with applied levels of attention.

Biological factors

Brain damage associated particularly with hypoxic types of insults during the neonatal period is linked with attention deficit and even hyperactivity (Cruickshank, Eliason and Merrifield 1988; O'Dougherty, Nuechterlein and Drew 1984). However, most children with symptoms of inattention do not have seizure disorders or brain damage so it is important to understand how attention develops and how it is linked with other cognitive processes and link that with our understanding of different areas of the brain.

Neurobiology of attention

The human brain appears to be the last to develop on the evolutionary ladder so far. The brainstem, which connects the brain to the spinal cord, is the most ancient part. It evolved 500 million years ago and is rather like the entire brain of present-day reptiles. Various clusters of neurones in the brainstem determine the brain's general level of alertness and regulate essential body processes, like breathing, heartbeat and blood pressure. Above the brainstem is the diffusely spread nucleus called reticular formation (RF), which plays a major role in maintaining and modulating attention. The thalamus in the midbrain is like a relay centre. It acts as a two-way gatekeeper between the 'conscious' parts of the brain like the cerebral corti (especially the frontal cortex) and 'unconscious' parts like the hypothalamus, RF, cerebellum, pons and brainstem. It is also intimately connected to the amygdala, hippocampus, caudate and putamen, which are parts of the limbic system sometimes called the emotional brain.

From a developmental perspective, myelination occurs from the inside of the brain spreading outwards as it develops from the embryonic stage onwards. Myelination makes electrical conduction more efficient and reduces short-circuiting. The deeper and more ancient parts get myelinated earlier and the outermost parts like the frontal and prefrontal cortex get fully myelinated only during adulthood. Interestingly, the RF gets fully myelinated at or after puberty. This can be reflected in the clinically observed finding that attention span improves after puberty and that many children (40–50%) seem to grow out of ADHD after reaching adulthood.

Hyperactivity and impulsivity has been found to be associated with hypofunction of frontostriatal neural pathways. Dopamine, and to a lesser extent noradrenaline, is involved in this process. More recent studies now show that children with ADHD do not have different attentional abilities, but a different response to reinforcement and external states. This can be due to suboptimal arousal, which is linked to the frontostriatal system. It can also be associated with a defect of activation, which is linked to the basal ganglia or the effort level, which is associated with the hippocampus. During evolution, vigilance and scanning of stimuli to watch out for threats and opportunities was more important and the ancient parts of the brain could perform such functions. However, as the frontal and prefrontal lobes developed in human beings and the limbic system became more sophisticated, executive functions in the brain like planning and inhibition of irrelevant responses or ignoring irrelevant stimuli became more and more important for survival. It is quite possible that in individual children, different aspects of these circuits are functioning suboptimally and influencing one deficit may have gainful effects on other circuits.

Psychosocial factors

Maternal stress during pregnancy has been associated with disregulated behaviour during early childhood (O'Connor et al. 2000). Poor quality and disrupted early caregiving has also been associated with either disruptive behavioural disorders or ADHD. Poverty can influence parenting by increasing stress on parents to meet their own and their children's basic needs. Educational status of parents and cultural style of bringing up children can affect early development of children in terms of their capacity to contain anxiety or soothe or regulate themselves when frustrated. Modelling calmness in moments of adversity and a positive and happy problem-solving attitude demonstrated to children can facilitate the same behaviour in children. However, even though we are considering these factors separately, they are always linked with the child's temperament and genetic, constitutional and other environmental factors that have affected the child's development.

Attention in relation to mental health

Attentional problems can be associated with many mental health disorders and not just ADD or ADHD. Intellectual or global cognitive disability is associated with reduced attention span. Children suffering from specific learning difficulties like dyslexia (specific reading disorder) or dyspraxia (developmental coordination disorder) are very likely to be inattentive and easily distracted. Emotional disorders including generalised anxiety disorders, depression and obsessive compulsive disorder (OCD) can lead to impaired concentration in children as internal worrying thoughts, ruminations and obsessions can interfere with attention. It is often a difficult clinical task to unpick these disorders and to see whether they have evolved as a secondary problem or are the core or primary problems leading to the symptom of lack of concentration. Pervasiveness of attentional problems in the absence of other disorders is found in pure cases of ADHD, but these form only about 20 per cent of the referred clinic population diagnosed to have ADHD. Comorbidity is a rule rather than an exception with children referred with symptoms such as 'Does not listen', 'Does not stay on task', 'He is very disorganised, easily distracted, ignores me completely', etc. (see below).

Features of ADHD from DSM-IV-TR (APA 2000)

- *Inattention*: carelessness with detail, fails to sustain attention, appears not to listen, does not finish instructed tasks, poor self-organisation, avoids tasks requiring sustained mental effort, loses things, easily distracted, and seems forgetful.

- *Hyperactivity/impulsivity*: fidgets, leaves seat when should be seated, runs/climbs excessively and inappropriately, noisy in play, persistent motor overactivity unmodified by social context, blurts out answers before question completed, fails to wait turn or queue, interrupts others' conversations or games, talks excessively for social context.

Improving attention and promoting mental health

As attentional apparatus develops from early on in life, the sooner a child is exposed to measures that promote attention span, the better. Even during pregnancy parents should be aware of harmful effects of smoking, alcohol and stress on the developing foetus and plan accordingly. During the neonatal period, a smiling friendly face and relaxed, contented parents can give the infant the message, 'I am okay, they are okay and the world is a happy and safe place.' It is amazing how this early sense of security can be a firm foundation for successful and satisfactory future adjustment in school, community and work place. This applies to all children irrespective of their innate differences.

Assessment of attention

Attention span and problems with attention can be assessed clinically during history taking by being aware of presenting symptoms as described earlier. One can use observation of the child in the clinic during an interview lasting at least one hour and reports from parents and teachers. Children above the age of 6 years and of at least average intellectual ability are usually able to count from 1 to 20 forwards and backwards. Older children need more demanding tasks like serial threes (substract 3 from 50 and keep subtracting 3 from the answers you get) or serial sevens (100 minus 7 and so on).

Questionnaires (Conners 1997) and tests can aid screening and diagnosis but should not be the sole diagnostic tests. In complex or doubtful cases more detailed tests like Test of Attention in Infants (TAI) (DeGangi 1995) or the Wechsler Intelligence Scale for Children (WISC-III: Wechsler 1991) and the Wechsler Preschool and Primary Scale of Intelligence (WPPSI: Wechsler 1990) can provide more detail and differentiated information for the clinician to help in the assessment of the child. Tests like the Continuous Performance Test (CPT), Paired Associate Learning Test and Porteus Maze are hardly ever used nowadays, as their value to clinical populations appears limited. Tests occasionally used in the UK include CPT (Conners 2000), Test of Everyday Attention for Children (TEA-CH: Manly, Robertson and Anderson 1999) and Cambridge Neuropsychological Test Automated Battery (CeNeS 2001).

Cultural aspects

Recently the author attended a workshop on media presentation. One of the journalists running the workshop informed the participants that the time required for someone to be counted as a TV viewer for statistical purposes has dropped from 30 minutes a few years ago to 3 minutes. This meant that people in the media business knew that attention span in general had dropped to 3 minutes. She blamed the remote control for this drop! There is no doubt that we live in a world of 'information over-load'. In a way, 'sensory deprivation' is a sought-after luxury and medita-tion classes are a booming business especially in the West. Just as raw material from the East was brought and processed in the West and mar-keted back into both markets during the colonial era, many Eastern practices (e.g. Vipassana, Yoga) are being marketed in appealing pack-ages for quick fixes all over the world. Technology has made this possi-ble or rather irresistible; whether the effects are beneficial or harmful (or both) on developing generations is an open question, but they are appar-ently unstoppable.

Whether inattentive or hyperactive children are normal and ADHD as a disorder is a social creation has been argued by a few authors (Kohn 1989; Schrag and Divoky 1975). However, Barkley (2002) has argued that ADHD is a real disorder on two counts:

- children with ADHD have significant, demonstrable deficits in behavioural inhibition and inattention (the executive functions) that are critical for self-regulation

- those with ADHD experience numerous domains of impairment during their lifespan.

Children with ADHD have been found in most cultures studied so far (Bhatia *et al.* 1991; Bu-Haroon, Eapen and Bener 1999; Kroes *et al.* 2001; Liu *et al.* 2000; O'Leary, Vivian and Nisi 1985), but in this age of globalisation it may be almost impossible to find cultures untouched by modern western influences.

Prevention of attentional problems

Pregnancy

Avoiding or reducing exposure to harmful toxins like nicotine, alcohol and lead during pregnancy will help prevent attention problems in the child. It is also recommended that stress is avoided and this can be pro-moted by prioritising work and home schedule and improving or build-ing supportive social networks. Midwives and obstetricians could probably benefit from increased awareness and further education in this area.

Postnatal period

Improved care of the newborn baby as well as the mother as far as technological advances are concerned is an actively ongoing process. However, reducing demands on the mother to get back to work, massaging the baby (Inger 2003) and the mother, and allowing them plenty of relaxed playful time together would probably do wonders for both. A securely attached happy infant and a contented happy mother can conceivably build on this solid start. Parents In Partnership Parent Infant Network (PIPPIN), Sure Start and Home Start are valuable national initiatives in the UK which mostly focus on supporting and improving the parent–infant relationship. PIPPIN's website www.pippin.org.uk offers more information on supporting the transition to parenthood.

Early childhood

It is probably now more important to resist the drive in most competitive communities to start the rat race very early on in life. Children should be able to enjoy their childhood and acquire basic cognitive skills through play in the context of secure attachment to a parent who is able to nurture a sense of wonder and joy for just existing in this world.

Middle childhood

This is the period of latency when the child should have resolved the Oedipal conflicts. In ancient India, this was the period when children used to be sent to a guru (a sage) in a residential school in a forest so that they could just concentrate on acquiring knowledge, skills and wisdom. A child's considerable energies and emerging cognitive processes make this a crucial period to lay down a firm foundation for the future, especially in terms of acquiring 'learning capacity'.

Adolescence

Emerging abilities of complex and abstract thinking along with issues of self-identity, sexuality and excitement or anxiety about becoming independent from parental family make adolescence the most complex period of the lifespan. Interventions that gently motivate the adolescent to formulate short- and long-term goals and focus attention on these while being able to incorporate other activities in life are needed. Peer group processes or individual support can promote such activities. Adolescents are probably the most needy and most neglected group as far as mental health is concerned. Professionals need to think of ways of liaising with schools and colleges to incorporate preventive efforts through psychoeducation, through age-appropriate groups like youth clubs, drop-in centres, confidential telephone lines and other accessible and creative ways to engage this 'difficult to engage' group.

Management

Psychopharmacology

In a child with attentional problems in context of another organic disorder, one should treat the underlying reason for the organic disorder, e.g. meningitis, encephalitis, pyrexia of any origin or metabolic imbalances. The child's attention will be impaired along with state of consciousness and the child would show either clouded consciousness or a hypervigilant/confusional state with illusions, and visual and auditory hallucinations. Measures such as a moderately lighted room, a few familiar people around the child and clear instructions are as important as medications. Short-acting benzodiazepines like lorazepam, 1 mg. orally or intramuscular, can be safe medications, but need judicious, short-term use.

Attention problems (inattention as well as distractibility) as a part of ADHD are responsive to stimulants like methylphenidate and dexamphetamine even when the child may have comorbid specific or global learning difficulties, social communication disorder or emotional disorders. However, the child should have initial or concurrent management interventions for these comorbid conditions in addition to stimulant medication. Tricyclic antidepressants like imipramine are also effective in approximately 60 per cent of these children and can be used as a second-line treatment. The dose can vary from 25 to 75 mg. One has to, of course, take into account possible side-effects especially cardiotoxicity, and monitor the child clinically. Atomoxetine shows promise of being an effective alternative at the time of writing this chapter. Medications to improve memory or concentration, including various tonics, fish oils, etc., have not been proved effective but may have placebo value.

Yoga

The ancient Indian practice of Yoga has taken a holistic view of the child. Distractibility and hyperactivity are viewed as the manifestation of an innate quality (trait) of the mind called *rajas guna*. Everyone is supposed to have bits of *tamas* (loosely translated as inertia), *rajas* (dynamic) and *sattvic* (balanced and illuminated by spirituality) *gunas* with predominance of one of the three *gunas*. Yogic exercises including those for the body (*asanas*) and the mind (meditation) can be tailored to suit the child. In general, practice of yoga is supposed to be beneficial to everyone and good quality research to see whether it can promote mental health and influence outcome for children with attentional impairments is lacking at present. Though self-help books are now becoming available (Lark 2003), it is advisable that a trained Yoga practitioner is approached for advice, before beginning to practise yoga.

According to Samkhya Yoga, ego or the sense of self is described as evolving into mind and senses. All these form what is called Citta (pronounced Chitta), which is the executive arm of one's personality. The mind has the function of focusing attention through intention and imagination and creating a conceptual cage for intellectual elaboration. Yogic practices like *pranayama* (proper breathing) and *shavasana* (resting like a dead body) have been well described and have been shown to help increase body awareness, concentration, self-reliance and inner peace and self-direction (Yogendra 1995). Relaxation techniques like *yoga nidra* (sleep) and *tratak* among others are used to tune and harmonise the right and left brains.

Physical exercise

Physical exercise on a regular basis has been shown to reduce stress and increase a sense of well-being and create higher level of alertness leading to improved attention.

Life skills education

This has been developed and used in many schools and includes information and experiential practices to improve emotional literacy, social skills, problem solving and in turn improved concentration. A further account of life skills education through schools is given in Chapter 8 by Coley and Dwivedi in this volume.

Organisation

Time management and planning, self-organising aids like keeping a diary and prioritising tasks for every day in advance, are very useful for children with either attentional or executive function problems. There are many resources available, one example being *The 'Putting on the Brakes' Activity Book for Young People with ADHD* (Quinn, Stern and Russell 1998).

Meditation

Meditation of any type including vipassana where one simply focuses one's mind on the experience of breathing and from time to time brings the wandering mind back to the breathing as a body sensation is very useful to raise attentional activity apart from other benefits. Progressive muscle relaxation with guided imagery or other particular types of meditation may be subjectively more appealing to others.

Group exercises and stories

Group exercises are very useful for children and parents together or in separate groups. Parents can be trained to demonstrate to the child the practice of planning and thinking. The parent can be given a problem from an everyday situation (e.g. what you will do if the teacher asks the class a question and you know the answer; however, the child next to you is telling you a joke, which is quite funny.) First, the therapist can demonstrate a problem-solving thinking style by talking aloud. Then the parent can use self-talk to describe the problem, possible outcomes for different solutions and which is the best solution. A child can be asked to use external self-talk as a tool, which can eventually become internal self talk. 'Stop.' 'What do I do next?' 'What will happen if I blurt out the answer?' 'What will happen if I laugh at the joke and ignore the teacher?' These are some questions, which can be included in the explicit self-talk. Children can be encouraged to develop strategies that work for them. Experiential learning is more lasting and effective, but the evidence base that these skills are generalised in the long term in children with ADHD is still absent.

Just like group exercises and self-talk, stories can be used to improve a child's self-esteem, motivation to concentrate on goals and self-direction.

Telling stories is an art and needs to be perfected by practice. One has also to collect or formulate many stories for different occasions (Dwivedi 1997; Rowshan 1997).

Summary

Attention is the act or ability of mental selection by which salient objects or ideas are located, examined and responded to. It can be of various types like focused attention or varied, flexible attention shifting over various objects or ideas. Complementary to focused attention is the ability to block out irrelevant or competing stimuli and select only the salient ones to attend to. Even a neonate shows selective attention though throughout the life span it develops and is used in different contexts in different ways. Many biological and psychosocial factors are linked to the development of attention and there are also factors which lead to either attention deficit (inattention) or distractibility and quite often to hyperactivity and poor impulse control.

Preventive approaches at community, group and individual levels can be used alongside promoting attention by actively treating its disorders. Though ADD/ADHD may be universal and often have a biological basis, pathoplastic effect of cultural contexts cannot be ignored in the expression, acceptance and management of the child suffering from ADHD.

Acknowledgements

I am grateful to my parents for reading a draft and making comments. I am also very grateful to Mary Battison for her patience and help in typing various drafts of this chapter.

References

Abravanel, E. (1968) 'The Development of Intersensory Patterning with Regard to Selected Spatial Dimensions.' *Monographs of the Society of Research in Child Development 333*, 527.

American Psychiatric Association (APA) (2000) *Diagnostic and Statistical Manual of Mental Disorders*, 4th edn., text revision (DSM-IV-TR). Washington, DC: APA.

Barkley, R.A. (2002) 'Attention-Deficit/Hyperactivity Disorder.' In E.J. Mash and R.A. Barkley (ed) *Child Psychopathology*, 2nd edn. New York: Guilford.

Bhatia, M.S., Nigam, V.R., Bohra, N. and Malik, S.C. (1991) 'Attention Deficit Disorder with Hyperactivity among Paediatric Outpatients.' *Journal of Child Psychology and Psychiatry 32*, 297–306.

Blondis, T.A., Snow, J.H., Stein, M. and Roisen, N.J. (1991) 'Appropriate Use of Measures of Attention and Activity for the Diagnosis and Management of ADHD.' In P.J. Accardo, T.A. Blondis and B.Y. Whitman (eds) *Attention Deficit Disorders and Hyperactivity in Children*. New York: Marcel Dekker.

Bu-Haroon, A., Eapen, V. and Bener, A. (1999) 'The Prevalence of Hyperactivity Symptoms in the United Arab Emirates.' *Nordic Journal of Psychiatry 53*, 439–492.

CeNeS (2001) *The Cambridge Neuropsychological Test Automated Battery (CANTAB)*. Cambridge: CeNeS Pharmaceutical.

Conners, C.K. (1997) *Conners Rating Scales – Revised*. Windsor: NFER.

Conners, C.K. (2000) *Conners Continuous Performance Test Version 3.0*. Toronto: Multi-Health Systems.

Cruickshank, B.M., Eliason, M. and Merrifield, B. (1988) 'Long-term Sequelae of Water Near-Drowning.' *Journal of Paediatric Psychology 13*, 379–388.

DeGangi, G.A. (1995) *The Test of Attention in Infants*. Dayton, OH: Southpaw Enterprises.

Dwivedi, K.N. (ed) (1997) *The Therapeutic Use of Stories*. London: Routledge.

Hill, P. and Taylor, E. (2001) 'An Auditable Protocol for Treating Attention Deficit/Hyperactivity Disorder.' *Archives of Diseases in Childhood 84*, 904–909.

Inger, A. (2003) 'The Tiny Tim Centre: Providing Massage for Children with Disabilities and Special Needs.' *Massage and Health Review* Spring, 6–8.

Kagan, J. (1970) 'Attention and Psychological Change in the Young Child.' *Science 17*, 826–831.

Kohn, A. (1989) 'Suffer the Restless Children.' *The Atlantic Monthly* November, 90–100.

Kroes, M., Kalff, A.C., Kessels, A.G.H., Steyaert, J., Feron, F., van Someren, A., Hurks, P., Hendriksen, J., van Zeban, T., Rozendaal, N., Crolla, I., Troost, J., Jolles, J. and Vles, J. (2001) 'Child Psychiatric Diagnoses in a Population of Dutch Schoolchildren Aged 6 to 8 Years.' *Journal of the American Academy of Child and Adolescent Psychiatry 42*, 199–210.

Lark, L (2003) *Yoga for Kids*. London: Carlton.

Liu, X., Kurita, H., Guo, C., Tachimori, H., Ze, J. and Okawa, M. (2000) 'Behavioural and Emotional Problems in Chinese Children: Teacher Reports for Ages 6 to 11.' *Journal of Child Psychology and Psychiatry 41*, 253–260.

Manly, T., Robertson, I.H. and Anderson, V. (1999) *Test of Everyday Attention for Children (TEA-CH)*. Bury St Edmunds: Thames Valley Test Co.

O'Connor, T.G., Heron, J., Golding, J., Beveridge, M. and Glover, V. (2002) 'Maternal Antenatal Anxiety and Children's Behavioural and Emotional Problems at 4 Years.' *British Journal of Psychiatry 180*, 502–508.

O'Dougherty, M., Nuechterlein, K.H. and Drew, B. (1984) 'Hyperactive and Hypoxic Children: Signal Detection, Sustained Attention, and Behaviour.' *Journal of Abnormal Psychology 93*, 178–191.

O'Leary, K.D., Vivian, D. and Nisi, A. (1985) 'Hyperactivity in Italy.' *Journal of Abnormal Child Psychology 13*, 485–500.

Piaget, J. (1954) *The Construction of Reality in the Child*. New York: Basic Books.

Piaget, J. (1970) 'Piaget's Theory.' In P.H. Mussen (ed) *Carmichael's Manual of Child Psychology*, 3rd edn., Vol. 1. New York: Wiley.

Prabhupada, A.C. Bhaktivedanta Swami (1986) *Bhagavadgita As It Is*. London: Bhaktivedanata Book Trust UK.

Quinn, P.O., Stern, J.M. and Russell, N. (1998) *The 'Putting on the Brakes' Activity Book for Young People with ADHD*. New York: Magination Press.

Rose, S.A. and Ruff, H.A. (1987) 'Cross-modal Abilities in Human Infants.' In J.D. Osofsky (ed) *Handbook of Infant Development*, 2nd edn. New York: Wiley – Interscience.

Rowshan, A. (1997) *Telling Tales*. Oxford: Oneworld.

Schrag, P. and Divoky, D. (1975) *The Myth of the Hyperactive Child*. New York: Pantheon.

Sohlberg, M.M. and Mateer, C.A. (1992) *Attention Process Training*. Puyallup, WA: Good Samaritan Hospital.

Taylor, E. (1980) 'Development of Attention.' In M. Rutter (ed) *Scientific Foundations of Development Psychiatry*. London: Heinemann.

Van der Meere, J.J. (1996) 'The Role of Inattention in Hyperactivity Disorders.' In S. Sandberg (ed) *Hyperactivity Disorders of Childhood*. Cambridge: Cambridge University Press.

Wechsler, D. (1990) *Wechsler Preschool and Primary Scale of Intelligence* (WPPSI), revised UK edition. London: Psychological Corporation.

Wechsler, D. (1991) *Wechsler Intelligence Scale for Children*, 3rd edn. (WISC-III). London: Psychological Corporation.

Wright, J.C. and Vliestra, A.G. (1975) 'The Development of Selective Attention: From Perceptual Exploration to Logical Search.' In H.W. Reese (ed) *Advances in Child Development and Behaviour*. New York: Academic Press.

Yogendra, J. (ed) (1995) *Cyclopaedia Yoga Vol. III*. Santacruz (East), Mumbai, India: The Yoga Institute.

Chapter 6

Addiction as a Mark of Adulthood

The enduring fascination of drugs and alcohol among adolescents

Allan Guggenbühl

> Those guys are really cool. That's also a place where you can experience true friendship and closeness; people help each other irrespective of their backgrounds!

This 15-year-old is not talking about a scout camp. He is describing 'Needle Park', the worst and most despicable spot of Zurich. Before the police raided the area hundreds of weary, appalling drug addicts sat huddled on park benches, lay drowsily on the ground or wandered around aimlessly not knowing whether it was day or night. Pale young women with bloodshot eyes were begging or offering their services in order to buy 'dope', while confused young men were emptying rubbish bins, hoping to find something to eat. A horrendous scene that thousands of people considered to be a public disgrace was an object of fascination for this adolescent. He dismissed the adult arguments and stuck to his own version: 'Yes of course they are drug addicts, but that is because of the system.' These poor souls were all victims of society. According to the adolescent they were being punished for being 'John Average'. Amazingly, he glamorized life on the streets. In his eyes the scene radiated a special quality. These people symbolized life in the underground. He believed they were an antidote for society. Where most people would react with sadness and disgust, this young man saw a hidden answer. Trying to persuade him of the misery and desolation of the 'junkie' was a vain endeavour. He was convinced that 'Needle Park' was a valid alternative to the stress and strivings of a boring life in normality.

The perception of this 15-year-old is of course an extreme one. Most young people are not so naive and they do not romanticise the heroin drug scene. 'Heroin is for losers' is the saying. However, the psychological trap behind the words of the young man is widespread. Behaviours and scenes that horrify adults are frequently attractive to young people. They often exhibit a strange fascination with the unusual, bizarre and dreadful. This is also common with addictions. Although teachers, psychologists, psychotherapists, parents and politicians warn adolescents of the dangers of drug and alcohol abuse, the risks are often discounted. Ecstasy (MDMA), cocaine, 'poppers', 'crack' and 'speed' are considered to be cool and are common in the party scene in Europe. Despite sound information and numerous campaigns, drinking, smoking and drugs fascinate many young people, provided they are presented to them in a social context. For many young people warnings about the dangers of drugs and alcohol seem to heighten their interest in them, a group of youngsters informing the author that 'to party, drink and get drunk is definitely cool' and 'only sissies don't smoke'. One young person indicated that at his school smoking was a matter of survival, commenting that the designated smoking zones were the places in which to meet all 'the interesting women'. This was obviously not what the teachers had intended. Following the imposition of restrictions on advertising, the percentage of adolescents who smoke has risen. In Switzerland and Austria 15 per cent of 14- to 24-year-olds regularly drink alcohol and 22.1 per cent of 15-year-old young people smoke, while 15 per cent have experienced taking cannabis (Schweizerische Fachstelle für Alkoholprävention 2003). The consumption rate is rising and young people continue to be attracted to cigarettes, alcohol and drugs. Warnings and more and more stringent laws appear not to have the desired effect. Many young people are determined to indulge in everything their teachers and parents fear, commenting that 'booze and drugs are great', despite the fact that those in authority relentlessly advocate a life without drugs and with modest alcohol consumption (Sielbereisen 1997). In one school in Berne nearly all the students of a particular class met before their lessons in order to share a joint, and in a grammar school in Basel everyone met during breaks for sessions of champagne drinking. This is not exactly the traditionally advised preparation for lessons!

The comments of young people and the behaviours mentioned above raise important questions about the deeper reasons for the enduring fascination for drugs, alcohol and smoking among young people, and the reasons why adolescents continue to harm themselves and dismiss the warnings of health experts.

Adolescence

Developmental psychology divides our lives into different phases (Trautnerm 1991). A phase is a period in life in which certain challenges and qualities dominate. Thinking in terms of phases is an intellectual tool that helps one to understand the situations and problems of people of different ages. Typical challenges and tasks, personality traits, interests and situations characteristic of the particular age group are generally identified when defining phases. However, thinking in phases can be problematic, particularly when individual traits and personality factors are disregarded. Individual traits remain the single most influential factor in the personal growth of young people. In order to understand the deeper meaning of the attraction of drugs and smoking it is necessary to reflect on the developmental challenges that adolescents face. In order to understand the fascination for drugs and alcohol, a full and comprehensive consideration is required.

Developmental psychology defines adolescence as a 'transitional phase' (Krampen and Reichel 2002). Adolescents have left childhood and are redefining their relationships with and perspectives of their parents and teachers. They do not yet have a definitive place in society, and essentially live in two worlds: childhood is emotionally close and participation in the world of adults is emerging. The young person usually lives at home and is fed and taken care of by parents while simultaneously wishing to join life 'out there'. Either willingly or begrudgingly, typical adolescents attend school or college and learn a profession. However, their hearts are somewhere else. Their situation demands adaptation and they are compelled to adapt to the rules, regulations and rituals of the system or institution to which they belong. Mentally adolescents are set for autonomy and it is not surprising that they usually perceive themselves as the 'underdog' in the conflict between external demands and internal wishes. In essence, adolescents are not yet really allowed to move freely in the world of the adult. They still have to prove that they are eligible for real life, though they may psychologically and physically be grown-up. Sexual maturity develops during adolescence and adolescents' cognitive abilities enable sufficient comprehension of most issues (given the appropriate education). Adolescents therefore perceive themselves as 'adults in waiting'. They want to participate in the activities around them, and judge the actions of others, yet they are held back. They are capable of personal opinions, views and perceptions, but are forced to live in dependency. Rationally adolescents may understand the situation, but emotionally it is difficult to accept. Adolescents detect the gaffes of their parents, the blunders of their teachers and the inadequacies of institutions, but are forced to remain mute. They fantasise about challenges, dangers and experiences, but most of these are beyond their reach. Their lives are restricted by the boundaries of school and family. However, the family and school codes cannot impede their thoughts and adolescents tend to visualise what they would do once their lives take off. The author was graciously informed by a 14-year-old that he was going to be 'the greatest Swiss-speaking Reggae Star of Zurich', while a 16-year-old girl was convinced that she would 'open a school for starving children in Somalia'. Adolescents often imagine themselves joining the crowd, having fun or confronting challenges. Healthy adolescents want to distance themselves from home and school and to step into what they believe to be real life. They no longer want to be just the son or daughter of their parents.

The deeper reason for this wish is the need for adolescents to construct an identity of their own during this transitional phase (Fend 1991). They have to broaden their individuality and gain a distinctive profile. It is no longer sufficient to be someone's son or daughter. Adolescents want to be listened to and recognised by others. They no longer wish to be the annex of a family, but are searching for a distinct persona. Adolescents are very rarely convinced of the achievements and lifestyle of the older generation. They have to refuse some of their parents' values because they are trying to be different. As a result of this desire they begin to interpret society and their personal surroundings anew. Their aspiration is to reinvent the world around them and to develop a new lifestyle. They are pushed by an archetypal desire to differentiate themselves from their parents and teachers, even though they may consciously agree with the opinions and principles of the adults. They have to follow the deep urge to prove themselves and to be distinct.

Compliance in school and at home becomes difficult as a result of the archetypal longing for detachment. The adolescent's relationships with parents and teachers become increasingly ambivalent. Although adolescents may appreciate their parents or teachers and want them to be there and take care of them, these understanding considerate adults are simultaneously considered to be pests. Adolescents' compulsion is to be different (Baacek 1994), and they do not want to be understood. It is the adult's duty to adopt an adversary role. Over-attentive adults jeopardise the adolescent's quest for autonomy. Adolescents want the adults in their lives to act as 'oldies' so that they can distance themselves from them. In the adolescent's eyes, adults represent history and have outdated attitudes (Guggenbühl 1993). Adults who present themselves as tolerant and understanding are viewed with suspicion. In the adolescent's perception they lure young people into *their* world and force them to comply with their values and lifestyles. Unless adolescents at least partially refuse the ideas of adults, their fragile autonomy is endangered.

For adults the situation is neither easy nor simple. It is natural to want to pass on accomplishments and to have the next generation consent to the values and goal of the previous generation. Everyone hopes to leave some mark on this world. The problem is that many adolescents start to provoke in response to adults' attempts to impose their values. This is exemplified by the comments of a 16-year-old girl who said 'All I wish for is to find a sexy man with loads of money to take care of me', in response to her teacher praising the achievements of feminism. In the adolescent view it is only 'bores' who identify with adults' ideas and follow their rules meticulously. For the adolescent it is important to reinterpret society and to respond to the call of 'the world out there'. This wanderlust or longing to indulge in new experiences is also the reason why adolescents decorate their rooms with idols and pictures from distant countries, and dream of travelling to Australia, the Sahara, Siberia or South America.

Symbols of autonomy

What the adolescent is actually looking for are scenes that convey independence. They project their quest for autonomy onto groups, scenes, trends and fascinating places. They become projection carriers. They live out their oppositional tendency by choosing a compatible scene in the outside world. These scenes become symbols of autonomy that help them to redefine themselves, and they hope that these might strengthen them in their oppositional tendencies. Adolescents therefore choose scenes that guarantee a reaction from adults. The scenes and behaviours are intended to provoke, to aggravate and annoy parents and teachers, and their reactions provide the proof that one has gained some autonomy.

Friends and colleagues constitute an important reference group in the quest for autonomy. Young people want to empower themselves and orientate themselves to their peer groups through their dress code and interests and use of jargon of the age group. Friends generally face similar psychological dilemmas and provide an important source of support for the adolescent. This archetypal need leads to collective trends and makes it easier to gain some distance from parents and teachers, and to develop a distinct and independent personal perspective. The orientation towards peers periodically results in a movement. Young people come together in order to share mutual ideals and a vision. These youth movements sometimes develop a new life style and a common approach to the predominant challenges of the period. Traditionally youth movements are not quiet and unpretentious; they strive for attention. Unless they are seen, heard and talked about they are not considered to have served their purpose. They usually develop outside of the mainstream culture because of the drive to redefine the core values of society. Some youth movements perceive themselves as an antidote to the problems of society whereas others are happy just to draw some attention or disturb everyone a little.

Some examples of youth movements

More than a hundred years ago the possibility of steel and technology was greeted with great enthusiasm in Europe. The potential achievements of steel were considered to be limitless. The Eiffel Tower was built, huge ships were constructed and trains connected the major cities of Europe. Many even believed that increased mobility brought the prospect of eternal peace closer. Urban societies started to develop and the narrowness of the Victorian and Biedermeier lifestyles was gradually left behind. Interestingly adolescents largely ignored this fervour. Instead of rejoicing with the adults they gathered in forests, sat in dirty places, gazed at trees, sang songs and cherished nature. The Youth Movement (*Jungendbewegung*) that believed in nature and ordinary life was born. Thousands of adolescents met in remote spots, sang songs about wanderlust and created formulae for peace and harmony. This movement was a clear antidote to the then dominant admiration of technology. These adolescents despised technology and haste, and opted for an easier lifestyle (Nohl 1970).

Some years later the jazz generation emerged. To the horror of teachers, professors and parents, young people started listening to 'atrocious Negro music'. This 'noise' was considered to be morally damaging and pedagogical authorities voiced their fears that the core values of society were in danger. It was their belief that jazz music would seduce young people to move their hips and clap their hands in a morally hazardous manner. During this period many young people crept out of their parents' homes and clandestinely listened to the music of Fats Waller, Duke Ellington or Louis Armstrong.

Wars can hamper young people in their search for identity or from defining their profile. When young people are sacrificed on the battlefields their need for history is fulfilled by the political agenda of the society. During the Vietnam war the young people's need for their own identity was therefore satisfied by the protest movement against the war. In the 1960s the hippy movement became centre stage. Drugs, sex and rock 'n' roll were the fashion and were advocated as the remedy against narrow-mindedness, intolerance and bigotry. 'Make love not war' was the message and bright dresses and long hair the dress code. Youth movements thrive on the adolescent's desire to differ from grown-up society and it is this archetypal need which provides the deeper reason why the majority of adolescents have difficulties in adaptation. Of course they know that they should follow the rules and regulations of school and the codes of conduct of society, but emotionally they yearn to be something different. Even when they unconsciously agree with the values and lifestyle of the adults, adolescents long to rehearse their own culture and live in their own myths. Normality seems unbearable to adolescents because it would mean giving in to the demands of grown-ups (Guggenbühl 1998a).

The adolescent rebellion

Adolescents' wish to be distinct makes it inevitable that they will disrespect boundaries. Everything of which parents and educators warn is bound to be cool, because this offers the possibility of creating a separate identity. Adolescents are constantly on the lookout for behaviours that will allow them to create their own identity. The primary adolescent task is to rehearse a modest rebellion and they are therefore unable to comply with the rules of 'normality'. While they may consciously agree with the core values of their parents and teachers, they are also forced to disrespect these axioms. Development in adolescence requires the breaking of some taboos. If adolescents followed all the conventions of society, this would mean the end of their psychic development. They would fail to develop the story of their generation and be deprived of a distinct myth of their own (Guggenbühl 1998b).

Drugs, alcohol and, to a minor degree, cigarettes, provide the possibility of becoming more autonomous. The nice, predictable world that the adults are preparing for their offspring can be disrupted. Adolescents can identify with these scenes and their respective behaviours because it provides them with the chance to develop and irritate. As a result they might dive into the party scene, 'rave' all night and possibly swallow speed or ecstasy. 'Everybody does it!' is the chant, and being 'high' also offers an existential quality to life. To lose the senses, feel dizzy and dive into a Dionysian frenzy all belong to life, and life can be unbearable if one is not able to forget oneself and relinquish self-control. Most adolescents conclude that a life without mind-blowing experiences is not an option. They are on the lookout for the extreme and therefore dismiss the considered warnings of the grown-up bores. This fascination for astounding, excessive experiences is the core of the problem of drug and alcohol abuse.

Drugs, cigarettes and alcohol promise an extra bonus: these addictions belong to the adult world. Adults are entitled to smoke and drink and they may even illicitly take drugs. In our society adults seem to be legitimised to engage in 'bad behaviour'. Grown-ups allow themselves what they outlaw for their children and teenagers. The result of this seeming contradiction is highly problematic. Alcohol, smoking and drugs become an initiation path into the adult world. When society offers few distinct initiation patterns (Van Gennep 1986), consumption of alcohol and smoking offer a route through which to acquire adult qualities – 'I smoke therefore I am an adult' – and by demonstrating such behaviours the adolescent obtains a ticket to enter the adult world. Naturally parents and teachers warn about the dangers of smoking, drinking and taking drugs. They may even impose laws and regulations to prohibit these activities. However, as many adults have already fallen foul of these addictions the message is ambiguous: 'Refrain from that behaviour…but actually it's great!' As a result adolescents become suspicious, thinking that adults want to cling to some kind of privilege. This double meaning makes drugs immensely attractive and young people take on the behaviours in order to break the rules of childhood and become autonomous adults. When adolescents are warned about the dangers of alcohol, drugs and smoking, the message is heard with two ears:

> Yes of course you are worried, because smoking and too much alcohol is definitely despicable, but aren't you just trying to define the boundaries? Perhaps you just want to prevent us from becoming

'real adults' If we want to enter adulthood we have to break the rules. Drinking and smoking makes us adults and gives us a distinct, fearful identity. Your warnings provide us with information about how to be initiated into society.

The quest for autonomy is strenuous and ephemeral. Adolescents want to demonstrate independence, but parents and teachers remain important and influential. Young people hear the warnings and understand the dangers, but the urge to join in the interesting scenes and the 'wild side' of life is often stronger. They long to disobey, but at the same time they do not want to cut themselves off completely from adults. Most adolescents are still very much related to them, are eager for their advice and want to be assured that the adults will be there for them when times get hard. Parents and teachers play a vital role in the lives of the majority of young people. The difficulty is that their wish to keep close emotional ties contradicts the desire for autonomy. It is difficult for adolescents to admit openly that they are still hoping to get attention. Autonomy is the primary agenda item, and adolescents are confronted with the dilemma of how to act autonomously without losing the love and care of their parents and the support of their teachers.

Attention through provocation

The answer to the adolescent dilemma is provocation. Adolescents get their emotional attention by infuriating or irritating adults from time to time. When parents and teachers get annoyed it means that they are still connected to the adolescent and care about them. Their anger proves their relatedness. Adolescents will often deliberately madden the grown-ups in an attempt to 'feel them out' and cast an eye beyond the adult persona or mask. Adolescents can provoke when they take drugs, join the party scene and smoke. When parents and teachers get nervous, start to worry and perhaps even rant, this signals to the adolescents that something important has happened. Finally they are being recognised because the adults are paying attention to them.

This is exemplified by the story of a student in a secondary school in Fribourg who pressed past a teacher in the corridor, pushing him slightly. The teacher immediately informed the student that he could at least apologise; instead, the student spat on the floor. Understandably the teacher was enraged and demanded that the young person should follow him to the headmaster's office. After some strong, loud words the interaction between the teacher and student began to develop satisfactorily. It turned out that the young man needed an emotional reaction from an adult in order to stabilise himself. The student was actually checking out whether or not his teachers cared.

It is the duty of parents and teachers to get annoyed with adolescents from time to time. When young people want adults to be angry, it is important that the adults play their role by showing their discontent and perhaps their anger. Adolescents don't want agreeing 'goody-goodies'. They need potent counter-figures. Grown-ups need to show their feelings periodically if they wish to maintain their relationships with their children or students. Aloofness or a detached attitude is not appropriate. During adolescence red faces and loud voices are part of normality. Disagreement with young people communicates to them that they are important. When adolescents choose an addiction they might therefore also be hoping for distinctive reactions from the adults in their lives.

The right to be misunderstood

Adolescents want to develop a distinct identity and cherish alternative myths. The danger is that they may choose scenes or behaviours that are destructive and may lead to addiction. It is the duty of adults to prevent them from becoming victims of alcoholism, and drug and tobacco addiction. In order to fulfil this duty it is important that adults play the psychologically important role of disagreeing. Adults need to take a counter-stance to the positions or opinions of adolescents. Adolescents do not want adults to agree with their lifestyles and interests. There is nothing more annoying for young people than to be surrounded by adults who tolerate everything. Remarks like 'I know how it is: during the 1960s we were also really outrageous' are unhelpful for the adolescent, who is justified to retort 'It's my turn to differ, move on, Dad'. Adolescents want adults to oppose their views, and adults are required to play their role as 'oldies'. No longer is it *their* task to interpret the world. Adults are required to reflect and to scrutinise the behaviour of young people before drawing conclusions according to their own world-view and taste. In many cases adults may have to shake their head and start a dispute. On other issues they may agree. The adolescent is seeking autonomy in opposition and needs opposing adults. Adolescents want to create their own myths and construct their own identity. They strive for a distinct profile, and often choose behaviours that are revolting for adults.

The adult's task is to frown, to be amazed and to not understand the behaviour of the adolescent.

A mutual challenge

Addictions are a serious problem. In undertaking preventive work young people should not be singled out for an exclusive focus. Drugs and alcohol remain a *mutual* challenge. We *all* need to fight alcoholism, drugs and smoking. Programmes and laws that merely focus on the adolescent are in danger of producing a counter-effect and promote addiction as a mark of adulthood. It makes no sense to forbid alcohol consumption in pubs for young people under the age of 18 (as in Britain) because it classifies alcohol consumption as an adult privilege. Such condescending adult positions often persuade young people to opt for the forbidden, because these behaviours and activities are seen to make the adolescent important, mature and supposedly autonomous. It is a prerequisite of protecting young people that they should share adults' ambivalence, struggle and fears. When adolescents realise that addictions are a reality and a constant existential challenge the issue may be dissociated from the quest for autonomy. Preventive work does not mean just laws and regulations, but should also strengthen the psychological defences which adults have to mobilise in order not to fall foul of addiction. This can be made possible by offering programmes in which adolescents themselves develop ways and means of prevention. Schools should be invited to participate in programmes where students think of and instigate preventive steps. Such bottom-up programmes have been shown to be most effective (Guggenbühl *et al.* 2003). Such programmes are more likely to be accepted by adolescents because they elude the psychological dilemma caused by the quest for autonomy. This type of preventive work is less affected by the ambiguous, antagonistic relationship between adults and adolescents. In Switzerland, Sweden and Germany the Institute of Conflict Management and Mythodrama (www.ikm.ch) demonstrates some evidence that using this approach offers the hope that drugs and alcoholism do not spread and that addictions decrease.

References

Baacek, D. (1994) *Die 13-bis 18jährigen*. Belz: Weinheim.

Bericht der Schweizerischen Fachstelle für Alkoholprävention (2003) Lausanne: SFA.

Fend, H. (1991) *Identitätsentwicklung in der Adoleszenz.* Berne: Huber.

Guggenbühl, A. (1993) *The Incredible Fascination of Violence.* Thomston, CT: Spring.

Guggenbühl, A. (1998a) *Wer aus der Reihe tanzt, lebt intensiver.* Munich: Kösel.

Guggenbühl, A. (1998b) *Men, Myth, Power.* New York: Continuum.

Guggenbühl, A., Boström, P., Hersberger, K. and Rom, T. (2003) *Implementation of Conflict Management Strategies and Evaluation of its Effectiveness from a Comparative International Perspective* (A Research Report). Zurich: IKM.

Krampen, G. and Reichel, B. (2002) 'Frühes Erwachsenenalter.' In R. Oerter and L. Montana (eds) *Entwicklungspsychologie.* Belz: Weinheim.

Nohl, H. (1970) *Die Pädagogische Bewegung in Deutschland und ihre Theorie.* Frankfurt am Main: Schulte-Bulmke.

Sielbereisen, R.K. (1997) 'Konsum von Alkohol und Drogen über die Lebensspanne.' In R. Schwarzer (ed) *Gesundheitspsychologie.* Göttingen: Hogrefe.

Trautnerm, H.M. (1991) *Lehrbuch der Entwicklungspsychologie.* Göttingen: Hogrefe.

Van Gennep, A. (1986) *Les Rites des passages.* Paris: Edition de la maison sciences et l'homme.

Chapter 7

Parenting

Annie Waldsax

Introduction

> ...you will be relieved to know that I am not going to tell you what
> to do. (Winnicott 1964, p.15)

In similar vein to Winnicott's statement, this chapter is not an instruction
manual. The intention is to provide the reader with alternative views
about parenting and to promote the maintenance of emotional well-being in the demanding task of parenting. The material is intended to stimulate skills of self-awareness, to offer evidence-based information, and to
provide useful resources for professionals who provide support for parents.

The importance of parenting in promoting positive mental health

The transition into parenthood and the ensuing adjustments that parents
are required to make can be an exciting time but however much parents
welcome parenthood it brings practical and emotional disturbance. This
disturbance can lead parents to question themselves to the point of
self-doubt, a process which is made more complex when parents have a
predisposition to mental health issues and social problems. Evidence
suggests that mental health issues are common and their origins are frequently to be found in infancy and childhood. Studies show that a
mother's psychosocial health

> can have a significant effect on the mother–child relationship, and
> that in turn can have consequences for the short and long-term

psychological health of the child. (Barlow, Coren and Stewart-Brown 2001, p.2)

The importance of parenting support to prevent the escalation of mental health issues

Studies have shown that there is improvement in children's behaviour when parents attend group-based parenting programmes. Grimshaw and McGuire (1998) and Barlow (1999) report benefit from group-based interventions that include the establishment of positive support networks and mutual learning. However, more extensive and large-scale trials are needed to evaluate 'the effectiveness of parenting programmes in the primary prevention of mental health issues' (Barlow, Parsons and Stewart-Brown 2002, p.34).

The importance of self-awareness

The emotional transition and adjustment to parenthood is a complex and significant process. Psychologically parents are adjusting their projected fantasies and expectations of being a parent to the reality of being a parent. Parents reveal their fantasies in such comments as 'I never thought the birth would be so difficult/easy.' 'I thought my partner would be useless at the birth. He was brilliant!' Some of the transitions to reality are a pleasant surprise while others may be disappointing. For some parents it can be disappointing to discover that young children are not born with an innate sense of right and wrong, safety, respect for personal space, sharing and other complex social interactions. It is at this stage that some parents struggle with what they perceive as behaviour problems. Their confidence levels fall and they can become anxious and doubt themselves. This is a time when a group-based parent programme can be beneficial.

Parenting programmes

There is a variety of published programmes. Facilitators find using them is reassuring as they provide a structure to guide them. It is important that facilitators choose a programme they enjoy and feel comfortable with. The skill of balancing the needs of parents with the delivery of a programme is vital and it is recommended that the programme is used as a flexible guide to containing as well as responding to the individual needs of the parents. Common aims linking many programmes are education, skills, relationships and self-esteem building.

Programmes offer the following topics for parents to discuss:

- expectations and experiences of being a parent
- feelings and emotions
- parents' childhood experiences
- styles of parenting
- communication.

Parenting programmes encourage open discussions aided by video vignettes, invented scenarios and psychological concepts explaining reasons behind behaviour. The Internet can be a useful resource for exploring different parenting programmes.

A selection of parenting programmes that may be of interest includes the following:

1. *The Parents and Children Series* (Webster-Stratton 1992). This therapeutic 'collaborative model' aims to identify particular strengths in the parents and to value their experience of their children. It provides the opportunity for parents to learn effective strategies by watching vignettes on video and practising new skills in role play and through homework tasks.

2. *Handling Children's Behaviour* (Finch 1994) focuses on the development of strategies to promote more effective behaviour management in young children.

3. *Parenting Matters* (Munro 1998) is based in family systems and social learning theory frameworks. It aims to teach skills and strategies, provide parental support and enhance the parent–child relationship using clear cartoons and examples that illustrate everyday situations.

4. *The Family Caring Trust* (Tym and Drury 2001). This programme is also underpinned by family systems and social learning theory models and provides clear strategies and opportunities for parents to share their experiences.

5. *The Solihull Approach* (Douglas 2001). This is a therapeutic training model designed specifically for primary health care

professionals in the skills of containment, reciprocity and behaviour management.

For parents to benefit from attending these programmes they need to be sufficiently emotionally robust to tolerate the uncomfortable emotions that can arise when being invited to reflect on their own practice of parenting and make personal disclosures.

Theoretical models underpinning many programmes include social learning theory, attachment theory, cognitive behavioural models, psychodynamic theory, family systems perspectives, Adlerian theory and humanistic approaches. Studies show that programmes contribute significantly in the short term to issues such as maternal anxiety and depression, maternal self-esteem as well as showing improvements in the children's social and emotional adjustment (Barlow *et al.* 2002).

The Northampton Model

The Northampton Model provides a community-based service offering support, education and information on the mental health aspects of parenting as suggested by Einzig (1997). By providing an early intervention service it aims to normalise and destigmatise the need for parenting support and thereby prevent the escalation of mental issues.

The facilitators are community mental health workers who are psychotherapeutically trained in models focusing on the parent–child relationship. They co-work parent groups with professionals such as health visitors, school nurses and midwives (Behr 1997). A particular emphasis of the model is on the delivery of parenting programmes and a focus on the professional–parent relationship. The facilitators provide ongoing training and consultation for community-based professionals working with children.

Theory informing the practice

There are four key elements used: support, information for parents and professionals, education and services (Einzig 1997, cited in Kordan 1999).

Principles used to deliver an effective service to parents and professionals are comparable to Riley's (1994) principles:

1.   They target specific ages of children and specific outcomes.

2.   They have clear goals.

3. Programmes focus on critical periods to prevent problems, i.e. they are provided at transition points such as pregnancy, the first, second and third years of life and puberty.

4. They build on parents' and professionals' existing strengths.

5. Parents are involved in choosing programme design and content.

6. Programme facilitators encourage supportive inter-agency collaboration.

7. They are long term in that it is possible for past group members of the parenting programmes to develop their support further within our service.

8. Group facilitators have excellent interpersonal and facilitative skills, are sensitive to individual's needs, and have good emotional health.

Understanding the dynamic impact of social, economic and cultural factors on parents and professionals is critical to the delivery of the service, and as suggested by Wysling (1995), 'single causal factors are not an adequate explanation for the developmental outcomes of attachment relationships between parents and children'.

The facilitators' psychotherapeutic training is in transactional analysis and the PIPPIN and Open College Network training (Parr 1995). However, their practice integrates ideas of Heinz Kohut's (1978) views of empathy and connection, Daniel Stern's (1977) concept of Caregiver's and Infant's repertoire and Martin Buber's (1996) ideas of the I–Thou relationship and the power of dialogue.

Transactional analysis (TA) is a model of psychotherapy developed by Eric Berne. It uses the accessible concepts of Parent, Adult and Child ego-states (Berne 1961) to describe the complex and dynamic ways in which people relate with each other. Ego-states can also be used to illustrate a person's intrapsychic world, the dynamic structure of his or her emotional well-being.

PIPPIN training is a humanistic/integrative approach used in supporting couples during the transition to parenthood. It is informed by an understanding of the need for containment, holding and reciprocity aimed at enhancing the parent–infant relationship, and promotes the inclusion of both parents.

The combined use of research collected by Einzig (1997) and Riley (1994) with psychotherapeutic models has encouraged the Northampton Model to focus on the significance of containment in the delivery of parenting programmes and support services for professionals. Evidence shows that the parent–child relationship has an important impact on children's emotional well-being (Barlow *et al.* 2002). In a similar way, the professional–parent relationship will have a dynamic impact on the emotional well-being of parents and their children.

As the Northampton Model has evolved, several issues have become apparent in the work with professionals and parents. These include the following:

1. Self-esteem does become fragile and people feel vulnerable; this is normal and can be useful rather than problematic. Although self-questioning sometimes sounds like self-doubt, when shared in a safe environment it can become a powerful tool for problem solving.

2. Parenting programmes are intended to encourage self-reflection, so it is to be expected that anxiety levels will rise and that parents will feel vulnerable. Like children, parents and professionals need 'good enough' holding to contain the anxiety they can experience during times of transition.

3. Parents with good self-esteem are better able to adjust to the changes that their children bring into their lives and will therefore be more robust. However, some parents attending programmes may not have been raised in environments offering 'good enough' holding. Often professionals will have limited knowledge of parents' childhood experiences and may discount the impact that programmes might have on them.

4. If parents are required to develop 'good enough' holding in their relationships with their children, they need to develop their own 'good enough' internal parent that was missing in childhood.

5. Some parents might require short-term individual work before or after attending a group programme.

6. In order for professionals to tolerate and respond appropriately to parent anxieties it is essential that they receive regular clinical supervision.

The interactions between the parent and child impact on each other's sense of self. Likewise the interactions between professionals and parents will impact on each other's sense of self. Professionals, parents and children have different needs and it is balancing the various needs that makes the delivery of parenting programmes challenging. This suggests that to deliver a service it can be useful to look at the complexities of human relationships.

What is meant by quality in relationship?

Stern (1985), Bettelheim (1987) and Bowlby (1988) have all emphasised the importance of attachment in early life and how the quality of early relationships is the key to the development of self-esteem.

Mother and baby stimulate and respond to each other so that the physical and emotional needs of the infant are met. Imagine a mother with her baby at the breast: they gaze into each other's eyes; perhaps baby pulls away or gives a short cry, so mother responds with an empathic murmur such as 'Oh…dear, uncomfortable…?' and gently repositions baby as well as adjusting the cushion for herself. Mother looks at baby, smiles and says 'That's better'. Baby relaxes and continues to suckle. This is understood as attunement (Erskine 1993). Attunement occurs when the parent is aware of his or her own feelings and sensations, and at the same time recognises how the child is likely to be responding and can communicate this awareness back to the child. Mother and baby each know that their feelings and needs are OK to experience and to express. This attuned relationship with the parent is an important prerequisite for the development of a robust sense of self.

The unconditional quality of attunement leads to a more positive sense of emotional well-being. If children have been adequately attuned to, then they will develop into individuals who accept themselves readily. Professionals and parents who are able to accept praise or criticism of their actions without letting it affect their essential sense of self-worth will have had such experiences. They will be able to challenge inappropriate behaviour in compassionate and confident ways, and be realistic about their achievements and shortcomings. They will be self-reflective and healthily self-questioning. They will not be dependent on the judgements of others, but open to receive the opinions of others. These are the parents and professionals who view 'mistakes' as opportunities for personal and professional development.

However, no one has had 'perfect parents' so it can be easy to forget that whether a professional, parent or both, we each have a positive and negative sense of self. Our genetic and neurological development, linked with our childhood experiences, will influence how we regulate the interaction between the positive and negative aspects of ourselves.

The creation of self-esteem

How people feel or what they believe about themselves, others or the world is an expression of their self-esteem or emotional well-being. This might be experienced as a core sense of being OK or not OK (Ernst 1971). Self-esteem results from individuals' interpretation of their experiences. The earliest life experiences are the most influential in this regard. The infant and child make sense of their environment by making assumptions about self, others and the world (Berne 1961). These form the basis of early decisions about how to survive (Beck 1989). The younger these are made, the more fixed they become in the psyche of the child and, later, the adult. Such early interpretations and decisions influence interactions and behaviour throughout life. These influences contribute to the repeated parenting patterns that get passed on in the parent–child relationship (Hendrix and Hunt 1977).

Without self-awareness, these early decisions are not subsequently revised in the process of growing up. However, with self-awareness people can learn to appreciate and acknowledge their positive and negative potential and become responsible for themselves and their actions. Reflection on behaviour or past memories promotes an awareness of internalised negative interpretations. This will trigger emotional energy experienced as discomfort such as shame, anger, grief or fear.

The power of emotional discomfort in the adult

The wish to avoid discomfort is understandable. However, personal change cannot be achieved by avoiding discomfort. For instance, a typical problem voiced by a parent in a parenting group might be: 'I am totally isolated. I can't get out because of Sam's behaviour and I don't want her eating so many biscuits.' This parent has a 3-year-old who has temper tantrums in the supermarket and at home in response to the setting of a limit. The parent feels ashamed because of what she imagines other shoppers might think. She believes herself to be bad and sees Sam as disrespectful and uncooperative. To stop Sam's crying she gives her another biscuit. The more group members encourage her to ignore other people and Sam's crying, the more the parent feels discomfort. Parents need support to tolerate feeling 'bad' at the same time as acknowledging the child's distress when maintaining boundaries. Professionals easily forget the strength of emotional discomfort associated with making behavioural changes. This parent will need the group to give her something to reassure her that she is OK when she says 'No' to Sam. When the parent has received sufficient support from the comments of group members e.g. 'You're right; Sam needs to eat healthily', 'Yes, you will feel uncomfortable when you see Sam upset', 'You might feel horrid but you're not', she might feel sufficiently strong to make a behavioural change and succeed.

Creating the 'good enough' holding environment in groups

Parenting programmes invite parents to discuss issues that involve disclosing personal information and invite parents to change their own behaviour. Consequently parents will experience some anxiety. This is a normal and appropriate response. This discomfort has a healthy component to it known as mistrust. Realistically we cannot anticipate how others will respond until we risk disclosure. Even when safe ground rules about confidentiality and non-judgemental responses have been made explicit in anticipation of anxiety, these agreements need to be tested out. This involves group participants taking a risk and is possible only when a 'good enough' holding environment is provided. A sensitive facilitator will tolerate people taking their time in opening up. The role of a facilitator is not only to disseminate information, but also to notice the dynamic impact of people on each other. As trust and safety increases in the group, parents generally feel able to share more and safety is gradually established. Once sufficient trust has been established the facilitator can risk encouraging parents to become more actively involved.

For some parents expressing an opinion in their family of origin was unsafe. Experiencing a satisfactory holding environment in a group provides the potential for a reparative experience. In any group trust is an intrinsic need for everyone, including the facilitator. Before setting up a group it is worth spending time on the groundwork to promote safety and this can be enhanced by undertaking initial individual assessments (Behr 1997).

Containing feelings in groups

The facilitator listens for certain elements when parents share their expectations. The style of communication conveys underlying emotions such as anxiety, anger, fear, sadness or excitement. If it is anxiety then reassurance and information will be required. If it is excitement, then a reflecting of excitement or joy is an appropriate response. Where there is a mixture of both then the task is to explore the events and expectations associated with each separate emotion. Often there is simultaneous expression of more than one emotion. For example if a couple is expecting a second child they might be not only excited at having another child because they have enjoyed the first one so much, but also anxious about the potential for sibling jealousy. They might question their ability to cope. An initial response would be to acknowledge the anxiety and then to ask about their projected fear of jealousy. Enquiring about how the parents are already supporting the first child through the transition helps parents become aware of the skills they already have. The first steps in containing any emotion are acknowledgement and validation of the emotion. The facilitator needs to be able to tolerate negative feelings in order to do this.

Some parents who have reactive or volatile responses towards their children have difficulty in thinking about how they are feeling before they lose their temper. Teaching parents certain protective behaviour techniques (West 1991) can help them to connect with their own body and eventually stay calm when handling stressful situations. One such technique involves asking parents to share a particular incident that irritated them and then ask them to describe the physical sensations they experience in that situation. Prickly skin and racing heartbeat are common responses. This can be done as a fun group exercise that develops parents' skills of containing their own feelings outside of the group. The technique can be used for different emotions. When parents are encouraged to express the personal significance of specific emotions such as anger, anxiety, sadness, fear or excitement it gives them the opportunity to find words to express their emotions, thus promoting emotional literacy.

A normal phenomenon in stressful situations is to feel and act younger than one's chronological age and revert to defensive behaviours used in childhood. This is true of adults as well as children.

Developmental needs in parents and children

Progression through the developmental stages of childhood provides psychological landmarks that help children answer questions such as 'Who am I? Who am I in relation to others? How do I acquire the skills that I need?' (Illsley-Clarke and Dawson 1989, p.109). Winnicott describes the needs of younger children:

> in the case of under-fives, each child of four is also an infant being weaned, or an infant just born, or even an infant in the womb. Children go backwards and forwards in their emotional age. (Winnicott 1964, p.179)

In other words children recycle or revisit their different emotional stages. This is similar to the idea of 'developmental cycles' (Levin 1988). For example when a 2-year-old sees his baby sister fed by his mother he might snuggle into the baby's Moses basket, pull up the blanket and pop his thumb into his mouth, just like a sleeping newborn. Then as if by magic he might jump up, take his mother a book and snuggle up with her and the baby. Anyone who has lived with young children will recognise this recycling, as will those living or working with teenagers. The teenager rapidly oscillates from grandiose independence to helpless dependency in the attempt to become interdependent. Revisiting different emotional stages promotes self-discovery and continues across the lifespan.

An understanding of developmental stages has the following implications:

1. Self-discovery cannot be completed in one go.

2. We usually revert to an earlier stage of development as a defensive process under stress.

3. Nobody had perfect parents. Consequently adults have unmet needs.

When parents respond to their children in less effective ways they are likely to be recycling the emotional experiences of an earlier developmental stage. It is important to recognise these times, as they are likely to be a response to stress. Living with children is stressful and there will be times when the needs of parents compete or conflict with those of the child.

Parents requesting support consistently want to know how to

- meet everybody's needs
- improve their relationship with their children
- respond 'correctly' when faced with conflicting advice
- gain cooperation from their children
- feel in control
- develop strategies to manage difficult behaviours such as tantrums, night-waking, verbal and physical aggression.

These requests indicate that parents recognise stress in themselves, question their parental practices and are motivated to improve their parental relationships. Stress from any cause affects interaction with the child, and this can influence sleep patterns, tantrums and verbal and physical aggression in the child.

The transition to parenthood

Effective early intervention begins with pregnancy and the provision of services to enhance and integrate the emotional and psychological aspects of becoming a parent has been shown to be effective (Parr 1994). In Northampton, alongside traditional antenatal and postnatal practice, there are such groups being co-facilitated for couples by primary mental health workers and midwives.

Using the same approach, postnatal groups co-facilitated with health visitors have been developed. These groups support parents adjusting to their new role. Parents are encouraged to recount the birth story and so to make emotional sense of it. Another aspect of the programme focuses on the baby's and parent's interactions with each other. Exploring their expectations and experiences generates a mixture of emotion in parents, and they learn something about their own identity as well as their changing role. One mother recounted: 'I was never a broody sort of woman, could never understand my girl friends cooing over babies, I even loathed dolls when I was a child. When my son was born I just melted.' This parent never really knew until then that she was a warm person.

The inclusion of fathers is vital to enhance a stable relationship in couples. Groups comprising couples can allow facilitators to divide into gender-based groups to enable fathers to share their experiences with other men, and to introduce the importance of skin contact for the baby with father as well as mother. This facilitates the bond between all parties (Montagu 1971).

Disappointment alongside joy can come with transition. One parent described the shock she felt at her new lifestyle. Her baby was 6 months old and previously the mother had enjoyed a successful business career. She was someone who took control and had 'everything in order'. She felt frustrated, guilty and inadequate when she realised that following the birth of her daughter she could not order her life in the same way. This parent understood and accepted that changes to her daily routine were inevitable, but she continued to feel inadequate. The challenge of her new role activated unpleasant beliefs such as 'I'm not an OK person when I am not in control'. This is a situation where the parent's unmet need to be heard and validated can be met. The parent might need the experience of having the loss of her old life listened to and validated before moving on. In such circumstances the facilitator will need to tolerate the parent's temporary discomfort and perhaps 'hold' the discomfort of other group members in order to allow time for the parent to feel heard.

Dealing with the challenge of becoming self-aware: different stages of awareness

Parents are at different stages of self-awareness. Some parents want to continue seeing the child as the problem so as not to have to 'look at' themselves. This is unconscious denial. Such parents are not being difficult, but their resistance indicates a low level of trust and it is likely that they needed to defend their sense of themselves during childhood. Signs of resistance are:

- the constant rejection of solutions and strategies offered by the group
- 'Yes but...tried that.'
- 'Tried that...it only worked the once.'

In these situations the professional will become aware of his or her own internal responses. For example, responses of being irritated, feeling inadequate and general stuckness are normal. These responses might also be clues to how the parent is feeling as he or she pushes away possible solutions. Again this might be a time for the professional to step out of problem-solving solutions and move into exploring the parent's feelings.

Working with resistance using the discount matrix

The discount matrix (Mellor and Sigmund 1975) is a useful schema for working with resistance. Persistently holding on to an untrue belief in the face of evidence to the contrary is called discounting (Schiff *et al.* 1975), for example, believing incorrectly that 'no one is able or willing to help'. Discounting is a normal human phenomenon, and occurs when we make something greater or less than it is in reality. Mellor and Sigmund (1975) describe four levels of discounting:

1. *Existence*: the problem is treated as if it does not exist. For example, a 2-year-old is allowed to run across the car park while the parent pushes the laden trolley towards the car. Discounting at this level may involve an incorrect belief that the world is safe.

2. *Significance*: here the significance of the problem is not recognised. For example, 'Yes, I know there are cars about but he's done this lots of times and never been hit.'

3. *Change possibility*: at this level the possibility of a solution is rejected. For example, 'Yes, I know there are cars but you can't stop kids running about.'

4. *Personal ability*: this level of discounting involves the person denying that he or she has the ability to solve the problem. For example, 'Well, I've told him what will happen but he won't hold my hand, he'll only behave for his Dad.'

Everybody discounts on at least one of these levels much of the time. The discount matrix can help parents and professionals reflect on their way of handling situations. For instance many people discount their ability to solve problems, especially when life is hard. Discounting occurs in relation to ourselves, others and the external world.

A knowledge of discounting will enable facilitators to detect in which areas parents might be discounting, e.g. ourselves: 'I can't get him to behave so what can I do?' Old beliefs here might be 'I'm powerless' or 'I'm not OK'.

Others: 'He'll only behave for his Dad.' Underlying old beliefs might include 'others are capable and powerful', or they might be more specific, such as 'men are powerful, women are victims' or 'I'm not OK, others are OK'.

The external world: i.e. the environment. 'This is our local car park, the drivers are careful here. This is a nice neighbourhood.' The old belief in this statement might be 'the world is always safe'.

Using the discount matrix

The aim is to enable the parent to stop discounting. Paradoxically, the best way to help is for the facilitator to explore the parent's current belief system and to understand the reasons behind the beliefs as they will have a function that benefits the parent in some way.

If the mountain won't come to Muhammad, then Muhammad must go to the mountain

Some of the parents enrolled on a parenting programme have been identified by another agency as having a problem. Unfortunately if parents do not recognise that they have a need, then it is understandable that they will be resistant to change. They might make a verbal agreement to enrol but not attend the groups, clinic appointments or home visits. They say they will come along and they don't. The parents may have difficulty in establishing trust. They might be discounting the existence and the solvability of the problem, or it might be that groups are not for them. Groups may unconsciously be seen as replicating their family of origin. For some, the family group will have been an unsafe or unsupportive environment. Although it is disappointing that some parents are resistant to joining groups, it is important to recognise potential developments in other provisions such as child health surveillance and health promotion programmes. Opportunities for the development of trust can be provided by child health and health promotion clinics, which parents attend usually for physical health reasons.

Promoting and empowering

The following incident illustrates how apparently trivial interactions between parent and professional can lead to a positive outcome. A health promotion event, open to anyone in the local community, was held in a school. Various professionals including school nurses, community nurses, a health visitor and a primary mental care worker were in attendance. Each professional had a display of information. Visitors to the event were predominantly young mothers and older men and women. Mothers were asking the school nurses how to get rid of nits; other people were having their blood pressure checked. The informal, busy yet convivial atmosphere helped to retain a sense of anonymity. The primary mental health worker's table contained a display of posters and handouts on anger management, temper tantrums and other parenting strategies. Mothers sifted through leaflets, and passed comments about the information to those nearby. The child and family psychotherapist stood back in order to allow people space to be curious about the posters. She did not want to be intrusive neither did she want her customers to feel ignored or abandoned. In order to let people know she was available for questions, she stopped sorting out pamphlets and indicated her willingness to clarify information. As a consequence parents asked questions and shared information about themselves and their children. In the conversation they gained useful information and, in some cases, a sense of their own competency. Their willingness to converse with the primary mental health worker provided the opportunity for validation of the parents and the strategies they were already using. The professional recognised behavioural clues in the parents' tone of voice and facial expressions that suggested she was reinforcing their sense of being 'good enough' in their role as a parent.

These same parents asked where they might obtain further guidance and took up the suggestion of starting a parents' group on the school premises. They approached the head teacher, who jointly explored the needs of local parents by providing a drop-in forum.

A tool to promote self-reflection

Here is a short exercise to illustrate the myriad of ways that the invitation to join a group can trigger memories of one's original family group.

Close your eyes and take your time to reflect on this:

1. A group is defined as two or more people collected together, so bearing this definition in mind, what was your first experience of being in a group?

2. Your family of origin was your first group. This was your tribe.

3. Reflect on your experience of that tribe. Notice the times you felt safe, notice the times you felt unsafe.

4. Were you the quiet person, the ringleader, the joker or did you have some other role in your tribe? What was it?

5.   Do you take on the same role in groups now?

6.   How might this limit your effectiveness?

7.   Imagine yourself in an unfamiliar role in a group. How do you feel? What would you need in order to do it?'

The impact of parenting work on professionals and self-esteem

Professionals and parents have demanding roles that can be a drain on their personal resources. The professional–parent relationship requires the professional to be nurturing and to be involved in a balancing of competing needs, and the willingness to be self-reflective. It is important that professionals find ways of self-nurturing to enable them to replenish their resources. Securing time in the diary to enjoy activities with family and friends, and spending time alone in activities that allow one to decelerate and stop are crucial to continued well-being. Professionals who are able to care for themselves in this way are likely to be more successful in their work with parents.

Supervision and professional development

Clinical supervision is an essential learning tool and also a valuable form of self-care for the professional. Supervision increases awareness of a professional's relationship with clients. This includes the impact that the client has on the professional's internal world. Supervision provides a holding environment that enables professionals to manage their feelings and maintain emotional well-being. This is particularly helpful when working with parents who are resistant to change. When the work with a family is difficult there is a tendency to question one's abilities and stress levels might increase. The 'good enough' supervision environment (Hawkins and Shohet 2000) is a safe place in which to explore self-doubts and discover ways forward. Supervision is essential for the safety and well-being of both worker and client, encouraging self-reflection and open discussion by the professional. Supervision helps identify needs for further training that enhances group facilitation.

Conclusion

Research evidence consistently indicates that supporting parents is worthwhile and is beneficial for the emotional well-being of parents and children in the short term. However, like parenting because of the complexity of human relationships, this task is not as simple as it first appears. Making parenting support available to all parents helps to develop respect and value this vital role. Professionals need the resources to extend support for parents who are motivated to develop skills they have acquired by attending programmes. It is essential that professionals undertaking this work have the same support, time and understanding as they offer to parents. A support service that has mental health expertise such as the Northampton Model is crucial in offering a holding environment to such professionals. Resources need to be in the form of expert supervision and training as well as giving time for self-reflection and self-nurture. Some parents are very resistant to accessing help and do not make changes, or the changes they make are very small and slow. Professionals require support in dealing with the disappointments inherent in this work if they are to maintain an appropriately high standard in their practice.

References

Barlow, J. (1999) *Systemic Review of the Effectiveness of Parenting: Programmes in Improving Behaviour Problems in Children Aged 3–10 Years.* Oxford: Health Service Research Unit.

Barlow, J., Coren, E. and Stewart-Brown, S. (2001) *A Review of the Literature on Parenting Programmes and Measures of Maternal Psychosocial Health.* Oxford: Health Service Research Unit.

Barlow, J., Parsons, J. and Stewart-Brown, S. (2002) *Systemic Review of the Effectiveness of Parenting Programmes in the Primary and Secondary Prevention of Mental Health Problems.* Oxford: Health Service Research Unit.

Beck, C.J. (1989) *Everday Zen.* Los Angeles: Harper and Row.

Behr, H.P. (1997) 'Group Work with Parents.' In K.D. Dwivedi (ed) *Enhancing Parenting Skills.* Chichester: Wiley.

Berne, E. (1961) *Transactional Analysis in Psychotherapy.* New York: Grove Press.

Bettelheim, B. (1987) *A Good Enough Parent.* New York: Alfred A. Knopf.

Bowlby, J. (1988) *A Secure Base.* London: Routledge.

Buber, M. (1996) *I and Thou,* 2nd edn. Edinburgh: T&T Clark.

De Mause, L. (ed) (1995) *The History of Childhood.* London: Jason Aronson.

Douglas, H. (2001) *The Solihull Approach.* Birmingham: School of Primary Health Care, University of Central England.

Einzig, H. (1997) *Promoting Successful Parenting. Report of a Ministerial Seminar. London: Home Office Special Conference Unit.*

Ernst, F.H. (1971) 'The O.K. Corral.' *Transactional Analysis Journal 1,* 4, 33–42.

Erskine, R.G. (1993) 'Inquiry, Attunement and Involvement in the Psychotherapy of Dissociation.' *Transactional Analysis Journal 23,* 4, 184–190.

Finch, G. (1994) *Handling Children's Behaviour.* London: NCH Action for Children.

Grimshaw, R. and McGuire, C. (1998) *Evaluating Parenting Programmes: A Study of Stakeholders' Views.* London: National Children's Bureau Enterprises.

Hawkins, P. and Shohet, R. (2000) *Supervision in the Helping Professions.* Philadelphia, PA: Open University Press.

Hendrix, H. and Hunt, H. (1977) *Giving the Love that Heals: A Guide for Parents.* New York: Pocket Books.

Illsley-Clarke, J. and Dawson, C. (1989) *Growing Up Again.* Center City, MN: Hazelden.

Kohut, H. (1978) *The Search of the Self: Selected Writings of Heinz Kohut 1950–1978, vol 1.* New York: International Universities Press.

Kordan, L.R. (1999) *Patterns of Parenting Support.* Glasgow: Mental Health Foundation.

Levin, P. (1988) *Becoming the Way We Are.* Deerfield Beach, FL: Health Communications.

Mellor, K. and Sigmund, E. (1975) 'Discounting.' *Transactional Analysis Journal 5,* 3, 295–302.

Montagu, A. (1971) *Touching: The Human Significance of the Skin.* New York: Harper and Row.

Munro, S. (1998) *Parenting Matters.* Stroud: Hawthorn Press.

Parr, M. (1994) 'Towards a Humanistic/Integrative Approach to Parent Infant Counselling and Supporting Men and Women in the Transition to Parenthood.' Unpublished master's dissertation. London: Regent's College School of Psychotherapy and Counselling.

Parr, M. (1995) *Why PIPPIN was Developed: Some Research Findings.* Stevenage: PIPPIN.

Riley, D. (1994) *Some Principles for Designing Effective Parenting Education/Support Programmes.* Wisconsin Family Impact Seminars Briefing Report. Madison, WI: University of Wisconsin.

Schiff, J.L., Schiff, A., Mellor, K., Schiff, E., Fishman, J., Wolz, L., Fishman, C. and Momb, D. (1975) *The Cathexis Reader: Transactional Analysis Treatment of Psychosis.* New York: Harper and Row.

Stern, D. (1977) *The First Relationship.* Cambridge, MA: Harvard University Press.

Stern, D. (1985) *The Interpersonal World of the Infant.* New York: Basic Books.

Tym, S. and Drury, D. (2001) *The Family Caring Trust.* Sheffield: Hallam Caring Services.

Webster-Stratton, C. (1992) *The Parents and Children Series.* Seattle, WA: Seth Enterprises.

West, P.F. (1991) *Risking on Purpose.* Burnside, South Australia: Essence.

Winnicott, D.W. (1964) *The Child, the Family and the Outside World.* Harmondsworth: Penguin.

Wysling, M. (1995) 'Attachment Relationship of Parent and Child – A Multi-Dimensional Model.' Unpublished workshop presentation.

Chapter 8

Life Skills Education through Schools

Judith Coley and Kedar Nath Dwivedi

The Life Skills Education Programme, developed by the World Health Organization (1997), aims at psychosocial competence in children and young people and can be delivered in a variety of settings including schools. Although it is essentially a mental health promotion programme the gains from it have been found to be far reaching in a variety of areas across education, health and welfare. Improvements have been found in teacher–pupil relationships, academic performance, school attendance, parent–child relationships, self-confidence, self-esteem, prevention of classroom behaviour problems and bullying, substance abuse, adolescent pregnancy, Aids and so on (World Health Organization 1997).

The programme is not in the form of a recipe book but comprises a set of guiding principles that can be used to develop tailormade details appropriate for the local circumstances. For example, in a school setting it can be implemented over a flexible period (such as one to three years). The essence of the programme is to create a learning environment in which the teacher can organise active and experiential learning activities. It consists of experiential (in small groups and pairs, using brainstorming, discussion, role play, games and debates) education in areas such as decision making and problem solving; creative thinking and critical thinking; communication and interpersonal relationships; self-awareness and empathy; coping with emotions and stressors (see Box 8.1).

These are planned to be taught at three levels. At level 1, there is teaching of basic components of core life skills, practised in relation to common everyday situations. At level 2, the focus is on application of life skills to relevant themes that are connected to various health and social

---

Box 8.1 Some examples of the components of life skills education themes

- Critical thinking (e.g. analysing influences)
- Creative thinking (e.g. meta-perspective)
- Decision making (e.g. being indecisive, impulsive, procrastinating or putting off, letting others decide, evaluating all choices and deciding)
- Problem solving (e.g. defining the problem, brainstorming choices, evaluating choices, deciding and implementing, re-evaluating and learning from experience)
- Effective communication (e.g. desomatisation, verbal/nonverbal, direct/indirect, clear/masked, meta-communication)
- Interpersonal relationships (e.g. conflict resolution, actions/words, assertiveness, coping with pressure, asking for help, respecting personal space, respecting difference)
- Self-awareness (e.g. recognition of strengths and weaknesses, likes and dislikes, recognition of one's mood or mental state, stress, etc., self-control, identity, esteem, confidence)
- Empathy (e.g. other's point of view, prosocial behaviour)
- Coping with emotions (e.g. different aspects of emotional development such as differentiation, desomatisation, self-regulation and utilisation, recognition of emotions, influence of emotions on thoughts, attention, memory, motivation and behaviour, responses to emotions and emotional expression, coping with intense emotions like misery, anxiety, anger, jealousy) (see Chapter 4 by Dwivedi in this volume for further discussion)
- Coping with stress (e.g. recognition of stress and its sources, environmental considerations, relaxation, cognitive help).

---

problems, and at level 3, there is application of skills in relation to specific risk situations that can give rise to health and social problems. The strength of the programme is its flexibility so that it can be implemented as extra-curricular (e.g. as a mental health promotion initiative), integrated (as a part of school curriculum, e.g. personal, social and health education – PSHE) and/or infused (as a part of academic subjects, e.g. communication skill as a part of language class).

The programme has been implemented in a variety of countries. In this chapter, the experience of its implementation in Northamptonshire is described.

The Northamptonshire experience

One of the authors (KD) submitted a proposal in 1999 to the local Inter-agency Child and Adolescent Mental Health Strategy Group to incorporate this programme into its schools. The local health authority as a part of its health improvement plan funded the initiative. An inter-agency management group was formed to oversee the project and a coordinator (JC) was appointed to facilitate it. After an initial pilot scheme, a detailed plan was developed to train and support schools in the county. Schools were invited to apply for places on three-day training courses. The training sessions were planned to raise awareness and build confidence in the staff attending, as well as to develop and share strategies for classroom use. The out-of-school training venue and the light-hearted approach also contributed positively to the atmosphere. An outline of the content is given in Box 8.2.

The training programme includes several experiential and small group exercises, for example, to consider ways of further developing and implementing each topic in school life. Experts (local and national) in the fields of child development, drama, PSHE curriculum and so on, all contribute to the programmes over three days (held several months apart to allow colleagues to reflect upon and practise techniques in the classroom). During the training days, good practice is shared by examining the strategies used in schools and by reflecting on them for adaptation by others. Presentations by experienced practitioners help to illustrate the value and authenticity of particular teaching strategies and inspire a common appreciation of the advantages or associated problems. As each day is evaluated, the comments and requests at the end of each evaluation form are considered and built in to the next day wherever possible. In the rare event of a school being unable to attend the centrally based courses, the programme (mirroring as far as possible the central one) is offered to the whole school staff in sessions on training days or after school. The advantages of having everyone trained together and a wide expertise developing among the staff overall as well as no teacher being taken out of the classroom must be weighed against the disadvantages of a lack of wide discussion opportunities with other schools, no release

Box 8.2 An outline content of the training programme

Day 1

- Life skills – what they are; why; when and how to teach
- Strategies for developing communication skills – verbal and nonverbal
- The emotional development of the child
- Using support resources in the PSHE curriculum
- Planning to support the curriculum.

Day 2

- The classroom climate
- Life skills concepts and contexts
- Developing and promoting emotional health and well-being
- Values and life skills education
- Specific strategies – circle time, storytelling
- Classroom evaluation of life skills.

Day 3

- Conflict – children's responses to conflict and divorce
- Dialogue and attention directing tools – classroom strategies
- Links with National Curriculum subject areas
- Emotional literacy – strategies and vocabulary
- Puppetry and drama strategies to support emotional literacy
- Common themes through PSHE
- Evaluation of the school programme.

from the classroom to develop professional expertise and extending an already demanding day.

After the training sessions, the coordinator supports schools in the implementation of their plans. The programme is still continuing at the time of writing this chapter. Any school on the Life Skills Programme receives resources to support the classroom development of the children. These include the Teachers' Advisory Council on Alcohol and Drugs Education (TACADE 2001) folder *I Am, I Know, I Can*, which helps plan and deliver a programme of PSHE and life skills across the primary curriculum. The Rotary (2001) compact discs *Coping with Family Change* and *Coping with Bullying* along with storybooks to help illustrate the issues like *Getting to School* and *Playing Out* by Clark and French (1997a, 1997b) for TACADE are shared to support school work. Leaflets including *Me and My Family* or *My Family is Changing* (published in 2001 by the Lord Chancellor's Department, now the Department for Constitutional Affairs) are given out so that schools can make them available to individual children or install them on the information technology (IT) network. Further support is available to individuals or to schools who request personal consultation after the training programme has been completed. It is hoped that this level of support will encourage and enthuse busy teachers in further developing life skills in their classrooms and throughout their schools.

Barriers to life skills education

Conflicting priorities

What do we mean by the statement 'We want our children to do well in school'? It depends on who is speaking. Parents often mean 'be happy, make friends, and master some useful skills' in that order of priority. Governors might mean 'master many skills that can be evidenced in the league tables and be part of a happy community'. Teachers often mean 'be happy learners'. From recent evidence it appears that the government, together with the Department for Education and Skills (DfES), might mean something very different. The plethora of exhortations and targets, tests, tick boxes, league tables and regulations might suggest there is little time for anything other than curriculum skills. There is a danger that under these pressures the development of life skills in the school day will be squeezed out. It has even been said that political expediency places short-term target setting above children's broad developmental needs. This stress also affects the teachers and their ability to relate creatively and spontaneously to their pupils. The preparation for tests not only takes time out of the wider educational curriculum (sometimes from the autumn term prior to the tests), but also causes stress in both adults and children. This stress in the classroom manifests itself as irritability and tiredness in the teacher and lack of concentration and distraction on the part of the child. The classroom becomes a less enjoyable environment for all.

The letters pages of the magazines of the professional associations feature cries from teachers agonising about how to redirect the learning experience into areas now neglected. 'Humans are body, mind and spirit. …Our society seems to have lost sight of the fact that education is about more than schooling', cries one letter in *Report* (the in-house magazine of the Association of Teachers and Lecturers) in January 2003 (p.9), and reflects that those with 'intellectual abilities' will do well in the current system but the rest will have to turn to 'optional ' or 'extra-curricular activities'. Many commentators and professionals in education are reflecting upon how little time there is in the school day now for music, swimming, art and drama. Curriculum areas that support creativity and health are being squeezed out of the school day. BBC Radio 4 broadcast a play in 2003 by Ryan Craig dealing with the subject. When the issue is as widely and publicly accepted as this, then perhaps it is time to examine the topic of the three Ts – tests, tables and targets – more closely. The outcome might support the call for more recognition and development of life skills in the classroom.

In an acknowledgement of the concerns held by many teachers and parents, the Education Secretary Charles Clarke announced changes to the regime for Key Stage 1 in May 2003 by introducing an 80-page document on the DfES Standards Site called 'Excellence and Enjoyment – A Strategy for Primary Schools' (www.dfes.gov.uk/primarydocument/). Schools would be given more ownership of the target-setting process and teacher judgements would play a major part in the assessments. He said, 'I do believe that breadth and diversity is at the heart of what a good primary school is like'.

Subjects outside the National Curriculum are implicitly devalued by the earliest contacts a teacher-to-be has with the educational system. Initial Teacher Training students can leave university to enter schools with little or no grounding in PSHE as it is not a National Curriculum subject and is not tested. (Herein lies an implicit message for the school timetabler, stressed to find a slot for extra literacy or mathematics. Time can be found in the day if other 'non-essential' subjects can be pared down.) Postgraduate Certificate of Education students, in their one year of training, rarely have any exposure to the issues at all. However, training has now started to develop the role of the PSHE teacher, giving recognition and status to that role.

Confusion in the meaning of the phrase 'Life Skills'

The World Health Organization's (1997) definition has already been described. However, there are already several programmes in education that also sound like 'Life Skills' but are not. For example, 'Skills for Life' is one course for later teenage years and includes 'Basic Skills' – IT, numeracy and literacy as well as budgeting and job skills. 'Key Skills', introduced in 2000 in the revised National Curriculum, are defined as communication, IT, application of number, problem solving, working with others, improving one's own learning and performance. In contrast life skills are built naturally into early school life as part of the affective curriculum where teachers encourage mutual respect, value a strong sense of identity and expect pupils to help each other, communicate clearly and develop good interpersonal relationships with everyone in the school community. The outcome of this will be reduced disaffection, truancy or violence and a more enjoyable classroom climate.

Testing

Life skills are not examined or levelled at any stage in a pupil's education. The test comes later and is harsher. If students fail (to achieve a C grade in GCSE) in mathematics or science at the age of 16 they can take the test again next year, succeed, and move on. If, however, that student is pregnant or on drugs or has acquired a criminal record by the age of 16, they cannot remedy that in one year – it is likely to have a huge enduring impact on their life, even if they are well supported in their remedial actions.

Added value of life skills in education

Children with poor psychosocial competence

Many experienced teachers have observed that more children are coming into school with poorly developed social skills. Collaborative learning is a long-term target for many children entering school before their fifth birthday – and some are nearly a year younger than their peers in class. The pressures on parents and the reliance that some homes place on computers and television to contain children's enthusiasms mean that interpersonal relationships are not as well developed as they need to be on school entry. A child (often a boy) may get attention at home only when he misbehaves. While he is quiet in front of his electronic game or TV programme he is ignored, so he attracts adult attention by misbehaving. Evidence is seen in curriculum initiatives like literacy where many children have poorly developed listening skills, and so are slow to develop communication skills.

Chronological age has a marginal bearing on emotional development and teachers find that a child with older siblings is a different being from another in the class – perhaps born in the same month, but who has younger siblings, or even none. Primary schools with children under 12 have seen that the interventions and opportunities they can offer might have some influence on the emotional development and mental well-being of their pupils. However, pupils in secondary school with already well-developed attitudes are harder to approach and influence in this area. Society and education systems hope they have already gained skills in critical thinking and decision making, to equip them with strategies they need in life. The older pupil spends little time each day with the same teacher, and so building that crucial relationship which nurtures the development of positive attitudes and skills for life is harder. In middle schools, which the pupil has attended since the age of 9 (or Key Stage 3) interventions can be successful, but different teaching strategies have to be applied. Early intervention is crucial to the success of developing and building effective social competencies. The arrangements and relationships in the primary school are more effective than later programmes in schools where the styles of schooling militate against lasting success.

Ensuring that they happen

Where life skills opportunities are planned into the school day, there is much more likelihood that they will actually happen and there will be some status attached to them – they are not accidental, but are valued alongside the other curriculum subjects. Coherence with other curriculum areas like literacy can be achieved – or the other curriculum areas can be used as opportunities to explore the skills we all need in life. Many teachers use stories like *The Rainbow Fish*, by Marcus Pfister (1995), a 'big book', some using the hand puppet that accompanies the series, to raise issues of friendship and sharing, pride and envy. These abstract words are 'context free' and are meaningless to young children, but all children recognise and can increasingly empathise with friendships and envy of possessions in the playground.

Self-actualisation

Maslow (1998) first defined his 'hierarchy of needs' in 1962 in *Towards a Psychology of Being* and we know that the cognitive needs of children cannot be addressed until the more basic needs of physiological essentials, safety and security, belonging and self-esteem are satisfied. Many children need to have their feelings of self-esteem and self-worth built up. The reward system of a school needs to be reflected and practised in every classroom consistently. Verbal praise and out-of-class recognition of achievement must be a regular feature of the playground or corridor. Gender plays a part here: many boys prefer the informal recognition to the public reward.

Some of the dominant cultural ideas that usually affect schools are discussed by Zimmerman and Beaudoin (2002). If learners can envisage themselves succeeding at a task – executing a three-point turn in the car, finishing an essay, solving an equation, or riding a bicycle – then learners stand a better chance at mastering that skill, as they can include that skill in their idea of the person they want to be. This self-actualisation, bringing the real self closer to the ideal self, relies on good self-esteem to support the individual's development of his or her full potential, and is dependent on early acquisition of life skills.

Ways of meeting children's needs for life skills

The PSHE and citizenship curriculum (which is non-statutory in the primary phase) sets out comprehensive guidelines covering three main learning outcomes, attitudes, skills and knowledge (naturally known as the 'ASK' model), over four strands of the framework and identifies an opportunity to

- develop confidence and responsibility and make the most of opportunities
- prepare to play an active role as citizens
- develop a healthy, safer lifestyle
- develop good relationships and respect the differences between people.

The Gulbenkian Foundation commissioned the *Passport* document (by J. Lees and S. Plant) in 2000. This is a useful resource and suggests ways in which these areas can be tackled. Mapping is a useful tool for auditing where a school is in the development of these opportunities. By examining the long- or medium-term planning document for one year group and matching it to the PSHE guidance, a teacher can see where the coverage in the lessons occurs, and where to focus more time and activities – say, in the recent introduction of citizenship. The short-term planning can then be supported using resources like TACADE's (2001) *I Am, I Know, I Can* which plots each activity against the four framework areas. This folder offers support activities for both Key Stage 1 and Key Stage 2. Other useful commercial resources include Wetton and Williams' (2000) *Health for Life* and *Blueprints for Health Education* by Lloyd and Morton (1992). In spite of the existence of much good support material, the auditing and planning task may seem onerous at first but not when agreement is reached that PSHE is happening all the time in school; it is the teachers' choice whether to manage and develop it or not.

Good planning will take into account all the opportunities that occur in school, and build on them. Many teachers are doing a lot of this work already and this will lead to a confident outlook when planning the coherence and progression into the programme. There may be different types of activities, some infused into other curriculum areas – for instance, religious education, or dance to express feelings, or art, e.g. drawing hands, which also considers the good and bad uses for our hands – or clearly identified timetable slots for PSHE.

Other extra-curricular activities, visits out of school, residential visits, visitors to the school, festivals, concerts, school fairs, sports day, all can offer huge opportunities for children to develop their life skills. These can be planned, and tasks assigned to specific classes, for example, meeting and greeting, answering the telephone, escorting parents, monitoring attendance, making lists of requirements, financial problem solving and decision making. Children who are familiar with strategies like circle time will develop skills and can progress to more complex activities like dialogue or more responsible roles later in their school life. Many of these activities will satisfy the need to extend our children's citizenship capabilities, as will areas of school life like the school council or planning and presenting assemblies.

The National Healthy Schools Standard (NHSS) includes criteria covering emotional health and well-being. A school would be encouraged to consider and develop strategies to support both children and adults in the school community in this respect. Not only is there a requirement to have the policies in place to support the children, but also the implementation of the policies is considered. The development of school councils, life skills programmes, having members of staff with recognised responsibilities, offering continuing professional development and appraisal for all staff, developing links with the community and pupils' homes, all contribute to meeting the standard.

Guidance documents that support staff include the booklet *Staff Health and Wellbeing* (NHSS 2002). This booklet promotes the reduction of anxiety and stress through 'The Wellbeing Process'. It outlines both big and small changes that can build to benefit all the adults working in the school community through consultation, continuing professional development, benchmarking, shared learning and other strategies.

Some case examples from the Northamptonshire experience
Staff support

The Northamptonshire Healthy Schools programme, accredited to the NHSS, is promoting courses for teachers in the county with Work Life Support Ltd, part of the Teachers' Support Network. The aim is to support the development of good work–life balance through effective change management, tackling workload, and personal well-being. Strategies that will result in improved mental well-being for adults in education and will make life more enjoyable and rewarding for all in the school community are discussed and further supported by follow-up in schools.

Home–school links

Parents, as always, need to be included and the usual ways of communicating with parents should include the life skills work we do in school. Most parents will appreciate these at least as much as the curriculum skills and they will see the fruits of them at home more clearly too! As the Life Skills Programme is being evaluated, using Goodman's (1997) 'Strengths and Difficulties Questionnaire', this too is shared with parents and they are involved in the evaluation. Some parents who visit the school as voluntary helpers or are employed as classroom learning assistants are successful in supporting classroom activities.

The Life Skills Programme has evolved in schools in different ways. For example, in Collingtree School, parents and voluntary helpers offer in-class support. Children are encouraged to find ways of dealing with problems in their circle time. Year 6 have class discussions on controversial topics like 'playing out on your own; use of a mobile phone; hours spent watching television', etc. Critical thinking is introduced by the challenge to children to consider why they think a certain way, and also to consider the opposite point of view, empathising with someone who might hold a different opinion.

Parental involvement is seen as particularly valuable, and parents of children in Year 6 come in to school to support teachers and share their strategies for coping with stress, peer pressure, and health and fitness. Lunchtime supervisors have received training and support: their handbook of guidance, games and conflict resolution strategies ends with the statement 'Keep calm and cheerful!!!' The children can report, confidentially, anything that they consider a worrying incident in playground or class. Children's work on feelings – what makes them excited, angry, happy, bored – shows they have a confident approach and can communicate in an area that many find hard. Communicating their feelings is a step on the way to managing them. Some work, recognising the conflict in their lives and how they resolve it, shows unexpected maturity. Ideas for relaxation, expressed as flow charts and maps, combine creative thinking with art and organisational skills.

The children's role in the school council is to represent both the class and schoolhouse, and whole school issues are discussed. Responsibility for costs – both financial and time – is acknowledged. The school rules are discussed and negotiated by each class in September then worded by the children and signed as an agreement. Recognition for good behaviour is promoted and children are encouraged to reflect: 'What have I done today that makes me feel proud?'

Comprehensive integration of life skills in the school curriculum

Similarities exist between all schools and many characteristics of the planning in Oundle and Kingscliffe Middle School will be recognised by teachers and PSHE coordinators. Here the importance of planning is reinforced since the school is on two sites.

Oundle and Kingscliffe Middle School has a rural catchment area with two sites seven miles apart. Staff work closely together under the same management team. The coordinator for PSHE has built on the work already done in Key Stage 2 and all the Key Stage 2 class teachers use the TACADE pack *I Am, I Know, I Can* alongside the programme already in place to support and supplement existing activities. Several members of staff from both sites have attended training in the Life Skills Programme, and a whole-school presentation to all the staff both enthused and motivated teachers to implement the activities.

The learning support assistants have close relationships with the children through class work and the bursar and school secretary are the children's first-aiders. Lunchtime supervisors have high profiles in the middle of the day and their relationships with the children are different again – children can relate to non-teaching staff in informal ways; there is no perception that they could influence the relationship with the teacher responsible for their mathematics or English.

In Key Stage 2 and Year 7 the life skills work is taught by class teachers in the timetabled lesson and links with curriculum areas – science, English, literacy – are made through the key stages. For instance the consideration of problems and decision-making skills are practised in science when health, smoking and drug abuse is studied. Letters of thanks and invitations are linked with literacy skills and English.

The Rotary (2001) CDs *Coping with Family Change* and *Coping with Bullying* (both primary and secondary) have been networked into the information technology room so that children can access them in their own time whenever they feel the need.

The programme over four years ensures progression across a range of issues, and incorporates visits by the children and by visitors to the school. In 'Hazard Alley' children in Year 7 experience a range of challenges in a mock-up urban setting and have to make decisions around safety issues. The Year 8 Italian and French exchanges both offer opportunities for developing communication skills, self-awareness, empathy as well as critical and creative thinking. The children have to cope with emotions and stresses and build interpersonal relationships – while living in a foreign land without their parents. Visitors to the school from the community offer further opportunities for life skills like communication and self-awareness enhancement. This includes the school nurse, who contributes to the PSHE curriculum.

Entry planners and personal 'Success Folders' in which to record all their achievements – from a local fishing competition to an academic award – follow children through to Year 8 and they keep them and take them to their next school. The self-esteem that a child develops from successes in all areas of hs or her life contributes to personal growth.

Beyond circle time

Many schools use circle time, some in a planned way, some as a response to events in the day. Schools can see the benefits of allowing the children to participate in discussions when they set up school councils. Children then can take responsibility for decision making, building on the foundations of empathising and critical and creative thinking laid down in earlier classes.

In Whitefriar's Junior School, personal and social education is taught alongside and within religious education on a two-year cycle for twelve hours in the lower school and eight hours in the upper part of the school. An audit confirmed the opportunities within the curriculum where life skills could be built in. So, for example, science covers the areas of sex education in Years 3 and 6 and changing and growing in Year 5. Visits to programmes like Northamptonshire's 'Essential World' (where health and safety issues are tackled by the children on an interactive site) widen children's decision-making experiences. Children also have the opportunity to nominate charities, and raise money themselves and mix with other year groups in the Friday afternoon club sessions allowing wider ranges of friendship and mutual support to develop.

The school is a holder of the Northamptonshire Silver Healthy Schools Award and is moving to align this with the National Healthy Schools Standard. Citizenship awards, organised in conjunction with the local police officers, have been in place for pupils since 2000 and pupils contribute to the assessment of their meeting the criteria for the award. Developing children's confidence and self-esteem are high on the agenda for all the adults in school, including visiting parents and governors. Involving children in the school council further develops self-esteem and decision-making. The most recent issue of playtime has resulted in reduced conflict and improved communication between the children in the playground.

'How my actions affect others' involved the children sitting in a circle giving examples of ways that other people's behaviour affected them. Many of the anecdotes were critically negative – as when someone shouted at them and made them feel unhappy. Their self-awareness of fear and confidence were evident at this stage. Nearly all the relationships used in discussion were familial and domestic. Their communication skills were used confidently in these contexts, but less so in the stress of more abstract situations and third person awareness. Gradually the pupils developed more empathy and related to how other people felt. When urged to consider things they could do now but could not do four years ago (to help them recognise they had developed more responsibility for their actions) they recalled athletic or coordination skills – concrete and reassuringly peer-acceptable. One child mentioned that she was now trusted to do some things she couldn't when younger.

Role-play activities then helped to develop their decision-making skills. The communication skills shown were of a different order, child to child, compared to the circle time discussions. Free talking, deciding,

critical thinking and creative thinking were all evident as the pupils ana-
lysed and considered the effects of their persuading. The challenge to
work in the medium that made them uncomfortable – some children admitted they preferred maths or English – or where their communication
skills were not up to the demands of resisting the persuader, meant the
children were working very hard.

The empathy that some children showed in the role play and in its
re-enactment was enhanced by the teacher asking pupils to reflect at the
end of the lesson on how it felt to be the persuader and how it felt to be
the refuser. So some children who found the lesson hard could hear their
peers reflect on their feelings and could empathise with them. Some
children's self-awareness was evident as they admitted to difficulties in
the role. They were confident in their success in other curriculum areas
and happy to discuss them.

There will be many aspects of the case studies of the
Northamptonshire schools that will be familiar to teachers. It is hoped
that these examples will encourage further development of life skills
teaching in all classrooms, and more children will benefit from opportunities to enhance their social competencies within the school community.

Networking

Many groups in the county contribute to the work carried out to ensure
and support children's mental well-being. The Inclusion and Pupil Support Service offers schools advice and guidance about children's mental
health and the role of teachers in promoting and intervening in its development. Where appropriate, support teachers and/or educational psychologists or education welfare officers work in schools as part of
Inclusion and Pupil Support. With the consent of the family, a referral
might be made to the Child, Adolescent and Family Service, which can
offer counselling and guidance. The education home–school liaison officer might be involved where issues are of access and support in terms of
language and culture.

Courses like 'Effective Pastoral Support and Mentally Healthy
Schools' run jointly by the child and adolescent mental health development officer and the curriculum adviser for healthy schools and PSHE
bring many of the support groups together. Evaluation of emotional development and the acquisition of life skills can be carried out in several
ways – ephemeral, subjective and objective and longer term. Teachers

can use the scales in the Qualifications and Curriculum Authority's (2001) booklet *Supporting School Improvement*, which defines the criteria against which to judge emotional and behavioural development.

Conclusion: life skills in the school context

Young people in the twenty-first century struggle to cope with different risks and problems often earlier in their lives than might have been the case a generation ago. However, the skills necessary for competent adulthood are still common to all. Teachers are struggling to cope with the demands of an imposed and tested curriculum, and in some cases, disaffected pupils. Society no longer holds the profession in the high regard it once did and the social rewards are scant. The Life Skills Programme is located within several competing challenges each giving rise to tensions in the school community.

When children see that their school life addresses issues that they themselves consider important in their lives, or in the lives of their friends, then school becomes a relevant part of their life, an essential and contributory part. This will reduce truancy and disaffection among pupils, especially those for whom academic success is rare. Most of us recognise that in order for mutual respect and social competencies to develop, a good foundation of skills for life is important. It is therefore important that we give at least as much attention to this as we do to curriculum subject areas, and build it into our school life. We will then be better able to support and encourage each other, and ensure the mental well-being of the whole community.

Acknowledgements

The authors are extremely grateful to all the schools participating in the programme, to the local Interagency Child and Adolescent Mental Health Strategy Group, to the former Northamptonshire Health Authority (particularly its public health director, Dr Jill Meera) for the initial funding, and to the management committee of the project (particularly its chairman, Derek Lucas) for their valuable support.

References

Clark, R. and French, J. (1997a) *Getting to School*. Salford: TACADE.

Clark, R. and French, J. (1997b) *Playing Out*. Salford: TACADE.

Craig, R. (2003) *Looking for Danny*. BBC Radio 4, Afternoon Play, 24 March.

Goodman, R. (1997) 'The Strengths and Difficulties Questionnaire: A Research Note.' *Journal of Child Psychology and Psychiatry 38*, 581–586.

Lees, J. and Plant, S. (2000) *PASSPORT: A Framework for Personal and Social Development*. London: Calouste Gulbenkian Foundation.

Lloyd, J. and Morton, R. (1992) *Blueprints for Health Education Key Stage 1 and Blueprints for Health Education Key Stage 2*. With Pupil Copymasters and Teachers' Resource Book. London: Stanley Thornes.

Lord Chancellor's Department (2001a) *My Family's Changing*. London: Lord Chancellor's Department.

Lord Chancellor's Department (2001b) *Me and my Family*. London: Lord Chancellor's Department.

Maslow, A. (1998) [1962] *Towards a Psychology of Being*. London: Wiley.

National Healthy Schools Standard (NHSS) (2002) *Staff Health and Wellbeing*. Wetherby, Yorkshire: Health Development Agency.

Pfister, M. (1995) *The Rainbow Fish*. New York: North-South Books.

Qualifications and Curriculum Authority (QCA) (2001) *Supporting School Improvement: Emotional and Behavioural Development*. London: QCA.

Rotary (2001) 'Coping with Life' series of programmes (CDs): *Coping with Bullying, Coping with Family Change, Coping with Citizenship*. Kent: SMS Multimedia.

TACADE (2001) *Skills for the Primary School Child: I Am, I Know, I Can*. Salford: TACADE.

Wetton, N. and Williams, T. (2000) *Health for Life*. London: Nelson.

World Health Organization (1997) *Programme on Mental Health: Life Skills Education in Schools*. Geneva: WHO.

Zimmerman, J.L. and Beaudoin, M.N. (2002) 'Cats under the Stars: A Narrative Story.' *Child and Adolescent Mental Health 7*, 1, 31–40.

Further reading

Children and Youth Partnership Foundation (CYPF) (2002) *Make a Connection: Life Skills*. London: CYPF.

Clay, D. with Gold, J. (2000) *Primary School Council Toolkit*. London: School Council UK.

Goleman, D. (1996) *Emotional Intelligence*. London: Bloomsbury.

Leach, B. (2003) *Personal, Social and Emotional Development in the Foundation Stage*. London: Scholastic.

Thorp, S. and Blount, J. (2002) *Working for Wellbeing*. Northampton: Northamptonshire County Council and Worklife Support Ltd.

Watts, D. (ed) (2000a) *Citizenship Resource File for Key Stage 1 and Early Years*. London: Language Centre Publications.

Watts, D. (ed) (2000b) *Citizenship Resource File for Key Stage 2*. London: Language Centre Publications.

Chapter 9

Prevention of Depression and Anxiety in Children and Adolescents

Claire Hayes

Rationale for focus on preventing depression and anxiety

The World Health Organization (2001) has warned that by the year 2020, depressive disorders are expected to rank as the second leading cause of disease and disability world wide. This is shocking and highlights the urgency for all, professionals, politicians and the general public, to work together to prevent this from becoming reality. As it is, between 5 and 10 per cent of adolescents manifest a major depressive disorder (Cicchetti and Toth 1998) and there is no doubt that the increase in the rate of depression and the early age of onset in adolescents represents a significant mental health concern for children (Compas 1997; Dwivedi and Varma 1997; Joshi 1998). The argument for prevention is strong, given evidence that the younger the child is at the time of onset of the episode of depression, the longer the recovery time is (Joshi 1998) and the more likely it is that the individual will experience recurring episodes of depression (Rao *et al.* 1993; Stark and Smith 1995).

Depression is not the only serious concern. Anxiety disorders are recognised as being the most common psychiatric conditions in the paediatric population, with prevalence estimates ranging from 5 to 18 per cent (Labellarte *et al.* 1999). Anxiety is comorbid with a wide range of disorders (Ollendick and Ollendick 1997) and is clearly recognised as being a risk factor for depression (Parker *et al.* 1999). Adolescents with anxiety disorders who develop major depression are at a high rate of suicide (Pawlak *et al.* 1999). Although it is difficult accurately to predict those who are at risk from suicide (O'Connor and Sheehy 2001), the rate of suicide among young people is also increasing at an alarming rate, so prevention measures are imperative.

Prevention of depression and anxiety in adolescents involves

- a clear understanding of the nature of these disorders and how they may manifest in adolescence

- an ease in applying basic prevention principles to individuals or groups by all those who work with young people

- a consistent long-term commitment to prevention.

The following section presents a summary of how depression and anxiety may affect adolescents. This is followed by an overview of cognitive-behavioural psychoeducational approaches to preventing depression and/or anxiety in children and adolescents. The chapter concludes with two case studies illustrating how these principles may be applied in practice.

Brief overview of how depression and anxiety may manifest in adolescents

There are many reasons why an adolescent might develop depression and/or anxiety. Internal or external pressures, loneliness, maltreatment, early insecure attachment, parents with depression, early experiences of loss, unemployment, ethnic affiliation and social and economic disadvantage have all been attributed to the onset of these disorders in adolescents (Cicchetti and Toth 1998; Ernst and Cacioppo 1999; Joshi 1998; Kendall 1993; Settertobulte 2000). Brockless (1997) noted that the biological components of the depressive processes are not yet fully established in childhood and adolescent depression. Gender differences exist. Early to middle adolescence has been identified as the developmental period when girls begin to experience significantly more depression than boys (Cyranowski et al. 2000; Frydenberg 1999; Rutter 1985). Girls tend to report greater numbers of anxiety symptoms and greater numbers of fear reactions than boys (Hayes 2001; Kendall 1993). However, boys, while reporting fewer concerns, are more inclined than girls to report that they worry considerably more than their peers (Hayes 2001).

Children with depression have been found to have lower self-esteem, to feel more hopeless about their future and to experience more negative thoughts about their lives in general (Stark and Smith 1995).

Cognitive explanations for depression hold that adolescents with depression experience a negative bias in their thoughts about the self, the world and the future which is referred to as the depressive cognitive triad (Stark and Smith 1995). Research on the cognitive characteristics of young people with depression has found distortions in attributions, self-evaluation, and perceptions of past and present events as well as harsh and critical views of the self (Kendall 1993; Moore and Carr 2000). Deficits in social skills have been linked with the development of depression in so far as they create difficulties in establishing and maintaining close interpersonal relationships (Bates 1999; Coyne 1976; Lewinsohn 1974; Stark and Smith 1995). Children with depression are less popular and are less liked and rejected by peers and experience a deficit in social skills which is characterised by an angry and withdrawn style of interaction (Stark and Smith 1995). People with depression routinely misread another's behaviour, 'mind-read' and 'jump to conclusions' in the absence of any real evidence. As a result, they are prone to recurrent attacks of anxiety, depression or anger when relating to others (Bates 1993).

As worry, fear and anxiety are part of normal development (Ollendick and Ollendick 1997) symptoms of an anxiety disorder are often dismissed in children and adolescents as being attributed to normal experiences of stress (Labellarte et al. 1999). Indeed, anxiety can be a normal and adaptive response to a variety of situations. Most childhood fears are transitory, emerge in the course of encounters with new challenges and are resolved by facing these demands (Ronan and Deane 1998). In contrast to normal anxious reactions, fears or anxieties that are excessive, occur beyond the developmental timetable, or disrupt the child's life are considered maladaptive (Kendall 1993). The DSM-IV (American Psychiatric Association 1994) classification system lists criteria for at least 13 separate anxiety-related disorders in youth. The appropriateness of this for children and adolescents has been questioned by Ollendick and Ollendick (1997), while Banghoo and Riddle (1999) have offered an alternative approach suggesting that these disorders are based on four main fears: specific fears, general worries, excessive anxious response to stress and repetitive thoughts and/or behaviour. Clinicians and researchers view childhood anxiety as a multidimensional construct manifested at physiological, behavioural and cognitive levels. Anxious children seem preoccupied with concerns about evaluations by self and others and the likelihood of severe negative consequences. They seem to misperceive characteristically the demands of the environment and routinely add stress to a variety of situations (Kendall 1993).

Overview of cognitive-behavioural approaches to preventing depression and/or anxiety in children and adolescents

Cognitive-behavioural approaches have been found to be effective in treating depression and anxiety (Kendall *et al.* 1997). Books such as *Depression in Children and Adolescents* (Dwivedi and Varma 1997), *Cognitive-Behaviour Therapy for Children and Families* (Graham 1998) and *Child and Adolescent Clinical Psychology* (Carr 1999) give clear descriptions of how this can be done. More recently, cognitive-behavioural approaches have been incorporated in psychoeducational prevention programmes. Research findings are mixed. While many school-based programmes have been found to be effective in reducing depression and anxiety, the long-term effects of these programmes are as yet unclear. It seems increasingly more likely that schools, once they are no longer participating in a research project, no longer prioritise helping the sad, worried students (Hayes and Morgan, in press). Therefore consistent community-based approaches to prevention are essential.

A first step in a psychoeducational programme is in establishing a safe environment for the participants. Cognitive-behavioural approaches generally use active procedures as well as cognitive interventions to produce changes in thinking, feelings and behaviour (Friedberg 1996; Kendall 1992; Stallard 2002; Weist and Danforth 1998). One of their essential features is helping the child to identify dysfunctional cognitions and to become aware of their impact on thinking and subsequent behaviour (Kendall *et al.* 1997). Other identified strategies include exposure, use of relaxation techniques and modelling (Labellarte *et al.* 1999). Recognition of emotions and an understanding of the relationship between thoughts, feelings and behaviours is the cornerstone on which other coping skills are built (Stark and Smith 1995). Based on the coping skills model of treatment, the goal is to teach adolescents to use their mood as a cue to engage in various coping activities. This involves teaching a vocabulary for describing affective experiences, monitoring of pleasant activities, teaching anger management, problem solving and social skills and teaching various strategies for identifying and altering maladaptive cognitions.

While many programmes are given in the form of a manual, it must be emphasised that the development of a respectful, trusting relationship is key to any success. In response to criticism of the perceived rigidity of manual-based treatments, Kendall *et al.* (1998) highlighted the necessity of training, professional judgement, flexibility and creativity in ensuring that the needs of the participants are kept to the forefront. Kendall and Flannery-Schroeder (1998) described some of the advantages of manuals as enhancing internal validity and treatment integrity. Other advantages of running psychoeducational programmes in small groups result from the positive peer group support, particularly as being able to form even one close friend or confidant seems to reduce the likelihood of loneliness in individuals at risk (Ernst and Cacioppo 1999; Holmbeck and Shapera 1999; Van Schoor, Schmidt and Ghuman 1981). Breton (1999) proposed that comprehensive, multilevel community programmes for a given age group comprise two subprogrammes. The first would be population-wide aimed at improving life skills, while the second could target young adolescents in specific settings or at risk.

A variety of school-based psychoeducational programmes have been designed delivered and evaluated. Compas (1994) has categorised coping skills development programmes into those targeted at generic stress, acute stress and chronic stress. The influence of Ellis's (1962) rational–emotive therapy and Meichenbaum and Goodman's (1971) self-instructional training is evident in many psychoeducational programmes. Examples of how diverse these programmes have become include helping young people at risk of dropping out of school prematurely (Christenson and Brooke Carroll 1999); changing young people's explanatory style from pessimism to optimism (Seligman 1995); coping with sexual transitions (Moore 1999); treating bullying (Olweus 1994); preventing sexual abuse (MacIntyre and Carr 1999; MacIntyre and Lawlor 1991); normalising eating behaviour (Braet 1999); treating conduct disorders (Waddell, Lipman and Offord 1999); preventing substance abuse (Rollin, Anderson and Buncher 1999); preventing teenage pregnancy (Nitz 1999); treating anxiety (Kendall 1993, 1994; Kendall and Southam-Gerow 1996; Stark and Kendall 1996); and preventing depression (Clarke *et al.* 1995; Cuijpers 1998; Lewinsohn *et al.* 1990; Reynolds and Coates 1986; Rice and Meyer 1994; Seligman, Schulman, and DeRubeis 1999; Stark and Smith 1995; Stark, Rouse and Livingston 1991).

School-based psychoeducational programmes have been shown to be successful when used as part of research projects (Hayes 2001). However, it appears that school professionals such as teachers, guidance counsellors and counsellors may be less likely to implement such programmes as part of the normal curriculum (Hayes and Morgan 2003). Psychoeducational programmes, even if made obligatory in schools, are not a panacea and involvement of parents and the wider community is important.

The author has long been involved in research, training and clinical practice to prevent depression and anxiety in children and adolescents. In the section on key psychoeducational prevention principles which follows, she presents her own structure for working with young people in a preventive way. Two case studies are then presented to illustrate how these principles may be applied in practice. While the stories are ficti-tious they are based on many children whom the author has worked with in a therapeutic way. For ease of reading the person working with the young people is referred to as 'she' while the young person is usually referred to as 'he'.

Key psychoeducational prevention principles
Clarity of purpose
As an essential first step the professional intending to work with chil-dren and adolescents to prevent depression and/or anxiety must ask her-self key questions.

- Why do I want to prevent depression and/or anxiety?
- What are my own beliefs about depression and/or anxiety?
- What are my own beliefs about children and young people with depression and/or anxiety?
- What are my biggest fears about doing this work?
- Am I trying to help them avoid all pain or am I helping them to cope with the pain they may have?

These questions are vital if the professional is actually to work with the child's best interests at the centre. Someone who experienced adoles-cence as an extremely lonely, troubled period may be drawn to ensure that no one else has to suffer in the same way. Lack of awareness of this motive might result in a young person who is struggling with normal ad-olescent difficulties being rescued or given labels such as troubled, de-pressed, anxious or even suicidal. The young person himself may add additional labels such as crazy, mad or nuisance and may begin to believe that his worries are abnormal.

Similarly the person who believes strongly that being sad and troubled is a natural part of adolescence could easily miss the warning signs of a young person who may be at serious risk of harming himself. Much has been written about the nature of childhood and adolescence. A simple truth is that every person's experience is unique. Without personal reflection we might assume, given some very stark facts, that a child's life is horrific and that he needs urgent professional help. Yet we might have missed totally the resilience within the child, the support structures around him, as well as the veil of our own perceptions which may distort our true understanding of the child. Ongoing personal reflection may be greatly supported by regular supervision and/or private personal work such as therapy. The book by Berry (1988) and the article by Hayes (2000) raise awareness of the dangers of the 'Helping Messiah'.

Develop a respectful relationship

Psychoeducational prevention work can be carried out with individual children, with a group of eight to ten children, or in a larger group, such as a class group. The level of the child's difficulty and ability to cope, the qualifications and experience of the person working with him and the particular setting in which the professional is working will all determine which of these is most appropriate. With each, however, it is essential that a strong, respectful relationship be built with the child. How this is achieved depends on the individual's personality, training and natural empathy with children. With increased awareness of child abuse, absolute confidentiality can no longer be guaranteed and it is important that the child is made aware of that. Parental consent is an important consideration and respect for the parents or caregivers must also be central.

Assess the need for preventive work

While it could well be argued that all children will benefit from help in preventing depression and/or anxiety it is obvious that the extent of the need varies according to many variables such as the individual child's temperament, family support, level of stress and coping methods. Professionals who have been trained in the use of psychometric testing can use good standardised measures such as the Children's Depression Inventory (Kovacs 1980, 1992), the Porteous Problem Checklist (Porteous 1997) and the Adolescent Coping Scale (Frydenberg 1997) either with individual children or with large groups as part of an overall screening process. These tests are all self-report measures and are a way of ascertaining children's own perceptions of their difficulties and ability to cope. One key advantage is that they can indicate children who may be at serious risk, who may then be referred to the appropriate professionals for a more thorough assessment, followed by treatment if necessary.

As with all tests, care must be taken to ensure that they are used properly and responsibly and that interpretation is made in full consideration of their limitations. None of these tests is absolute and there is also the possibility that children might deliberately falsify their responses. Extreme care must be taken not to label the child as it is dangerous and unhelpful to label a child as being depressed or anxious. Instead it is recommended that the term 'might be in need of some extra help in coping' be used to explain why a particular child is being included in a preventive programme.

If the person working with the student is not trained and skilled in the use of psychometric tests he or she can employ different methods of assessing the extent of the student's need for prevention work. Key people in the child's life, such as parents and teachers, can provide valuable information and it is important to pay particular attention to three areas: intensity, frequency and duration. Rather than accepting that he is 'depressed' or 'anxious', help the parent or teacher to give concrete examples to illustrate their concerns about the child. It is necessary to have as clear a sense as possible as to whether this behaviour is new, sudden, out of character, or typical of a pattern of behaviour evident over a long period of time. Is the parent or teacher able to give some logical explanation to explain the child's behaviour, such as a reaction to a major loss or trauma? What are the parent's or teacher's own concerns about the child? Why are they alarmed? What is their biggest fear? This is important as the adult may be unconsciously projecting her own fears onto the child. What have they already done to try to help the child?

Assessing a child's risk for depression and/or anxiety is an ongoing process and occurs at every meeting with the child. The professional must listen carefully and pay particular attention to the following:

1. Emotional

    (a) How does the child seem to be feeling?

    (b) Does his expression seem consistent with the content of the story?

    (c) Does he seem to be fighting back tears?

    (d) What is his biggest fear?

2.   Cognitive

    (a) What seems to be the meaning of the difficulties for the child and for the parents?

    (b) Are there definite patterns in his speech which may give clues to his thinking patterns, such as:

        I should…be able to sort this out myself/be doing better/have lots of friends.

        Everything…I do turns out wrong/always is hard for me/is easy for everyone else.

        I'm…useless/no good/stupid/ugly.

        I'm letting down my parents.

        It's all my fault.

        What's the point? I'll never be able to do it.

3.   Behavioural

    (a) How does the child behave while telling the story?

    (b) Is he fidgety, does he hold eye contact or avoid it?

    (c) Are there patterns of avoidance behaviour while he is telling his story?

    (d) Has the child's behaviour changed recently?

    (e) Is he engaging in unhelpful or harmful behaviours such as drinking excessively and/or taking drugs?

    (f) Is he isolating himself from his family and his peers?

    (g) Is he eating a lot of high-calorie, sugar foods?

    (h) Does he sleep well or tend to lie late in bed at weekends?

    (i) How is he getting on at school?

    (j) Is he indulging in gloomy thoughts about the past, present and/or future?

4.   Coping

    (a) How is the child currently coping?

(b) Does he have a sense of strong family and/or peer support available which he is able to access?

(c) Is he involved in sport?

(d) Does he have at least one good friend he can be himself with?

(e) Is there anything positive he can see in the current difficulty?

Teach core psychoeducational prevention principles

Emotions

In an effort to ensure that children are happy, society may have taught them that it is wrong to be unhappy. They may have learned at a very young age that their parents and teachers do not like it when they get upset, angry or frightened and therefore they have become experts at blocking their true feelings. The occasional flash of temper from a 'good' child or sudden, unexplained tears from the 'happy' child may cause discomfort and anxiety in parents as well as the child. Has life got to the stage where children and young people are not allowed to feel miserable? Not allowed to feel scared? Or not allowed to feel angry?

Educating children and young people about emotions is essential. While babies instinctively cry if they want something, children and young people often are judged and judge themselves harshly for expressing emotions. It is vital that they be helped understand that feelings are messages from their body – neither good nor bad – and that if they make sense they are OK. Therapeutic stories such as 'The Volcano' are particularly helpful in helping young people make sense of their feelings in a safe way. 'The Volcano' is a story which was made up by the author years ago and is described in the context of the case studies in the next section of this chapter. Other stories which may be helpful are described in Sunderland (2000).

Cognitions

Careful attention to what young people say about themselves and others can give important information as to how they are thinking. Use of cartoons and drawings can be very concrete ways of helping children to become aware of their thoughts. They can then be helped to examine these for accuracy. One example is to ask the young person to see himself entering the hall of his school and notice a group of his peers at the other end laughing. When asked what his automatic thought might be, he is very likely to respond 'They are laughing about me'. This can then be used as an example to teach him not automatically to believe what he thinks. He can be helped to make links between his thoughts, his feelings and his behaviours in concrete ways such as 'If I think that they are laughing at me, then it makes sense that I will feel upset, but going up and hitting them, or sneaking away to cry might not be the most helpful things to do'. When working with young people's cognitions it is very important to help them to become aware of what they believe. The fact that years ago people really believed that the world was flat is a great example to help them see that even if a belief is not true, if it is believed, it can shape a person's thoughts, feelings and behaviours. The song 'No matter what' sung by Boyzone (1998) has a line 'No matter what they tell us…what we believe is true'. Playing this song to children and young adolescents and helping them become aware of the meaning of the words can be very beneficial. Other practical exercises are to be found in Stallard (2002).

Behaviours

The example of the young people laughing in the school hall can be used to help the vulnerable child or adolescent to examine what he normally does when he feels hurt, upset or anxious. The next step is to help him decide if this way of behaving is helpful or unhelpful and to look at possible alternative ways of behaving. It may be incredibly difficult for a sensitive 13-year-old who really believes that his peers are laughing at him to go up and very casually ask what the joke is. Training in assertiveness skills may be necessary and it is recommended that he be helped rehearse appropriate ways of behaving in a safe environment, before gently moving in a graded way to become exposed to more difficult situations. It is also important that he be helped to learn and practise basic relaxation exercises such as breathing slowly, and tightening and relaxing key muscles. As well as actually helping him relax, this exercise will distract him from his feelings and help him to feel more in control of his own emotions.

Coping

Helping a young person who may be at risk of developing depression and/or anxiety to become aware of his feelings, thoughts and behaviours is an important first step. It may well be that his feelings of distress are natural and appropriate and that what is needed is for him to relax about how he is feeling and to make sense of it. His attention can then turn to how he is thinking and what he is doing to determine whether he is coping in the most helpful way he can. One way of helping him to do this is to teach him how to use the following tool 'I feel…because… but…' (Hayes 1999). This helps him to acknowledge his feelings, make sense of them and then turn to focus on how best to cope with the situation. It is vital that whatever comes after 'but…' is true and will always be true. The example 'I feel worried because of the exam tomorrow but I have done my best' will not work if the young person really knows that he did not do his best. A better 'but…' might be 'I feel worried because of the exam tomorrow but my dog thinks I am wonderful'. This will probably bring a smile to his face although, depending on the child, other endings such as 'but I am doing my best' might be more helpful. The important thing is to help the child develop the ability to feel relaxed about however he is feeling and then to focus on what actually to do to help him cope.

The following case examples illustrate how these principles can be used in practice to help a sad 12-year-old and an anxious 15-year-old cope and to help them develop healthy ways of thinking and behaving to prevent them developing more serious depression and anxiety.

Case Example: Sam

Sam is a 12-year-old child who is at risk of depression. He feels sad a lot of the time and as he has no way of understanding this, he interprets it as stupid, selfish or crazy. He gives himself many reasons why he should be happy – he is from a lovely home, with lovely parents and lovely friends. He has always judged his feelings of sadness as 'wrong'. Lately Sam has begun to hide that he feels sad and now smiles almost constantly. The eldest of three children, he believes that his parents are overworked and are not happy. He does his best to keep his younger sister and brother quiet and will often play with them rather than join his own age group in a game of football near their house. He also spends a lot of time on his own and likes keeping busy by playing with his parents' computer. At school he tries very hard to do his work, but never has a sense that he has achieved his best. Regardless of his parents' response to his tests he always feels that he has let them down. Over the past year he has put on a lot of weight and eats an enormous amount of sugar throughout the day. He tends to get to sleep very late and is constantly tired during the day. His biggest fear is that he is 'depressed' and will either have to take tablets every day, like his friend's mother, or that he will commit suicide when he is 19 years old, like another friend's cousin.

Case Example: Annie

Annie is 15 years old and has lately become a worrier. A minor car accident six months ago made her realise how vulnerable she and her family actually are. Her father is a long-distance lorry driver and for the past month she has sat up at night praying that he will not have an accident. If the phone rings late at night she is convinced that he is dead, and twice was so upset that it took her older sister 15 minutes to calm her enough to tell her that the phone call was from their eldest sister to say that she had missed the bus and was staying with a friend. Annie is known as the baby in the family and her parents openly admit that they worried more about her than about their other two girls. She has always worked incredibly hard at school, but has never been pleased with her performance in school tests. She consistently says that she could have done better and she spends a lot of time in her room studying. State exams are coming up in a few months and Annie has been to the doctor three times in the last month with severe headaches and stomach pains. She does not agree with the doctor's view that she is suffering from stress and worries that she has some form of stomach cancer. She often spends time daydreaming about what chemotherapy would be like and pictures her classmates at school feeling sorry for not having been nicer to her. Recently these daydreams have ended with her observing her own funeral. Annie's biggest and totally secret worry is that she is 'mad' and not normal.

It is clear that both Sam and Annie are distressed by their feelings. They are misinterpreting them and both have exaggerated their significance and are secretly worried that they have serious problems. Their ways of thinking and of behaving are not helpful and they are locked into a victim, rather than a coping pattern. Using the template outlined above they can both be helped to cope in the following way.

Helping Sam and Annie cope with their emotions

1. Teach them that feelings are messages their bodies are giving them. They are neither right nor wrong in themselves, but they can respond to them by thinking in a helpful or unhelpful way and/or by doing helpful or unhelpful things.

2. Use an example of 'Our ancestor the cave man out hunting the bear' – how is he feeling? Relaxed? Hopeful? Peaceful? Scared? Worried? Lonely? Hungry?

3. Ask Sam and Annie if it makes sense for the cave man to feel that way and explain to them that 'If a feeling makes sense it is OK'.

4. Use 'The Volcano' story to illustrate what people do with their feelings. This is a particular story that the author made up a number of years ago and uses over and over when working in a therapeutic way with children and adults. She finds it particularly helpful when working with people who are closed to their feelings and who prefer not to acknowledge that they might be feeling angry, sad, worried or whatever.

The volcano story

This is how the story goes:

Claire: Do you know what a volcano is?

Sam/Annie: Yes, it is a mountain which explodes with lava when it gets too hot.

Claire: Well, let's suppose that this drawing is a picture of a volcano.

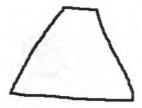

Claire: I've a theory that people are like volcanoes, but instead of lava inside, we have feelings, which we keep in 'feelings cabinets'. Any feelings we have about anything that happens to us get pushed into one of the drawers of the feelings cabinets.

Claire: If we open the Christmas drawer, what feelings might we see in there?

Sam/Annie: Happy, excited.

Claire: Suppose you really, really wanted something for Christmas and your sister got it, how might you feel? (Note: it generally takes a little prompting before a child will give a 'negative' feeling such as jealousy.)
             Is it OK to feel jealous?

Sam/Annie: Hmmm.

Claire: The feeling itself is OK – it is just giving us a message, but it would not be OK to hit her because we felt jealous.
             Sam, how might you feel if one of your classmates called you names?
             Annie, how might you feel if you had an exam in the morning?
             Do those feelings make sense?

'Boy sneering drawer':
sad, upset, cross

'Christmas drawer':
happy, excited

'Exam drawer':
worried, scared,
upset

Claire: So, what do we do with our feelings?
            Some people close up the cabinets, put a big block on the
            top, pretend that they are not there and put a big smile on
            their face, like this.

Claire: Others also close up the cabinets, put a big block on the
            top, pretend that the feelings are not there, but instead of a
            smile put on a frown and become 'yes, but people' – so if
            someone says 'it is a lovely day', they immediately say 'yes,
            but it is going to rain!'

Claire: But what happens to the feelings? They have to go some-
                where, and just as a volcano erupts when it gets too hot,
                people can explode when their buried feelings push out
                and explode. Or maybe, they stay inside, banging away in
                the feelings cabinets, causing tummy pains, headaches or
                even more serious illnesses. The thing is they have to come
                out some way.
                So how can we help? First by acknowledging that they are
                there and that it is OK to have them. Then if we put little
                pinholes into the top of the volcano we can let some steam
                out, so if we feel sad and cry, that is us letting some steam
                out!

In the case of Sam, this meant helping him look at his feelings of being
the eldest, being slow at games, having no friends. With Annie, this involved helping her look at her feelings of worrying about her father and
about exams. The next step is to help Sam and Annie to think of a specific incident and to list their feelings about that incident.

Helping Sam and Annie become aware of their cognitions

It is clear that both Sam and Annie think a lot of unhelpful thoughts.
They refer to themselves as stupid or mad. They are very harsh judges of
themselves. They both magnify what they do wrong and minimise what
they do well. They see themselves and their world in terms of absolutes
and they use a lot of 'should' statements. To help prevent them developing more serious depression and anxiety it is crucial that they first begin
to become aware of what they are thinking, and then examine it to see
whether their thoughts are in fact true. Ask them to picture themselves
walking into their school hall. They see a group of their classmates
laughing loudly – what do they think they are laughing about? The
most likely response is that both Sam and Annie will think that they are
laughing about them.

The next step is for Sam and Annie to become 'detectives' and to
catch what they are thinking and to write down their thoughts. Once
they begin to tune into what they are thinking it is possible to teach them
strategies to examine their thoughts for truth such as:

How sure am I that I am right? Am I 100 per cent sure, or might I
only be 99 per cent sure?

Suppose that it is actually true, what is the worst thing that could possibly happen and could I cope with that?

Helping Sam and Annie become aware of their behaviours

The third step in this psychoeducational prevention model is to help the child focus on his behaviours and to help him see this as something which he has control over. For example, Sam's excessive eating of junk foods and his isolating himself from his peers are behaviours which are probably not helpful for him in the long term. Similarly Annie's compulsive worrying is not the most helpful behaviour for her. Instead of telling herself 'not to be stupid and stop worrying', Annie could be encouraged to allow herself to worry, if that was what she wanted to do – but to gain some control over her worries, so that they would not take over her life. One suggestion is that she chooses a box to be her worry box, and a worry spot in her home (a chair, the stairs, or somewhere else) and that each day for a set ten minutes she worries. When she feels herself worrying at other times she is to write down her worries on a piece of paper, fold it up and put it into her worry box until her next worry time. This is a very simple technique but it works.

Both Sam and Annie would benefit enormously from learning some basic relaxation principles to help them when they are feeling sad or anxious. Paradoxically encouraging them to feel whatever they feel, for a fixed period of ten minutes, allows them to have control over their emotions and helps them to stop labelling themselves as stupid or crazy. Raising their awareness of the importance of fun in their lives is also important and they might need help in developing their social skills. It is important that they be helped to 'do' activities rather than talk about doing them. With children and young people who are anxious, reassurance is not helpful. Rather than telling Annie that her father will be fine, it is more honest and ultimately much more helpful to acknowledge that he might have an accident, but that worrying about it is not going to stop it happening. Sometimes rather than staying at the level of the worry it can be much more effective to ask children about their worst fears and to help them look at them, rather than trying to run away from them.

Helping Sam and Annie develop a coping approach to life

This aspect brings together the feelings, thoughts and behaviour in a simple framework which can be very helpful for the child. The coping sentence is intended to help the child access a quick way of making sense of his feelings, without feeling demoralised, blaming himself, or blaming others.

Sam's coping sentence:

I feel puzzled because there is no reason for me to be sad, but that's OK.

Annie's coping sentence:

I feel worried because my Dad might crash his lorry, but I am not in charge of keeping him safe.

Conclusion

Sam and Annie are entitled to feel worried, sad, angry, disappointed, rejected and/or lonely. None of these mean that they have depression or anxiety. Yet, statistics and everyday experience tell us that it is becoming tragically easy for anyone, young or old, to develop these conditions. Medical science has proven that inoculation works in preventing physical diseases. A vast amount of research evidence demonstrates that inoculation in the form of psychological preventive methods also work. However, there is a catch. They will work only if they are used. Earlier in this chapter prevention of depression and anxiety in adolescents was described as involving

- a clear understanding of the nature of these disorders and how they may manifest in adolescence
- an ease in applying basic prevention principles to individuals or groups by all those who work with young people
- a consistent long-term commitment to prevention.

The remainder of the chapter addressed the first two points. The challenge lies in the third: in order to prevent depression and anxiety developing in children and adolescents, a consistent long-term commitment is essential. The increase of these disorders and the rapid decrease in age of onset sends a very clear signal: this commitment is needed now.

References

American Psychiatric Association (1994) *Diagnostic and Statistical Manual of Mental Disorders*, 4th edn. Washington: APA.

Banghoo, R.K. and Riddle, M.A. (1999) 'Pharmacologic Treatment of Anxiety Disorders in Adolescents.' In A. Eisman (ed) *Adolescent Psychiatry*. Hillsdale, NJ: Analytic Press.

Bates, T. (1999) *Depression: The Common Sense Approach*. Dublin: Newleaf.

Berry, C.R. (1988) *When Helping You is Hurting Me*. New York: HarperCollins.

Boyzone (1998) 'No Matter What.' In *Where We Belong* (compact disc). Dublin: Polygram Ireland.

Braet, C. (1999) 'Treatment of Obese Children: A New Rationale.' *Clinical Child Psychiatry 4*, 4, 579–591.

Breton, J.J. (1999) 'Complementary Development of Prevention and Mental Health Promotion Programs for Canadian Children Based on Contemporary Scientific Programs. *Canadian Journal of Psychiatry 44*, 227–234.

Brockless, J. (1997) 'The Nature of Depression in Childhood: Its Causes and Presentation.' In K.N. Dwivedi and V.P. Varma (eds) *Depression in Children and Adolescents*. London: Whurr.

Carr, A. (1999) *Handbook of Child and Adolescent Clinical Psychology: A Contextual Approach*. London: Routledge.

Christenson, S.L. and Brooke Carroll, E. (1999) 'Strengthening the Family–School Partnership through "Check and Connect".' In E. Frydenberg (ed) *Learning to Cope: Developing as a Person in Complex Societies*. New York: Oxford University Press.

Cicchetti, D. and Toth, S.L. (1998). 'Perspectives on Research and Practice in Developmental Psychopathology.' In W. Damon, I.E. Sigel and K.A. Renninger (eds) *Handbook of Child Psychology*, 5th edn, vol. 4. New York: Wiley.

Clarke, G.N., Hawkins, W., Murphy, M., Sheeber, L., Lewinsohn, P.M. and Seeley, J.R. (1995) 'Targeted Prevention of Unipolar Depressive Disorder in an At-risk Sample of High-school Adolescents: A Randomised Trial of a Group Cognitive Intervention.' *Journal of the American Academy of Child and Adolescent Psychiatry 34*, 312–321.

Compas, B.E. (1994) 'Promoting Successful Coping during Adolescence.' In M. Rutter (ed) *Psychosocial Disturbances in Young People: Challenges for Prevention*. New York and Cambridge: Cambridge University Press.

Compas, B.E. (1997) 'Depression in Children and Adolescents.' In E.J. Mash and L.G. Terdal (eds) *Assessment of Childhood Disorders*. London: Guilford.

Coyne, J.C. (1976) 'Toward an Interactional Description of Depression.' *Psychiatry 39*, 28–40.

Cuijpers, P. (1998) 'A Psychoeducational Approach to Treatment of Depression: A Meta-analysis of Lewinsohn's "Coping with Depression" Course.' *Behaviour Therapy 29*, 521–533.

Cyranowski, J., Frank, E., Young, E. and Shear, M.K. (2000) 'Adolescent Onset of the Gender Difference in Lifetime Rates of Major Depression.' *Archives of General Psychiatry 57*, 21–27.

Dwivedi, K.N. and Varma, V.P. (1997) *Depression in Children and Adolescents.* London: Whurr.

Ellis, A. (1962) *Reason and Emotion in Psychotherapy.* New York: Lyle Stuart.

Ernst, J.M. and Cacioppo, J.T. (1999) 'Lonely Hearts: Psychological Perspectives on Loneliness.' *Applied and Preventive Psychology 8,* 1–22.

Friedberg, R.B. (1996) 'Cognitive-behavioural Games and Workbooks: Tips for School Counsellors.' *Elementary School Guidance and Counselling 31,* 11–20.

Frydenberg, E. (1997) *Adolescent Coping: Theoretical and Research Perspectives.* London: Routledge.

Frydenberg, E. (ed) (1999) *Learning to Cope: Developing as a Person in Complex Societies.* New York: Oxford University Press.

Graham, P. (ed) (1998) *Cognitive-Behaviour Therapy for Children and Families.* Cambridge: Cambridge University Press.

Hayes, C. (1999) 'A Simple Approach to Coping with Stress.' *Journal of the Institute of Guidance Counsellors 23,* 70–72.

Hayes, C. (2000) 'Hope for the "Helping Messiah".' *Journal of the Institute of Guidance Counsellors 24,* 3–10.

Hayes, C. (2001) 'A Psychoeducational Approach to Helping Adolescents Cope.' *Irish Educational Studies 20,* 97–106.

Hayes, C. and Morgan, M. (in press) 'A Psychoeducational Approach to Preventing Depression and Anxiety.' *Journal of Adolescence.*

Holmbeck, G.A. and Shapera, W.E. (1999) 'Research Methods with Adolescents.' In P.C. Kendall, J.N. Butcher and G.N. Holmbeck (eds) *Handbook of Research Methods in Clinical Psychology,* 2nd edn. New York: Wiley.

Joshi, P.T. (1998) 'Affective Disorders in Children and Adolescents.' In H.S. Ghuman and R.M. Sarles (eds) *Handbook of Child and Adolescent Outpatient, Day Treatment and Community Psychiatry.* New York: Taylor and Francis.

Kendall, P.C. (1992) *Coping Cat Workbook.* Ardmore, PA: Workbook Publishing.

Kendall, P.C. (1993) 'Cognitive-behavioural Therapies with Young: Guiding Theory, Current Status, and Emerging Developments.' *Journal of Consulting and Clinical Psychology 61,* 235–247.

Kendall, P.C. (1994) 'Treating Anxiety Disorders in Children: Results of a Randomised Clinical Trial.' *Journal of Consulting and Clinical Psychology 62,* 100–110.

Kendall, P.C. and Flannery-Schroeder, E.C. (1998) 'Methodological Issues in Treatment Research for Anxiety Disorders in Youth.' *Journal of Abnormal Child Psychology 26,* 27–39.

Kendall, P.C. and Southam-Gerow, M. (1996) 'Long-term Follow-up of a Cognitive-behavioural Therapy for Anxiety-disordered Youth.' *Journal of Consulting and Clinical Psychology 64,* 724–730.

Kendall, P.C., Panichelli-Mindel, S.M., Sugarman, A. and Callahan, S.A. (1997) 'Exposure to Child Anxiety: Theory, Research and Practice.' *Clinical Psychology: Science and Practice 4*, 29–39.

Kendall, P.C., Chu, B., Gifford, A., Hayes, C. and Nauta, M. (1998) 'Breathing Life into a Manual: Flexibility and Creativity with Manual-based Treatments.' *Cognitive and Behavioural Practice 5*, 177–198.

Kovacs, M. (1980) 'Rating Scales to Assess Depression in School-aged Children.' *Acta Paedopsychiatry 46*, 305–315.

Kovacs, M. (1992) *Children's Depression Inventory.* New York: Multi-Health Systems.

Labellarte, M.J., Ginsburg, G.S., Walkup, J.T. and Riddle, M.A. (1999) 'The Treatment of Anxiety Disorders in Children and Adolescents.' *Biological Psychiatry 46*, 1567–1578.

Lewinsohn, P.M. (1974) 'A Behavioural Approach to Depression.' In R.J. Friedman and M.M. Katz (eds) *The Psychology of Depression: Contemporary Theory and Research.* Washington, DC: Winston-Wiley.

Lewinsohn, P.M., Clarke, G.N., Hops, H. and Andrews, J. (1990) 'Cognitive-behavioural Treatment of Depressed Adolescents.' *Behaviour Therapy 21*, 385–401.

MacIntyre, D. and Carr, A. (1999) 'Helping Children to the Other Side of Silence: A Study of the Impact of the Stay Safe Programme on Irish Children's Disclosures of Sexual Victimisation.' *Child Abuse and Neglect 23*, 1327–1340.

MacIntyre, D. and Lawlor, M. (1991) *The Stay Safe Programme.* Dublin: Department of Health.

Meichenbaum, D. and Goodman, J. (1971) 'Training Impulsive Children to Talk to Themselves: A Means of Developing Self-control.' *Journal of Abnormal Child Psychology 77*, 115–126.

Moore, M. and Carr, A. (2000) 'Depression and Grief.' In A. Carr (ed) *What Works with Children and Adolescents?* London: Routledge.

Moore, S. (1999) 'Sexuality in Adolescence: A Suitable Case for Coping?' In E. Frydenberg (ed) *Learning to Cope: Developing as a Person in Complex Societies.* New York: Oxford University Press.

Nitz, K. (1999) 'Adolescent Pregnancy Prevention: A Review of Interventions and Programs.' *Clinical Psychology Review 19*, 457–471.

O'Connor, R. and Sheehy, N.P. (2001) 'Contemporary Perspectives on Suicide.' *The Psychologist 14*, 20–25.

Ollendick, T.H. and Ollendick, D.G. (1997) 'General Worry and Anxiety in Children.' *In Session: Psychotherapy in Practice 3*, 89–102.

Olweus, D. (1994) 'Annotation: Bullying at School – Basic Facts and Effects of a School Based Intervention Program.' *Journal of Child Psychology and Psychiatry 35*, 1171–1190.

Parker, G., Wilhelm, K., Mitchell, P., Austin, M.P., Roussos, J. and Gladstone, G. (1999) 'The Influence of Anxiety as a Risk to Early Onset Major Depression.' *Journal of Affective Disorders 52*, 11–17.

Pawlak, C., Pascual-Sanchez, T., Rae, P., Fischer, W. and Ladame, F. (1999) 'Anxiety Disorders, Comorbidity, and Suicide Attempts in Adolescence: A Preliminary Investigation.' *European Psychiatry 14*, 132–136.

Porteous, M.A. (1997) *Porteous Problem Checklist.* Cork, Ireland: Psychometrica International.

Rao, U., Weissman, M.M., Martin, J.A. and Hammond, R.W. (1993) 'Childhood Depression and Risk of Suicide: A Preliminary Report of a Longitudinal Study.' *Journal of the American Academy of Child and Adolescent Psychiatry 32*, 21–27.

Reynolds, W.M. and Coats, K.I. (1986) 'A Comparison of Cognitive-behavioural Therapy and Relaxation Training for the Treatment of Depression in Adolescents.' *Journal of Consulting and Clinical Psychology 54*, 653–660.

Rice, K.G. and Meyer, A.L. (1994) 'Preventing Depression among Young Adolescents: Preliminary Process Results of a Psycho-educational Intervention Program.' *Journal of Counselling and Development 73*, 145–152.

Rollin, S.A., Anderson, C.W. and Buncher, R.M. (1999) 'Coping in Children and Adolescents: A Prevention Model for Helping Kids Avoid or Reduce At-risk Behaviour.' In E. Frydenberg (ed) *Learning to Cope: Developing as a Person in Complex Societies.* New York: Oxford University Press.

Ronan, K.R. and Deane, F.P. (1998) 'Anxiety Disorders.' In P. Graham (ed) *Cognitive-Behaviour Therapy for Children and Families.* Cambridge: Cambridge University Press.

Rutter, M. (1985) 'Resilience in the Face of Diversity: Protective Factors and Resistance to Psychiatric Disorders.' *British Journal of Psychiatry 147*, 589–611.

Seligman, M. (1995) *The Optimistic Child.* Sydney: Random House.

Seligman, M.P., Schulman, P. and DeRubeis, R.J. (1999) 'The Prevention of Depression and Anxiety.' *Prevention and Treatment 2*, Article 8, http://journals.apa.org/prevention/volume2/pre0020008a.html

Settertobulte, W. (2000) 'Family and Peer Relations.' In C. Currie, K. Hurrelmann, W. Settertobulte, R. Smith and J. Todd (eds) *Health and Health Behaviour among Young People.* WHO Cross-National Study (HBSC) International Report. Copenhagen: WHO Regional Office for Europe.

Stallard, P. (2002) *Think Good – Feel Good: A Cognitive Behaviour Therapy Workbook for Children and Young People.* Chichester: Wiley.

Stark, K.D. and Kendall, P.C. (1996) *Treating Depressed Children: Therapist Manual for 'Taking Action'.* Ardmore, PA: Workbook Publishing.

Stark, K.D. and Smith, A. (1995) 'Cognitive and Behavioural Treatment of Childhood Depression.' In H.P.J. Van Bilsen (ed) *Behavioural Approaches for Children and Adolescents.* New York: Plenum Press.

Stark, K.D., Rouse, L.W. and Livingston, R. (1991) 'Treatment of Depression during Childhood and Adolescence: Cognitive-behavioural Procedures for the Individual and Family.' In P.C. Kendall (ed) *Child and Adolescent Therapy: Cognitive-behavioural Procedures.* New York: Guilford.

Sunderland, M. (2000) *Using Story Telling as a Therapeutic Tool with Children.* Bicester, Oxfordshire: Winslow Press.

Van Schoor, E.P., Schmidt, K. and Ghuman, H.S. (1998) 'Group Psychotherapy with Children and Adolescents: Key Issues.' In H.S. Ghuman and R.M. Sarles (eds) *Handbook of Child and Adolescent Outpatient, Day-Treatment and Community Psychiatry.* New York: Taylor and Francis.

Waddell, C., Lipman, E. and Offord, D. (1999) 'Conduct Disorder: Practice Parameters for Assessment, Treatment and Prevention.' http://www.cpa-apc.org/publications/archives/cjp/1999/oct/suppl2/chapter 1.html

Weist, M.D. and Danforth, J.S. (1998) 'Cognitive-Behavioural Therapy with Children and Adolescents.' In H.S. Ghuman and R.M. Sarles (eds) *Handbook of Child and Adolescent Outpatient, Day Treatment and Community Psychiatry.* New York: Taylor and Francis.

World Health Organization (2001) Speech. www.who.int/director-general/speeches/2001/english/20011025_copingwit hstressbrussels.en.html

Chapter 10

Prevention of Eating Disorders

Anne Stewart

Introduction

The prevalence of eating disorders in the Western world is high. Approximately 1–2 per cent of young women have a diagnosis of anorexia nervosa or bulimia nervosa, and the prevalence of eating disorders which do not meet diagnostic criteria is even higher (Fairburn and Beglin 1990; Killen *et al.* 1994; Lucas *et al.* 1991). Many eating disorders start in the adolescent years or even younger. Since the early 1980s there has been an increase in the prevalence of eating disorders in childhood and adolescence (Goldman 1996; Hoeck *et al.* 1995). A focus on thinness and dieting is becoming increasingly common in young children (Levine *et al.* 1994).

Eating disorders can have a devastating effect on a child's development with serious physical, psychological, educational and social consequences, including impairment of identity. Family members, including siblings, may also be adversely affected with impairment of relationships and abnormal focus on the child with the eating disorder (Perring, Twigg and Atkin 1990).

Treatment of a serious eating disorder can be time-consuming and costly. Outpatient treatment may last a year or more, and inpatient treatment, if necessary, will result in a lengthy period of withdrawal from family, school and social life. A significant number go on to relapse, which may impair their life for many years. A good outcome varies between 36 and 76 per cent (Herzog, Rathner and Vandereycken 1992). Mortality can be high (5–15%: Russell 1992).

With this in mind, it is crucial to develop effective ways of preventing eating disorders. This chapter will, first, review the risk factors for eating disorders, an understanding of which is essential for the development of prevention programmes. The range of school-based primary prevention interventions that have been developed and evaluated will then be described. The areas of secondary and tertiary prevention will also be discussed, including the challenges for primary care and dealing with high-risk groups. The important role of families across all levels of prevention is emphasised. Finally, there will be discussion on the way forward, and directions for future research.

Prevention model

It is useful to conceptualise prevention at three levels. Primary prevention involves reduction or elimination of key risk factors which lead to eating disorders; secondary prevention involves early identification and intervention; tertiary involves establishing effective treatments to prevent chronicity and secondary complications. At each level there is scope for a range of preventive interventions (see Figure 10.1). Most attention in research has been towards tertiary prevention e.g. through specialist Children and Adolescent Mental Health Services (CAMHS), although there is now increasing interest in primary and secondary prevention.

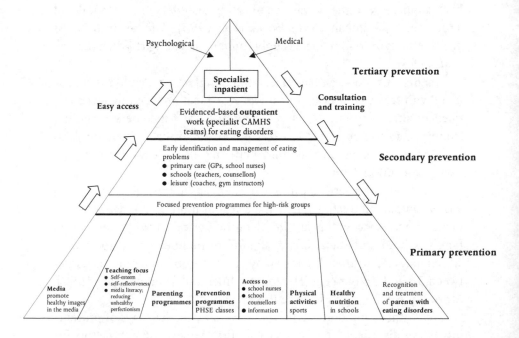

Figure 10.1 Model for prevention

Integration between the three levels is essential. Early identification is useful only if there are competent treatment centres with easy access to them. Expert treatment resources may be swamped if large numbers of young people develop serious eating disorders due to inadequate primary and secondary levels of prevention. Ideally specialists should provide training and consultation to the primary and secondary levels, to assist in the process of preventing the development of eating disorders.

Risk factors and protective factors: implications for prevention

Our understanding of how eating disorders develop is still far from complete; however, research has begun to identify some of the factors that increase the likelihood of developing an eating disorder.

Individual risk factors

A number of studies have found high levels of body dissatisfaction among children and adolescents (Wood, Becker and Thompson 1996) which can lead to dieting and eating problems. It is now well established that perfectionism and low self-esteem can increase the risk of an eating disorder (Button *et al.* 1996; Fairburn *et al.* 1999; Pliner and Haddock 1996; Williams and Currie 2000). Young people with a history of depression or obesity are also more at risk (Fairburn *et al.* 1997).

A number of researchers have found that early puberty is associated with disordered eating (Attie and Brooks-Gunn 1989; Williams and Currie 2000). Cauffman and Steinberg (1996) suggested that it is not early puberty itself that predicted disordered eating, but rather the combination of early puberty and socialising with boys and dating.

The role of temperament has been examined. Martin *et al.* (2000) found that negative emotionality (high levels of negative reactivity, inflexibility, irritability and low levels of cooperativeness) increases the risk of eating problems.

Dieting and sociocultural influences

The commonly held belief in western society that thinness is linked to attractiveness, success and happiness leads many young females to diet (Hill, Weaver and Blundell 1990; Smolak and Levine 1994). Not all who diet develop eating disorders; however, a number of studies have shown that dieting is a significant risk factor (Patton 1999; Patton *et al.* 1990). It is of concern that the prevalence of dieting is rising and is seen at increasingly younger ages (Bryant-Waugh and Lask 1995; Levine *et al.* 1994; Smolak and Levine 1994).

A number of studies have looked specifically at the role of mass media in contributing to dieting. It is likely that the negative impact of images of thin women in the media is more pronounced in young women who already have poor body image and low self-esteem (Levine and Smolak 1996; Martin and Kennedy 1993; Shaw and Waller 1995).

Some writers have explored more generally the influence of society. Since the early 1980s there has been an increasing breakdown in family cohesion, resulting in less connectedness between family members, less support within families and fewer family meals together. Katzman and Lee (1997) argue that disconnection of young women is an underlying problem linked to development of eating disorders. They emphasise the role of cultural values and norms in contributing to this disconnection and highlight the importance of development of self-awareness and competency in young women.

Developmental transitions

Normal adolescent development involves a number of tasks and challenges that can be difficult to negotiate, particularly for girls. These include adjusting to the biological changes of puberty, establishing relationships, developing skills, becoming independent, and developing a sense of identity. Physical changes of puberty may lead to body dissatisfaction and a wish to lose weight, particularly if puberty is early (Williams and Currie 2000). The other developmental tasks necessitate taking responsibility and making decisions, which can be difficult for some girls, particularly those with low self-esteem and perfectionism. Losing weight can become a way of avoiding these challenges (see Stewart 1998; Striegel-Moore 1993).

Family risk factors

Family and twin studies have indicated that eating disorders are familial, with contribution from both genetic and environmental factors (Strober *et al.* 2000). Shared environmental effects appear less important than non-shared environmental effects (Bulik, Sullivan and Kendler 2000).

A number of studies have looked at the links between specific family factors and the development of eating disorders. Daughters of overweight or weight-concerned mothers may be at an increased risk of development of eating problems (Fairburn *et al.* 1997; Fairburn *et al.* 1999).

Vincent and McCabe (2000) found that parental comments about their child's weight and encouragement to lose weight was associated with dieting, disordered eating and body image dissatisfaction. A number of researchers have found that there is a link between dieting behaviour in young females and dieting behaviour in their mothers (Hill *et al.* 1990; Pike and Rodin 1991). However, some studies have found that dieting behaviour in parents and pressure to diet did not influence body image and dieting behaviour (Byely *et al.* 2000; Keel *et al.* 1997).

Some studies have indicated the role of poor family relationships as a risk factor for disordered eating and body image dissatisfaction (Attie and Brooks-Gunn 1989; Byely *et al.* 2000; McVey *et al.* 2002).

Peer influences

There is growing evidence that peer relationships can influence dieting behaviour in adolescent girls (Paxton 1999). Vincent and McCabe (2000) found that peer discussion about weight loss and peer encouragement to lose weight were associated with eating problems and poor body image in girls. For boys, peer encouragement to lose weight was associated with disordered eating.

Lieberman *et al.* (2001) found that having a high social status among peers, being pressured or teased by peers about weight, and modelling of concern about weight by peers all play an important role in the development and maintenance of negative body image and disordered eating.

High-risk pursuits

A number of researchers have found that there is an increase in prevalence of eating disorders among athletes (Thompson and Sherman 1993). Although involvement in sport can lead to high self-esteem, disciplines such as gymnastics, which rely on thinness for enhanced performance, can foster eating disorders. Moreover, if the young person is a perfectionist, the need of the sport may become stronger than the risk of poor health. Coaches can have a negative effect on self-esteem and can put pressure on young people to lose weight. Similarly, dancers have an increased risk for eating disorders (Garner *et al.* 1987).

Protective factors

Knowledge of protective factors can help in the design of prevention programmes; however, there is little research in this area. It is likely that high self-esteem is a key protective factor.

Two longitudinal studies found that positive family relationships can protect young people from developing eating disorders (Byely *et al.* 2000; Swarr and Richards 1996). McVey *et al.* (2002) found that higher levels of paternal support could protect young people from developing eating disorders when under stress.

Positive family relationships could help in a number of ways; parents could provide support when a young person is under stress, provide opportunities for expressing emotions and communicating difficulties and contribute to the development of positive self-esteem. More research is needed in this area.

Positive peer relationships have also been suggested as a protective factor. Belonging to a peer group that accepts a range of body types can be helpful; having positive peer relationships and engaging in social activities can foster self-esteem (Paxton 1999). Tiggermann (2001) found that being involved in organised sport can be protective.

Model for development of eating disorders

In developing a primary prevention programme the first task is to identify the modifiable risk factors. Using this knowledge, an intervention then needs to be designed which has the potential to change attitudes and behaviour, is developmentally appropriate, and practically feasible.

Figure 10.2 shows a model for the development of eating disorders taking into account known risk and associated factors. Body image dissatisfaction, low self-esteem and feelings of loss of control are at the core of this model. A number of influences such as peer, family, puberty, sociocultural and school pressures can contribute to these factors. Whether an individual progresses to dieting may depend on underlying personal and family risk factors. Not all dieting leads to eating disorders, but those at higher risk are more likely to develop eating disorders. Factors that are potentially modifiable through a primary prevention programme are dieting, negative body image, low self-esteem, perfectionism, response to media images, reaction to critical comments about weight and shape, stressful life events and reaction to puberty (particularly early puberty). Potential risk factors for eating disorders, such as a family history of eating disorders and obesity, or a previous history of depression and obesity are more difficult to address through a school-based programme.

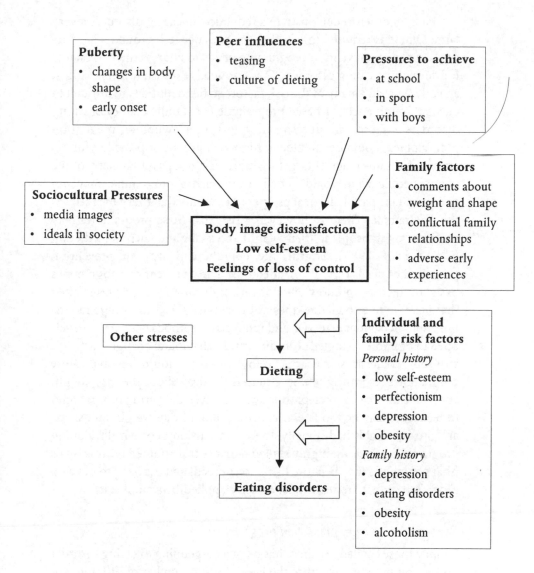

Figure 10.2 Factors involved in development of eating disorders

Primary prevention of eating disorders

School-based programmes: methodological challenges

Schools are an ideal place to base prevention programmes; however, there are a number of methodological issues and challenges for researchers.

First, in order to demonstrate a reduction in eating disorders a very large sample is required (given that the prevalence is around 1%). Second, a primary prevention programme needs to address the risk factors for developing eating disorders. Our knowledge of risk factors is still at an early stage and many of the risk factors so far identified are difficult to tackle through a school-based programme (e.g. family history of eating disorders). Third, an unresolved question is whether prevention programmes should be targeted at high-risk groups or provided for everyone. A disadvantage of targeting high-risk groups is that many of the young people who would benefit from such a programme may not choose to take part. Universal programmes ensure that everyone receives the programme. There is, however, a risk that these programmes may sensitise young people to their weight and shape and encourage dieting (Carter *et al.* 1997). Fourth, the content and style of prevention programmes needs careful consideration. Early prevention programmes based on increasing knowledge of eating disorders have demonstrated that increase in knowledge does not necessarily lead to change in attitudes and behaviour. Creative and innovative methods need to be developed to promote sustained attitudinal and behavioural change. Fifth, it is still not clear at what age young people should receive these programmes. Exposing young children to ideas about dieting, weight and shape may be counter-productive. However, delivering programmes to teenagers may be too late, if concerns about body weight and shape are already established. Finally, there is a tension between developing programmes requiring highly skilled delivery from trained professionals (that potentially may be more likely to succeed) and the need to develop programmes that are realistic and easily applied by school staff.

Strategies for primary prevention programmes

Despite these challenges, there has been a burgeoning of eating disorder prevention programmes since the late 1980s. A number of different approaches to prevention have evolved.

Psychoeducation has been a key focus, particularly in earlier programmes (Moreno and Thelen 1993; Shisslak, Crago and Neal 1990). Strategies include increasing knowledge of nutrition, healthy eating and lifestyle, changes in puberty, factors associated with body dissatisfaction, the negative effects of dieting, and the nature and consequences of eating disorders. It is hypothesised that increasing knowledge will lead young people to seek help for eating problems and deter others from developing them.

Given that a major risk factor for eating disorders in developed countries is the sociocultural pressure to diet, there has been a significant focus in prevention programmes on teaching young people to become more aware of unhelpful messages in the media and to challenge these messages (Killen et al. 1993). Another key risk factor is low self-esteem. This has led to a number of programmes focusing on the promotion of positive self-esteem (O'Dea and Abraham 1999).

Review of eating disorder prevention research

Over 30 school-based prevention programmes have been evaluated to date. Earlier studies (Killen et al. 1993; Moreno and Thelen 1993; Moriarty, Shore and Maxim 1990; Paxton 1993; Rosen 1989; Shisslak et al. 1990) generally involved psychoeducation and, in some cases, media literacy training. Most of these studies showed a change in knowledge about eating disorders and related topics, but this did not lead to a change in attitudes and behaviour (not all these studies actually measured eating behaviour).

Since the early 1990s there has been increasing interest in developing more innovative ways of delivering prevention programmes. The more successful programmes tend to use interactive methods with a focus on building self-esteem.

Neumark-Sztainer, Butler and Palti (1995) developed a programme which included a focus on self-esteem and coping with stress. They showed that the onset of unhealthy dieting and bingeing behaviours could be prevented at long-term follow-up, although pre-existing dieting showed no change following the programme. Springer et al. (1997) found that a body image curriculum for college students improved body image and reduced disordered eating. Huon et al. (1997) showed no difference in drive for thinness or body dissatisfaction following a six-week programme. However, when the highest scoring subjects were examined there was a reduction in body dissatisfaction at post-test. Irving, Dupen and Berel (1998) developed a media literacy programme for high school girls and found that following the programme, the index girls perceived media messages as less realistic: they found no differences in body dissatisfaction. Santonastaso et al. (1999), in a programme which focused on body image and self-esteem, showed an improvement in body dissatisfaction scores at one-year follow-up among low-risk subjects, although high-risk subjects showed no change compared to controls. O'Dea and Abraham (1999) have developed a new approach to the prevention of eating disorders. In their study an interactive school-based self-esteem programme that did not refer to eating disorders produced improvements in body image and in eating behaviour. However, these changes were not fully sustained in the long term.

Our own intervention (Stewart *et al.* 2001) was designed to take account of the normal process of development in young adolescent girls (Stewart 1998). It addresses the developmental challenges for girls, sociocultural pressures, negative thinking and responses to stress and adverse comments about shape and weight, all of which can lead to low self-esteem, disturbed body image and eating problems in some girls. The overall aim was to prevent the development of eating disorders by reducing dietary restraint and concern about shape and weight. The programme focused on encouraging the development of skills and behavioural change by incorporating active involvement by the students. Skills were developed through a variety of strategies, such as identifying and challenging negative automatic thoughts, including those concerning shape. A key strategy throughout was to help students feel good about themselves. Results demonstrated a short-term improvement in the target behaviour in the index group compared to the control group, which showed little change. However, at six-month follow-up the positive changes were not fully maintained. Both index and control groups showed an increase in dietary restraint from post-intervention to follow-up. However, in the index group the follow-up levels of some measures (Eating Attitudes Test and Shape Concern subscale of the EDE-Q) remained significantly lower than at base line, and the index group had both lower EAT and dietary restraint scores at follow-up, compared to the control group. A major limitation of this study was the lack of randomisation.

A systematic review of randomised controlled trials (RCTs) of prevention programmes (Pratt and Woolfenden 2003) has shown disappointing results overall. This review was based on eight studies and concluded that there was insufficient evidence that the included prevention programmes were effective in promoting healthy eating attitudes and behaviour in young people. Pooled evidence did not indicate that harm resulted from the included programmes.

Problems with current approaches

A number of studies in existence are flawed by methodological difficulties, such as small numbers, lack of a controlled group or lack of randomisation. The systematic review of RCTs (Pratt and Woolfenden 2003) has highlighted that there is a long way to go in developing effective school-based prevention programmes. Studies have shown that it is relatively easy to increase knowledge. Changing attitudes and behaviour even in the short term is difficult; sustaining any changes is even more difficult.

Need for comprehensive approaches to primary prevention

The lack of demonstrated effectiveness of school-based programmes has prompted a number of researchers to suggest a more comprehensive approach to prevention. Neumark-Sztainer (1996) suggested an ecological approach involving the whole school in creating an environment that fosters healthy eating attitudes and behaviour.

Some researchers have taken on board this approach and have moved away from entirely student-focused interventions. Chally (1998) devised an intervention which was targeted at adult school staff and demonstrated an improvement of behaviour following the intervention. Piran (1999b) and Gresko and Rosenvinge (1998) have developed interventions which are directed at a social/environmental level. As well as preventive sessions for young people over a prolonged period of time, these interventions also targeted teachers and parents in an attempt to modify the school and home environment. Although both of these interventions showed positive change in improvements of eating attitudes, neither of these interventions had a comparison group.

Ideally, a more comprehensive approach would involve parents, teachers and students in a strategy that starts at primary school and continues through secondary school, adapting the focus of teaching to the developmental level. Strategies could focus on building self-esteem, managing stress, problem solving, resisting sociocultural pressures and promoting healthy lifestyle, rather than just providing information on the development and consequences of eating disorders. It should involve the school in a broad-based way, including attention to school meals, physical education and creating an environment that fosters self-esteem. Such strategies could be developed in collaboration with other prevention programmes e.g. suicide prevention, drug and alcohol abuse prevention. Access to counselling would be an important element, given that emotional difficulties can increase the risk of developing eating disorders.

Alongside this general school strategy, parenting programmes may be a useful way to encourage parents to help children develop healthy eating patterns, as well as tackle the difficulties of bringing up adolescents. Many parents find it hard coping with the demands of adolescents. Changes in the parent–adolescent relationship can be difficult to adapt to and questioning of authority may lead to conflict. Where there is secure attachment it may be easier to resolve these conflicts and develop healthy relationships. Swarr and Richards (1996) noted that girls who spent less time with their mothers in early adolescence were more likely to develop eating problems. The role of fathers has received very little attention in the literature (Levine 1994), but fathers may play a significant role in helping their teenage daughters develop healthy attitudes about body weight and shape. Parenting programmes may be easier to establish if linked in to programmes for young people within schools. It would be helpful if parents had access to information on normal adolescent development and issues related to parenting of teenagers, as well as healthy nutrition. Parents might usefully be helped not to focus on the weight and shape of their offspring, to encourage appropriate independence while at the same time continuing to provide love and stability, to praise their child for small achievements but not put undue pressure on them to achieve in the future, to encourage social interaction and to provide them with experiences that help to foster identity.

To date there has been no evaluation of the effectiveness of parenting programmes in the reduction of eating disorders.

The comprehensive universal strategy for prevention is based on a health promotion model. This general approach could go alongside specific interventions for high-risk groups. Stewart *et al.* (2001) found that there was greater change in the high-risk subgroup in their sample. With this high-risk group, the issues of who and how to select, as well as how to motivate this group to make changes, are crucial.

Other strategies for primary prevention

Having a parent with an eating disorder leads to a greater chance of developing an eating disorder and there is evidence that both genetic and environmental factors can contribute. Treatment of adult eating disorders may reduce the likelihood of eating disorders developing in offspring; however, this has not yet been substantiated by research. Genetic counselling could potentially play a part in prevention, with identification of families at risk, and provision of guidelines for parents to minimise the risk of their offspring developing an eating disorder.

Alongside school-based prevention programmes it is important to consider the influence of the media, and encourage the promotion of healthy messages about shape and weight.

Secondary prevention of eating disorders

It is generally thought that the prognosis for eating disorders is improved if there is early identification and management of eating problems (Herzog, Rathner and Vandereycken 1992; Morgan and Russell 1975), although there is no strong evidence for this to date. Ideally, strategies should be established within primary care and within schools to detect and effectively manage early eating disorders.

Primary Care

General practitioners (GPs) play an important role in health promotion and early identification of eating problems. However, GPs may lack the knowledge to diagnose and intervene appropriately. Epidemiological research suggests that eating disorders are under-diagnosed in primary care (Whitehouse et al. 1992). Bryant-Waugh et al. (1992) found that diagnosis of early onset eating disorders is often delayed. This may be because of a number of factors. First, young people with eating disorders may delay going to see their doctor due to fears of the outcome, or denial that they have a problem. Second, eating disorders can be hard to recognise in children and young people, particularly as GPs may only rarely see patients with eating problems. If eating disorders are recognised, poor communication between the patient (and family) and the GP may make it hard to proceed with further help (Newton, Robinson and Hartley 1993). Finally, once eating disorders are suspected and the diagnosis is conveyed sensitively, GPs need the confidence to be able to proceed effectively.

It is important that GPs are aware both of the risk factors for developing eating disorders and the early warning signs of eating disorders (Table 10.1). Where risk factors are present, sensitive counselling and education at this stage may help prevent eating problems developing. For those at risk, simple questions such as 'Do you think you have an eating problem?' or 'Do you worry about your weight?' may clarify the presence of an eating problem. Where there is an eating problem, an early intervention by the GP may be helpful. This should include education about the negative consequences of developing an eating disorder, nutritional advice, encouragement to develop alternative ways of addressing problems, and providing an opportunity to discuss adolescent fears and difficulties, along with regular weight monitoring. Improving the motivation to make changes is an essential component of this approach. In addition, the GP should involve the family, wherever possible, in order to provide education and encourage re-establishment of healthy eating. There are a number of very useful books for young people and their parents which may assist the task, e.g. Bryant-Waugh and Lask (1999), Palmer (1996) and Treasure (1998). Regular follow-up is important and if weight continues to be lost or a healthy weight is not achieved despite intervention, then an early referral to a child and adolescent mental health team is indicated.

A brief cognitive-behavioural approach by GPs has been piloted with adults with bulimia nervosa and found to be helpful (Waller *et al.* 1996); however, there are no studies exploring the efficacy of GP interventions with young people.

For those with a history of eating problems or significant risk factors, annual check-ups in primary care which involve measurement of height and weight as well as checking other physical indices and emotional health could be an important aspect to secondary prevention. However, to date, there is no research evaluating this approach. A screening tool such as the SCOFF questionnaire (Morgan, Reid and Lacey 1999) may assist GPs in identifying eating disorder pathology, although more research is needed to evaluate it.

Education for GP registrars should include a component on identification and early management of eating disorders, and trained GPs should have access to continuing education addressing this problem. Where there is shared care with mental health services, attendance at case reviews can be a useful way of sharing information.

Finally, self-help literature has been shown to have a significant effect on recovery from binge eating disorder in adults, particularly guided self-help (Carter and Fairburn 1998). There may be scope for using self-help literature with adolescents with mild forms of bulimia nervosa, although there is no evidence to date.

Box 10.1 Early warning signs of eating disorders

Physical signs

- feeling the cold, wearing baggy clothes
- dizziness
- lethargy
- weakness
- poor sleeping
- low body-mass index (BMI)/poor growth
- menstrual disturbance or amenorrhoea
- repeated vomiting
- gastrointestinal symptoms

Behavioural changes

- eating alone
- hiding food
- secretiveness
- missing meals

Psychological changes

- low mood/anxiety
- irritability
- poor concentration

Educational changes

- poor concentration
- difficulty in attention to school work
- absence from school due to physical weakness

Social changes

- disturbance in family relationships
- loss of interest in friends

Teacher Training

Teachers are in an ideal position to identify young people at risk and those who have early warning signs. Teacher training could usefully include a module on awareness and management of eating problems and other mental health disorders. Continuing education of teachers by way of in-set training days could also address these issues.

Prevention in high-risk groups

Some groups are at particularly high risk and warrant consideration, for example athletes, dancers and young people with diabetes.

Dancers

There is evidence that in professions such as dancing, which focus on appearance, there is a higher risk of eating disorders (Garner *et al.* 1987). The pressures to achieve a thin, pre-pubertal body shape, particularly in top ballet companies, are immense. Because this drive for thinness can be perpetuated by the trainers and examiners, eating disorders in a trainee may not be addressed until they are severe. Piran (1999a) has described consultation work with ballet schools and prevention programmes within this setting. As well as specific programmes, Piran's work has helped to shape the culture of the institution.

Elite athletes

A number of studies have shown an increase in eating disorders in athletes, particularly those in sports that emphasise a thin body such as running, lightweight rowing, gymnastics and figure skating (Rosen and Hough 1988; Thompson and Sherman 1993). The widely held belief among coaches that achieving a low body fat percentage will enhance performance complicates preventive efforts. Prevention therefore needs to be focused towards coaches as well as athletes themselves. Kratina (1996) drew up guidelines for coaches in order to increase the awareness among this group. Since the late 1990s some major international sporting organisations have recognised that this problem needs addressing.

Diabetes

Eating disorders in people with diabetes may pose considerable risk to diabetic control, therefore prevention of eating disorders developing is a high priority for this group. There has been an attempt to develop prevention programmes with groups of young women with diabetes.

Olmstead *et al.* (2002) conducted a controlled study of a psycho-educational intervention with young women with diabetes attending a paediatric clinic. They found significant reduction on the restraint and eating concern subscales of the Eating Disorder Examination (EDE) and on the drive for thinness and body dissatisfaction subscales of the Eating Disorder Inventory (EDI). However, there was no reduction in frequency of insulin omission or improvement in glycaemic control. More work needs to be done with this high-risk group.

The use of the Internet

The Internet has become a widespread and uncontrolled way of obtaining and disseminating information. There are over 200 websites relating to eating disorders, some of which promote rather than prevent eating disorders. Adolescents with early symptoms of eating disorders may access the Internet for information. In view of this, there is growing interest in developing the use of the Internet for health promotion (Fawcett *et al.* 2000).

Tertiary prevention of eating disorders

Prevention of chronic problems and complications of eating disorders: Evidence-based treatment in CAMHS services

For established eating disorders it is essential that there are services available providing effective treatment to minimise the risk of chronic problems developing.

Available evidence suggests that family-based approaches with anorexia nervosa are important with children and adolescents (Dare *et al.* 1995; Eisler *et al.* 2000; Robin *et al.* 1999). Family therapy in bulimia nervosa has also been explored (Dodge *et al.* 1995) although there are no convincing data as yet. Specialist teams for treating eating disorders should be available at a local level in order to prevent chronic problems developing and minimise the need for inpatient admission. Many young people with established eating disorders are reluctant to have treatment. Motivational approaches have been found to be useful with adults with eating disorders (Treasure and Ward 1997) and are increasingly being used with young people.

Eating disorders can lead to a number of serious physical, psychological, social and educational consequences. It is important that treatment approaches minimise these risks by careful assessment and management of physical state as well as competent psychological treatment.

Appropriate inpatient care

There will always be a small minority of young people that need inpatient care for severe eating disorders. Gowers *et al.* (2000) conducted a follow-up study of adolescents receiving inpatient care. The outcome was poor on a number of measures, although this was not a controlled study. The risks of inpatient care need to be minimised as far as is possible, for example encouraging continuing links with family and friends to minimise the social impact of inpatient care.

Role of families within prevention

Families are an essential component of primary, secondary and tertiary intervention. Parents can help promote positive self-esteem and healthy eating and are also in a good position to identify problems and seek help as early as possible. If their daughter or son develops an eating disorder, parents may be a crucial part of the recovery process. Services at all levels need to be aware of the important role that families have and work with them to develop this resource.

Summary and way forward

Eating disorders carry significant mortality and morbidity. Research is currently exploring the best ways to intervene to prevent these problems developing, and to identify and treat early to prevent long-term consequences. School-based programmes have been evaluated in many countries, although the outcome so far has been disappointing. Awareness is growing of the important role of schools in helping to prevent various mental health problems. The previous narrow approach to prevention is being widened from disease prevention to a health promotion model (Rosenvinge and Børreson 1999). It is likely that the most effective approach within schools is a comprehensive one, including a focus on building self-esteem; providing counselling; encouraging a critical enquiry in young people; monitoring of health by school nurses; providing a school environment where students are listened to and valued and there is an effective anti-bullying policy; and a considered and sensitive emphasis on personal and social education and nutrition. Alongside this approach there may be a need for more focused interventions for those at high risk. In addition, accessible information, counselling and programmes for parents may prove to be essential.

Further research is needed to explore the role of primary care in identifying and treating those with early symptoms of eating disorder. Specialist CAMHS teams need continuing development in order to provide the most effective treatment for established eating disorders in order to prevent chronicity. Consultation and training at all levels is an essential aspect of prevention. Finally, alongside these prevention measures, addressing the cultural dimension is essential, including establishing links with the media and encouragement of the promotion of a preventive perspective at a sociocultural level.

Acknowledgements

I am grateful to Debbie Waller for her very helpful comments on an earlier draft.

References

Attie, L. and Brooks-Gunn, J. (1989) 'Development of Eating Problems in Adolescent Girls: A Longitudinal Study.' *Developmental Psychology 25*, 70–79.

Bryant-Waugh, R.J. and Lask, B.D. (1995) 'Eating Disorders in Children.' *Journal of Child Psychology and Psychiatry 36*, 191–202.

Bryant-Waugh, R.J. and Lask, B.D. (1999) *Eating Disorders – A Parents' Guide.* Harmondsworth: Penguin.

Bryant-Waugh, R.J., Lask, B.D., Shafran, R.I. and Fosson, A.R. (1992) 'Do Doctors Recognise Eating Disorders in Children?' *Archives of Diseases in Childhood 67*, 103–105.

Bulik, C.M., Sullivan, P.F. and Kendler, K.S. (2000) 'Twin Studies of Eating Disorders: A Review.' *International Journal of Eating Disorders 27*, 1–20.

Button, E.J., Sonuga-Burke, E.J.S., Davies, J. and Thompson, M. (1996) 'A Prospective Study of Self-esteem in the Prediction of Eating Problems in Adolescent School Girls.' *British Journal of Clinical Psychology 35*, 193–203.

Byely, L., Archibald, A.B., Graber, J. and Brooks-Gunn, J. (2000) 'A Prospective Study of Familial and Social Influences on Girls' Body Image and Dieting.' *International Journal of Eating Disorders 28*, 155–164.

Carter, J.C. and Fairburn, C.G. (1998) 'Cognitive-behavioural Self-help for Binge Eating Disorder: A Controlled Effectiveness Study.' *Journal of Consulting and Clinical Psychology 66*, 616–823.

Carter, J.C., Stewart, D.A., Dunn, V.J. and Fairburn, C.G. (1997) 'Primary Prevention of Eating Disorders: Might it Do More Harm than Good?' *International Journal of Eating Disorders 22*, 167–172.

Cauffman, E. and Steinberg, L. (1996) 'Interactive Effects of Menarcheal Status and Dating on Dieting and Disordered Eating among Adolescent Girls.' *Developmental Psychology 32*, 631–635.

Chally, P.S. (1998) 'An Eating Disorders Prevention Programme.' *Journal of Child and Adolescent Psychiatry Nursing 11*, 51–60.

Dare, C., Eisler, I., Colahan, M., Crowther, C., Senior, R. and Asen, E. (1995) 'The Listening Heart and the Chi Square: Clinical and Empirical Perceptions in the Family Therapy of Anorexia Nervosa.' *Journal of Family Therapy 17*, 31–57.

Dodge, E., Hodes, M., Eisler, I. and Dare, C. (1995) 'Family Therapy for Bulimia Nervosa in Adolescents: An Exploratory Study.' *Journal of Family Therapy 17*, 59–77.

Eisler, I., Dare, C., Hodes, M., Russell, G., Dodge, E. and Le Grange, D. (2000) 'Family Therapy for Adolescent Anorexia Nervosa: The Results of a Controlled Comparison of Two Family Interventions.' *Journal of Child Psychology and Psychiatry 41*, 727–736.

Fairburn, C. and Beglin, S.J. (1990) 'Studies of the Epidemiology of Bulimia Nervosa.' *American Journal of Psychiatry 147*, 401–408.

Fairburn, C.G., Welch, S.L., Doll, H.A., Davies, B. and O'Connor, M.E. (1997) 'Risk Factors for Bulimia Nervosa: A Community-based Case-control Study.' *Archives of General Psychiatry 54*, 509–517.

Fairburn, C.G., Cooper, Z., Doll, H.A. and Welch, S.L. (1999) 'Risk Factors for Anorexia Nervosa: Three Integrated Case-control Comparisons.' *Archives of General Psychiatry 56*, 468–476.

Fawcett, S.B., Francisco, V.T., Schultz, J.A., Berkowitz, B., Wolff, T.J. and Nagy, G. (2000) 'The Community Tool Box: A Web-based Resource for Building Healthier Communities.' *Public Health Report 115*, 274–278.

Garner, D., Garfinkel, P., Rockert, W. and Olmstead, M. (1987) 'A Prospective Study of Eating Disturbances in the Ballet.' *Psychotherapy and Psychosomatics 48*, 170–175.

Goldman, E.L. (1996) 'Eating Disorders on the Rise in Preteens and Adolescents.' *Psychiatry News 24*, 10.

Gowers, S.G., Weetman, J., Shore, A., Hossain, F. and Elvins, R. (2000) 'Impact of Hospitalisation on the Outcome of Adolescent Anorexia Nervosa.' *British Journal of Psychiatry 176*, 138–141.

Gresko, R.B. and Rosenvinge, J.H. (1998) 'The Norwegian School-based Prevention Model: Development and Evaluation.' In W. Vandereycken and G. Noordenbos (eds) *The Prevention of Eating Disorders*. London: Athlone Press.

Herzog, W., Rathner, G. and Vandereycken, W. (1992) 'Long-term Course of Anorexia Nervosa: A Review of the Literature.' In W. Herzog, H.C. Deter and W. Vandereycken (eds) *The Course of Eating Disorders. Long term Follow-up Studies of Anorexia Nervosa and Bulimia Nervosa*. Berlin and Heidelberg: Springer-Verlag.

Hill, J.A., Weaver, C. and Blundell, J.E. (1990) 'Dieting Concerns of 10-year-old Girls and their Mothers.' *British Journal of Clinical Psychology 43*, 445–449.

Hoeck, H., Bartelds, A.I., Bosveld, M.A., van der Graaf, Y., Limpens, V.E., Maiwald, M. and Spaaij, C.J.K. (1995) 'Impact of Urbanisation on Detection Rates of Eating Disorders.' *American Journal of Psychiatry 152*, 1272–1278.

Huon, G.F., Roncolato, W.G., Ritchie, J.E. and Braganza, C. (1997) 'Prevention of Dieting-induced Eating Disorders: Findings and Implications of a Pilot Study.' *Eating Disorders 5*, 280–292.

Irving, L.M., Dupen, J. and Berel, S. (1998) 'A Media Literacy Programme for High School Students.' *Eating Disorders: The Journal for Treatment and Prevention 6*, 2, 119–131.

Katzman, M.A. and Lee, S. (1997) 'Beyond Body Image: The Integration of Feminist and Transcultural Theories in the Understanding of Self-starvation.' *International Journal of Eating Disorders 22*, 385–394.

Keel, P.K., Heatherton, T.F., Harnsden, J.L. and Hornig, C.D. (1997) 'Mothers, Fathers and Daughters: Dieting and Disordered Eating.' *Eating Disorders 5*, 216–228.

Killen, J.D., Barr Taylor, C., Hammer, L.D., Litt, I., Hammer, L., Wilson, D.M., Rich, T., Hayward, C., Simmonds, B., Kraemer, H. and Varady, A. (1993) 'An Attempt to Modify Unhealthful Eating Attitudes and Weight Regulation Practices of Young Adolescent Girls.' *International Journal of Eating Disorders 13*, 369–384.

Killen, J.D., Taylor, C.B., Hayward, C., Wilson, D.M., Hammer, L.D., Robinson, T.N., Litt, I., Simmonds, B.A., Varady, A. and Kraemer, H. (1994) 'The Pursuit of Thinness and Onset of Eating Disorder Symptoms in a Community Sample of Adolescent Girls: A Three Year Prospective Analysis.' *International Journal of Eating Disorders 16*, 227–238.

Kratina, K. (1996) 'Ten Things Coaches can do to Help Prevent Eating Disorders in their Athletes.' *National Eating Disorders Organisation (NEDO) newsletter 6*.

Levine, M.P. (1994) 'Beauty Myth and the Beast: What can Men Do and Be to Help Prevent Eating Disorders.' *Eating Disorders 2*, 101–113.

Levine, M.P. and Smolak, L. (1996) 'Media as a Context for the Development of Disordered Eating.' In L. Smolak, M. Levine and R. Striegel-Moore (eds) *The Developmental Psychopathology of Eating Disorders: Implications for Research, Prevention and Treatment*. Mahwah, NJ: Erlbaum.

Levine, M.P., Smolak, L., Moody, A.F., Schuman, M.D. and Hessen, L.D. (1994) 'Normative Developmental Challenges and Dieting and Eating Disturbance in Middle School Girls.' *International Journal of Eating Disorders 15*, 11–20.

Lieberman, M., Gauvin, L., Bokowski, W.M. and White, D.R. (2001) 'Interpersonal Influences and Disordered Eating Behaviour in Adolescent Girls: The Role of Peer Modelling, Social Reinforcement, and Body Related Teasing.' *Eating Behaviours 2*, 215–236.

Lucas, A.R., Beard, C.M., Faloon, W.M. and Kurland, L.T. (1991) '50 Year Trends in the Incidence of Anorexia Nervosa in Rochester: A Population Based Study.' *American Journal of Psychiatry 148*, 917–922.

McVey, G.L., Pepler, D., Davis, R., Flett, G.L. and Abdolell, M. (2002) 'Risk and Protective Factors Associated with Disordered Eating during Early Adolescence.' *Journal of Early Adolescence 22*, 75–95.

Martin, G.C., Wetheim, E.H., Prior, M., Smart, D., Sanson, A. and Oberklaid, F. (2000) 'A Longitudinal Study of the Role of Childhood Temperament in the Later Development of Eating Concerns.' *International Journal of Eating Disorders 27*, 150–162.

Martin, M.C. and Kennedy, P.F. (1993) 'Advertising and Social Comparison: Consequences for Female Pre-adolescents and Adolescents.' *Psychology and Marketing 10*, 513–530.

Moreno, A.B. and Thelen, M.H. (1993) 'A Primary Prevention Programme for Eating Disorders in a Junior High School Population.' *Journal of Youth and Adolescence 22*, 109–124.

Morgan, H.G. and Russell, G.F.M. (1975) 'Value of Family Background and Clinical Features as Predictors of Long-term Outcome in Anorexia Nervosa: 4 Year Follow-up Study of 41 Patients.' *Psychological Medicine 5*, 355–371.

Morgan, J.F., Reid, F. and Lacey, J.H. (1999) 'The SCOFF Questionnaire: Assessment of a New Screening Tool for Eating Disorders.' *British Medical Journal 319*, 1467–1468.

Moriarty, D., Shore, R. and Maxim, N. (1990) 'Evaluation of an Eating Disorder Curriculum.' *Evaluation and Programme Planning 13*, 407–413.

Neumark-Sztainer, D. (1996) 'School-based Programs for Preventing Eating Disturbances.' *Journal of School Health 66*, 2, 64–71.

Neumark-Sztainer, D., Butler, R. and Palti, H. (1995) 'Eating Disturbance among Adolescent Girls: Evaluation of a School-based Primary Prevention Programme.' *Journal of Nutrition and Eating 27*, 24–31.

Newton, T., Robinson, P. and Hartley, P. (1993) 'Treatment for Eating Disorders in the UK. Part 2. Experiences of Treatment: A Survey of Members of the EDA.' *Eating Disorders Review 1*, 10–21.

O'Dea, J.A. and Abraham, S. (1999) 'Improving the Body Image, Eating Attitudes and Behaviours of Young Male and Female Adolescents: A New Educational Approach that Focuses on Self Esteem.' *International Journal of Eating Disorders 28*, 43–57.

Olmstead, M.P., Daneman, D., Rydall, A.C., Lawson, M.L. and Rodin, G. (2002) 'The Effects of Psychoeducation on Disturbed Eating Attitudes and Behaviour in Young Women with Type 1 Diabetes Mellitus.' *International Journal of Eating Disorders 32*, 230–239.

Palmer, R.L. (1996) *Understanding Eating Disorders.* London: Family Doctor Publications.

Patton, C.G. (1999) 'Onset of Adolescent Eating Disorders: Population Based Cohort Study over 3 Years.' *British Medical Journal 318*, 765–788.

Patton, C.G., Johnson-Sabine, E., Wood, K., Mann, A.H. and Wakeling, A. (1990) 'Abnormal Eating Attitudes in London School Girls – A Provective

Epidemiological Study: Outcome at Twelve Month Follow-up.' *Psychological Medicine 20*, 383–394.

Paxton, S.J. (1993) 'A Prevention Programme for Disturbed Eating and Body Dissatisfaction in Adolescent Girls: A One Year Follow-up.' *Health Education Research 8*, 43–51.

Paxton, S.J. (1999) 'Peer Relations, Body Image and Disordered Eating in Adolescent Girls.' In N. Piran, M.P. Levine and C. Steiner-Adair (eds) *Preventing Eating Disorders: A Handbook of Interventions and Special Challenges*. Philadelphia, PA: Taylor and Francis.

Perring, C., Twigg, J. and Atkin, K. (1990) *Families Caring for People Diagnosed as Mentally Ill: The Literature Re-examined*. London: HMSO.

Pike, K.M. and Rodin, J. (1991) 'Mothers, Daughters and Disordered Eating.' *Journal of Abnormal Psychology 100*, 198–204.

Piran, N. (1999a) 'On the Move from Tertiary to Secondary and Primary Prevention: Working with an Elite Dance School.' In N. Piran, M.P. Levine and C. Steiner-Adair (eds) *Preventing Eating Disorders: A Handbook of Interventions and Special Challenges*. Philadelphia, PA: Taylor and Francis.

Piran, N. (1999b) 'Eating Disorders: A Trial of Prevention in a High Risk School Setting.' *Journal of Primary Prevention 20*, 75–90.

Pliner, P. and Haddock, G. (1996) 'Perfectionism in Weight-concerned and -Unconcerned Women: An Experimental Approach.' *International Journal of Eating Disorders 19*, 381–389.

Pratt, B.M. and Woolfenden, S.R. (2003) 'Interventions for Preventing Eating Disorders in Children and Adolescents (Cochrane Review).' In *The Cochrane Library, Issue 3*. Oxford: Update Software.

Robin, A.L., Siegel, P.T., Moye, A.W., Gilroy, M., Dennis, A.B. and Sikand, A. (1999) 'A Controlled Comparison of Family Versus Individual Therapy for Adolescents with Anorexia Nervosa.' *Journal of the American Academy of Child and Adolescent Psychiatry 38*, 1482–1489.

Rosen, J.C. (1989) 'Prevention of Eating Disorders.' *National Anorexic Aid Society Newsletter 12*, 1–3.

Rosen, L.W. and Hough, D.O. (1988) 'Pathogenic Weight Control Behaviours of Female College Gymnasts.' *Physicians and Sports Medicine 16*, 141–146.

Rosenvinge, J.H. and Børreson, R. (1999) 'Prevention of Eating Disorders: Time to Change Programmes or Paradigms? Current Update and Future Recommendations.' *European Eating Disorders Review 7*, 6–16.

Russell, G.F.M. (1992) 'The Prognosis of Eating Disorders: A Clinician's Approach.' In W. Herzog, H.C. Deter and W. Vandereycken (eds) *The Course of Eating Disorders: Long-term follow-up Studies of Anorexia Nervosa and Bulimia Nervosa*. Berlin and Heidelberg: Springer-Verlag.

Santonastaso, P., Zanetti, T., Ferrara, S., Olivotto, M.C., Magnavita, N. and Favaro, A. (1999) 'A Preventive Intervention Programme in Adolescent Schoolgirls: A Longitudinal Study.' *Psychotherapy and Psychosomatics 68*, 46–50.

Shaw, J. and Waller, G. (1995) 'The Media's Impact on Body Image: Implications for Prevention and Treatment.' *Eating Disorders: The Journal of Treatment and Prevention 3*, 115–123.

Shisslak, C., Crago, M. and Neal, M.E. (1990) 'Prevention of Eating Disorder among Adolescents.' *American Journal of Health Promotion 5*, 100–106.

Smolak, L. and Levine, M.P. (1994) 'Towards an Empirical Basis for Primary Prevention of Eating Problems with Elementary School Children.' *Eating Disorders: The Journal of Treatment and Prevention 2*, 293–307.

Springer, E.A., Winzelberg, A.J., Perkins, R. and Barr Taylor, C. (1997) 'Effects of a Body Image Curriculum for College Students on Improved Body Image.' *International Journal of Eating Disorders 26*, 13–20.

Stewart, D.A. (1998) 'Experience with a School-based Programme.' In G. Noordenbos and W. Vandereycken (eds) *Prevention of Eating Disorders*. London: Athlone Press.

Stewart, D.A., Carter, J.C., Drinkwater, J., Hainsworth, J. and Fairburn, C.G. (2001) 'Modification of Eating Attitudes and Behaviour in Teenage Girls – A Controlled Study.' *International Journal of Eating Disorders 29*, 107–118.

Striegel-Moore, R.H. (1993) 'Aetiology of Binge Eating: A Developmental Perspective.' In C.G. Fairburn and G.T. Wilson (eds) *Binge Eating: Nature, Assessment and Treatment*. New York: Guilford.

Strober, M., Freeman, R., Lampert, C., Diamond, J. and Kaye, W. (2000) 'Controlled Family Study of Anorexia Nervosa and Bulimia Nervosa: Evidence of Shared Liability and Transmission of Partial Syndromes.' *American Journal of Psychiatry 157*, 393–401.

Swarr, A.E. and Richards, M.H. (1996) 'Longitudinal effects of adolescent girls' pubertal development, perceptions of pubertal timing and parental relations on eating problems.' *Developmental Psychology 32*, 636–646.

Thompson, R.A. and Sherman, R.T. (1993) *Helping Athletes with Eating Disorders*. Champaign, IL: Human Kinetics.

Tiggerman, M. (2001) 'The Impact of Adolescent Girls' Life Concerns and Leisure Activities on Body Dissatisfaction, Disordered Eating and Self-esteem.' *Journal of Genetic Psychology 162*, 133–142.

Treasure, J. (1998) *Anorexia Nervosa: A Survival Guide for Families, Friends and Sufferers*. Hove: Psychology Press.

Treasure, J. and Ward, A. (1997) 'A Practical Guide to the Use of Motivational Interviewing in Anorexia Nervosa.' *European Eating Disorder Review 5*, 102–114.

Vincent, M.A. and McCabe, M.P. (2000) 'Gender Differences among Adolescents in Family and Peer Influences on Body Dissatisfaction, Weight Loss and Binge Eating Behaviours.' *Journal of Youth and Adolescence 29*, 205–221.

Waller, D., Fairburn C.G., McPherson, A., Kay, R., Lee, A. and Nowell, T. (1996) 'Treating Bulimia Nervosa in Primary Care: A Pilot Study.' *International Journal of Eating Disorders 19*, 99–103.

Whitehouse, A.M., Cooper, P.J., Vize, C.V., Hill, C. and Vogel, L. (1992) 'Prevalence of Eating Disorders in Three Cambridge General Practices: Hidden and Conspicuous Mortality.' *British Journal of General Practice 42*, 57–60.

Williams, J.M. and Currie, C. (2000) 'Self-esteem and Physical Development in Early Adolescence: Pubertal Timing and Body Image.' *Journal of Early Adolescence 20*, 129–149.

Wood, K.C., Becker, J.A. and Thompson, J.K. (1996). 'Body Image Dissatisfaction in Preadolescent Children.' *Journal of Applied Developmental Psychology 17*, 85–100.

Chapter 11

Promotion of Prosocial Development and Prevention of Conduct Disorders

Kedar Nath Dwivedi and Sachin Sankar

Introduction

Promotion of order and good conduct has intrigued humankind since writing began. Some of the earliest writings, such as the tablets of Hamurabi, are about what constitutes good conduct and were written to promote social behaviour. The field was brought into the realm of child psychiatry in 1968 when the category of 'Unsocialised aggressive reaction of children' was included in the DSM-II (American Psychiatric Association 1968).

ICD-10 (World Health Organization 1992) contains a group of disorders described as 'Behavioural and emotional disorders with onset usually occurring in childhood and adolescence' and includes conduct disorders, hyperkinetic disorders, disorders of social functioning and so on. Conduct disorders are characterised by a repetitive and persistent pattern of antisocial, aggressive or defiant conduct such as disobedience, provocative behaviour, severe temper tantrums, excessive fighting or bullying, cruelty, destructiveness, stealing, lying, truancy and fire setting. Such behaviours should amount to major violations of age-appropriate social expectations to meet the diagnostic threshold.

In ICD-10, conduct disorders have six subcategories: (a) conduct disorder confined to the family context, (b) unsocialised conduct disorder (with isolation), (c) socialised conduct disorder, (d) oppositional defiant disorder, (e) other, and (f) unspecified. In addition, there is a category of mixed disorders of conduct and emotions.

In DSM-IV (American Psychiatric Association 1994), the diagnosis is based on the presence of specific criteria such as for aggression to people or animals (seven criteria), destruction of property (two criteria), deceitfulness or theft (three criteria) and serious violations of rules (three criteria). In order to make the diagnosis, three or more criteria must be present for more than twelve months and at least one for six months. There are three subtypes depending on the onset: (a) childhood onset type, (b) adolescent onset type and (c) unspecified onset. 'Disruptive behaviour not otherwise specified' and 'oppositional defiant disorder' are separate diagnostic categories.

Juvenile delinquency is a legal concept for children with antisocial behaviour who are involved in breaking the law.

Conduct disorders are very common in children and one of the most frequently diagnosed conditions. The prevalence in Western countries has increased fivefold since 1929 (Robins 1999). In a survey of 5–15-year-old children by the Office of National Statistics (Meltzer *et al.* 2000) 5.3 per cent of children (7.4% of boys and 3.2% of girls) in Great Britain were found to have conduct disorder. The rates were higher in poorer areas, in unemployed households and in lone parent families.

A very useful distinction between life-course persistent conduct disorder and adolescence-limited conduct disorder has been made (Moffit 1993a). The former begins in early childhood with disobedience, aggressiveness and bullying, is associated with difficult temperament, severe family dysfunction and educational failure and persists to adolescent offending and adult criminality. The latter begins in adolescence after an unremarkable earlier childhood, may involve some quite serious antisocial behaviour, but is not associated with serious family dysfunction or persistence into adult criminality.

Once established, conduct disorders are difficult to treat and have a poor prognosis; 27 per cent of behaviourally disturbed children between the ages of 8 and 10 years go on to become delinquent adolescents (West and Farrington 1973). Conduct disorders are associated with key developmental failures and have very detrimental outcomes for the well-being of the child. These outcomes include juvenile delinquency, educational underachievement, substance misuse and dependence, anxiety, depression and deliberate self-harm. Between 25 and 40 per cent develop dissocial personality disorder in adulthood and become vulnerable to marital disharmony, mental health problems, offending, higher mortality rate and transmission of the disorder to their children (A. Scott, Shaw and Joughin 2001). S. Scott *et al.* (2001) estimated the cost for individuals with conduct disorders by the age of 28 to be ten times higher (involving many agencies) than for those without conduct disorder. These problems are, therefore, not only common, but also persistent, difficult to treat, expensive for the society and have poor prognosis (Kazdin 1993; Robins 1991). In this context, understanding, preventing and treating childhood conduct disorder can have long-term benefits in improving the well-being of children, adults, families and communities.

Risk and protective factors

Development of conduct disorders can best be understood by a risk-resilience model. Accumulation of risk with the absence of protective factors leads to an increased probability that a conduct disorder will develop (Farrington 1999). Thus, conduct disorders are generated and maintained by a large number of factors in a variety of ecologically nested systems.

1. Individual factors include difficult temperament (with poor emotion regulation), early separation experience, poor social skills, poor learning of prosocial behaviour from experience and academic underachievement. These also include neurodevelopmental and cognitive risk factors such as attention problems, executive function deficits, language delay, lowered intelligence and social information processing showing hostile attribution bias.

2. Family factors include a family history of criminal behaviour, violence at home, use of physical methods of punishment, child abuse, coercive parenting, ineffective parental monitoring and supervision, providing inconsistent consequences for rule violations, failing to provide reinforcement for prosocial behaviour, family disorganisation, attachment difficulties, marital discord, parental psychopathology (especially maternal depression and paternal antisocial personality disorder), smoking in pregnancy, parental alcohol and substance abuse.

3. School factors include being a 'failing' school, with discipline problems, attainment difficulties, and lack of educational resources, teacher and peer rejection, delinquent peer affliction, early onset of youth drug and alcohol misuse.

4.   Important social factors include involvement with deviant
      peers, drug abuse and psychosocial adversity such as
      unemployment, poverty, overcrowding and institutional care.

The major protective factors include secure attachment and positive
parenting, at least one positive relationship with an adult, positive school
and community ethos promoting prosocial behaviour, association with
non-delinquent peers, participation in recreational activities, easy temperament and higher intellectual ability (IQ).

Causal mechanisms

In conduct disorder there are multiple contextual levels of influence so
that various sociocultural factors interact with individual biological, genetic and cognitive factors throughout the developmental process. A
number of theories to explain the causative mechanisms have been
prompted by this multiplicity of causative factors.

Biological theories

Biological theories have explored the role of genetics. Males are more
likely to suffer from conduct disorder than females. Genetic factors also
require the presence of environmental risk for their expression. The role
of genetic factors in autonomic hyper-reactivity and under-arousal, defi-
ciency in neurohumoural regulation, and neurophysiological deficits in
executive control has already been identified. Autonomic under-arousal
can lead to impairment of one's capacity for responding to the positive
reinforcement that often follows prosocial behaviour or for avoiding
punishment associated with antisocial behaviour. Deficits in verbal reasoning and executive functioning are associated with self-regulation difficulties (Moffit 1993b; Shapiro and Hynd 1995).

Social learning theories

Social learning theories examine the role of modelling and reinforcements. Thus, behaviour problems may arise due to imitation of others'
(e.g. parents, siblings, peers, teachers, media characters) behaviours. Parents or teachers can reinforce (often negatively) such behaviours by confronting or punishing the child briefly. However, when the child
escalates the antisocial behaviour, the parent or teacher may withdraw
their confrontation or punishment and the child learns that the escala-

tion of antisocial behaviour leads to parental or teacher's withdrawal. Many children learn to continue their antisocial behaviour as they are positively reinforced by their peer group.

Cognitive theories

Similarly there are cognitive theories accounting for the development of conduct disorder. In social situations where the intentions of others are ambiguous, children with conduct disorder tend to exhibit aggressive behaviour. According to social information processing theory, this is intended to be retaliatory because they attribute hostile intentions to others in such situations (Crick and Dodge 1994). According to social skills deficit theory children with conduct disorder lack the skills to generate alternative solutions to social problems and to implement such solutions (Spivack and Shure 1982). Psychodynamic theories have highlighted the role of impoverished superego functioning (due to overindulgent, punitive or negligent parenting) and of disrupted attachments.

Systems theories

Systems theories emphasise the role of characteristics of various systems (e.g. family system, broader social network and social systems) in the causation and maintenance of behaviour problems, for example, confusing and unclear rules, roles, routines and communication in a family or a school. The sociological theory of anomie highlights the illegitimate means used by members of a socially disadvantaged delinquent subculture to achieve material goals valued by mainstream culture (Cloward and Ohlin 1960).

Some key mediators

Thus, there seem to be numerous mediators which can be targeted for the purpose of preventive interventions. However, some selected ones of these are outlined below.

Empathy (and prosocial behaviour)

Empathy, 'sharing the perceived emotion of another – feeling with another' (Eisenberg and Strayer 1987, p.5), is an important mediator of other interpersonal responses (Barnett 1987), notably prosocial behaviour, helping and altruism. Empathy is an important aspect of the development of 'theory of mind' in children (please see Chapter 4 by Dwivedi in this volume) and can be affected by both biological and psychosocial environmental factors. For example, in autistic spectrum disorder there is an impaired development of the 'theory of mind' including empathy. Development of empathy in children is also influenced by a variety of environmental factors (Walley 1993).

An environment that satisfies children's own emotional needs (so that they are not preoccupied with satisfying their own needs) helps them to become more responsive to the feelings and needs of others. An expressive family environment can encourage the child to identify, experience and express a broad range of emotions. Therefore, a child requires an environment that provides numerous opportunities for the child to observe and interact with others such as grandparents or pets who, through their words and actions, encourage emotional sensitivity and responsiveness to others. Children have been found to emulate television characters who display prosocial actions such as offering sympathy and assistance to others in need. Discouraging excessive interpersonal competition and encouraging children to perceive others as similar to self also contributes to the development and expression of empathy. The peer group, because of similarity, plays a vital part in the development of empathy and related responses. An intimate friendship in childhood in particular helps an individual to develop a sense of humanity (Sullivan 1953). Children who are treated in a harsh and unloving way are less empathic and those who are encouraged to feel good about themselves are more inclined to empathise with others than those with poor self-esteem.

There are numerous exercises and games that can also be used to develop self-acceptance and self-regard and then regard for others. Many have been derived from Rogerian counselling and from Buddhist practices, for example, visualisation exercises to rehearse feelings of warmth and acceptance gradually of oneself and then certain others extending to almost all others (Nelson-Jones 1983, 1989; Walley 1987, 1990; Welwood 1979). Meditation techniques have traditionally been used to develop compassion, loving kindness, sympathetic joy and equanimity with an appreciation of the fact that lives, expectations and experiences of others are very similar to our own.

Emotion regulation

Psychological development in a child also includes a shift from other-control to self-control with the emergence of the capacity for self-regulation. Thus, refraining from antisocial behaviours involves affective, cognitive, behavioural and motivational processes (Kochanska 1993). Poor development of emotional management skills so as to result in anxiety, anger, jealousy, sadness and so on (Dwivedi 2002; Dwivedi and Varma 1997a, 1997b) can easily contribute to behaviour problems and other mental disorders. Chapter 4 by Dwivedi in this volume explores various developmental aspects of emotion regulation and dysregulation. Development of emotional dysregulation in the context of emotionally rejecting parenting and maternal depression has been found to be predictive of subsequent conduct disorder, particularly in boys (Raine, Brennan and Mednick 1994, 1997a).

Attachment

Early attachment experiences are of great importance in the subsequent development of children, including the development of empathy. Empathic responsiveness in children is associated with their involvement with the emotional life of the care givers. Securely attached children are less preoccupied with satisfying their own needs and more responsive to the feelings and needs of others.

Attachment disorders are clearly characterised by behaviour problems. Children with persistent conduct disorder are often 'disconnected' from individuals and norms of the society within which they live. Thus, interventions for the prevention of conduct disorder or treatment need to establish meaningful connection with the child, and with the key individuals in the child's life (Moore, Moretti and Holland 1998). For further exploration of attachment issues, see Chapter 3 by Bailham and Harper in this volume.

Trauma and Arousal

Many children with conduct disorder have a history of emotional trauma (Dwivedi 2000). Level of arousal plays an important role in social learning. Children with conduct disorder have difficulty in learning prosocial behaviour or avoiding antisocial behaviour, as they have an impaired capacity to respond to positive reinforcement (of prosocial behaviour) and negative reinforcement (for antisocial behaviour) due to their low arousal levels, such as lower levels of electrodermal activity, lower mean resting heart rate, lower heart-rate reactivity and lower heart-rate variability (Raine, Venables and Mednick 1997b). Early trauma leads to dysregulation of the hypothalamo-pituitary-adrenal axis and associated problems with the regulation of arousal and aggressive behaviour (McBurnett, Lahey and Rathauz 2000).

Cognitive bias

Conduct disordered children have been found to have not only cognitive deficits but also cognitive bias. For example, when they are in conflict with others they underestimate their own level of aggression and responsibility in the early stages of a disagreement (Lochman 1987). In ambiguous situations, they tend to attribute the behaviour of others to hostile intentions, recall high rates of hostile cues in social situations and attend to few cues when interpreting the meaning of others' behaviour (Dodge 1986). Thus, a cognitive behavioural approach has enormous potential in the management and prevention of conduct disorders (Bailey 1998).

Parenting

Ineffectual parental behaviour may be due to a variety of factors, such as their own experiences of inadequate parenting, stressful living conditions, lack of social support, personality disorder, substance abuse, learning disability, serious mental illness and so on. Several aspects of parenting have been found to contribute to children's behaviour problems, for example, poor supervision, erratic harsh discipline, parental disharmony, rejection and low involvement in child's activities. Lower levels of mother–child joint activity have been found to be associated with behaviour problems in preschool children (Galboda-Liyanage, Prince and Scott 2003).

Through coercive parenting the basic training of children's aggressive behaviour can take place within the family. The primary mechanism is that of negative reinforcement. Negative reinforcement of a child's aggressive behaviour occurs when the parent makes a request, the child responds negatively and the parent backs down. An irritable temperament or hyperactivity in a child makes it more difficult for the parent to handle this behaviour. The child learns to avoid the parent's demands by persisting noisily with their own, while parent learns to give in. Thus, the child learns to gain control over a chaotic or unpleasant family environment. Both parent and child are negatively reinforced for their behaviour, by learning how to switch off the other's annoying behaviour. Thus, disciplining is inconsistent and ineffective and there may also be a lack of supervision and positive involvement as well. As children learn the success of coercion, they may take this behaviour outside the home, where it may be reinforced by teachers and peers (Patterson 1982).

Comprehensive parenting programmes spanning the preschool to early school years and given at critical transitional phases in later years can reduce conduct disorders and prevent delinquency (Dwivedi 1997a; Webster-Stratton 1998). Behavioural parent training programmes are sufficiently well researched and show good results in treating conduct disorders (Richardson and Joughin 2002). However, the relationship programmes may be more effective than the behavioural types in producing changes in parental attitudes, self-esteem and psychopathology (Barlow 1999).

Educational difficulties

A substantive proportion of the school population suffers from school failure and in turn exhibits a variety of emotional, behavioural and physical problems and frequently engages in risky behaviours (including dangerous sexual practices) and substance abuse. In an Isle of Wight study, one-third of children with conduct disorder were severely behind in their reading. Similarly, one-third of children with severely delayed reading levels had conduct disorder (Rutter, Tizard and Whitmore 1970). Children with conduct disorder often have delays in language development and cognitive functioning (Hinshaw 1992). Mother–child interactions and the home environment have also been found to be good predictors of language skill by the age of 3 years (Bee, Barnard and Eyres 1982). Similarly, the teacher's style of classroom management has a significant influence on classroom discipline. An authoritarian style does not seem to be conducive of promoting desirable behaviour.

Treatment

As the aetiology of conduct disorders is multifaceted, the interventions also need to be multidimensional. The treatment strategy therefore needs to use a variety of methods such as family therapy, parent training and behavioural management, depending on the nature and extent of the problem. In very resistant situations, medication or institutional placements have also been used. Findings from research on parent training programmes for the management of young children with conduct disorders is available in a systematic review (Richardson and Joughin 2002). Behavioural parent training for children aged 3 years and upwards (Barlow 1999) and behavioural parent training combined with child-focused problem-solving skills training for children aged 5 and above have been found to be an effective intervention for preadolescent conduct disorders (Webster-Stratton 1993). Combined programmes are more effective and group-based programmes more cost-effective (Behan and Carr 2000).

Brosnan and Carr (2000) reviewed studies of approaches to family intervention for adolescent conduct disorders and found that each of the four approaches studied (behavioural parent training, functional family therapy, multisystemic therapy and therapeutic foster care) was effective for a proportion of cases. According to the continuum of care suggested, less severe cases may be offered parent training or functional family therapy, moderately severe cases multisystemic therapy and extremely severe or unresponsive cases therapeutic fostering.

Preventive interventions

The prevention of conduct disorder is an attractive proposition as this causes multiple and complex problems and impacts on many individuals such as the child, parents, family and community. It has an exorbitant cost to society. Treatments are inefficient and expensive. Only a small proportion of children needing treatment receive it because many fail to seek it and there is a general lack of adequate treatment resources. Conduct disorder is difficult to treat, particularly where it is severe.

Prevention focuses on building social competence and resilience as a way of promoting adaptive functioning, therefore helping to avert multiple problems rather than ameliorating a single problem in a surgical manner. There is sufficient evidence that preventive programmes, unlike treatment programmes, can reduce the onset of conduct disorders and can reach large numbers. However, their long-term effect is not yet known. There is also a need to understand the critical components of the programmes that produce change and also the optimal time for intervention.

Early interventions can have an impact on multiple factors. Because of the role of parenting in the development of self-regulatory capacity from infancy and the role of early trauma in the development of arousal dysregulation and the disabling nature of early onset life course persistent conduct disorders, it is important to adopt the strategy of early intervention. Studies have shown that maternal rejection before the age of 1 year predisposes the child to serious and early onset of violence in 18-year-olds (Raine *et al.* 1997a). In older children the emphasis is primarily on treatment and therefore prevention programmes are less prominent.

Early interventions

The early interventions are usually family-based with some daycare opportunities and are focused on parenting and child development. Interventions before the child is born have the advantage of targeting some important risk factors for conduct disorders such as certain family characteristics and disadvantages, lack of support, early pregnancy, smoking, alcohol and drug abuse, prenatal and perinatal complications and so on. Early emotional dysregulation can be predicted in case of rejection and coercive parenting (Morrell and Murray 2003). Promotion of maternal health therefore needs to start from pregnancy, for example, to address the fact that maternal smoking during pregnancy increases the risk of conduct disorders in children (Cresses, Laudenback and Morret 2003).

Programmes aimed at parenting enhancement (see also Chapter 7 by Waldsax in this volume), parent education and support through home visits, parent groups, etc. have already been used to demonstrate their usefulness (see for example Campbell and Ramey 1994; Johnson 1988; Lally, Mangione and Honig 1988; Olds, Henderson and Cole 1998a; Olds, Henderson and Kitzman 1998b; Provence and Naylor 1983; Schweinhart and Weikert 1988, 1989). These projects found that such interventions can reduce a number of risk factors that have an important influence on conduct disorder (and several programmes measured this impact). Most of these programmes also included direct interventions with children such as day nursery experiences with stimulating playful educational opportunities. Such early interventions through a set of developmental priming mechanisms can increase school readiness and increase the child's ability both to meet the academic expectations and to adapt behaviourally to the school setting (Ramey and Ramey 1998).

School-based interventions

There are numerous possibilities for school-based interventions supplemented by additional contacts with parents to prevent conduct disorders in children. Schools have a central role not only in the academic development of children but also in their social and psychological development. A three-pronged approach to a school development programme, aimed to (a) identify school problems, (b) develop and implement appropriate solutions and mental health initiatives and (c) involve parents in all aspects of school life, has demonstrated promising results (Comer 1985). The Positive Action Through Holistic Education (PATHE) is another programme of school development through organisational change strategies and the provision of services to high-risk students (Gottfredson 1986).

The Linking the Interests of Families and Teachers (LIFT) programme is based on the ecological model and targets both prosocial and antisocial behaviour with multicomponent interventions in three settings: home (parent training), classroom (social problem solving) and playground (a version of Good Behaviour Game, see the end of this section) (Capaldi and Eddy 2000; Reid et al. 1999).

The Seattle Social Development Project aimed to increase opportunities, skills and rewards to develop prosocial bonding to conventional social institutions (such as family, school, peer groups), values and consequently social competence (Hawkins et al. 1999). The Fast Track approach has multiple foci (child, family, school, peer group and community) and includes academic skills, social skills, parenting skills, family support and the Promoting Alternative Thinking Strategies (PATHS) curriculum (Conduct Problems Prevention Research Group 1999a, 1999b). The PATHS curriculum includes skills in self-control, emotional awareness and social problem solving.

As a way of increasing prosocial behaviour and strengthening resilience, mentoring has become popular because it is seen as a way of promoting the positive rather than decreasing the negative. As the demand for services for children with externalising behaviour far outstrips the number of professionals working in the field, national and local organisations have created opportunities for non-clinically trained adults and adolescent volunteers to participate in direct service programmes within the framework of mentoring (Hurley and Lustbacker 1997; Rogers and Taylor 1997). These schemes provide children with a positive role model (usually of the same gender) and a supportive relationship.

Mentoring programmes differ as regards the length, type and quality of mentorship. They extend from simple coaching of a direct skill (e.g. reading) to a long-term mentorship with the goal of directing youngsters towards self-awareness and other prosocial behaviours (Freedman 1988). Studies present a mixed picture of the usefulness of mentors. This may be due to differing definitions and durations of mentoring. Brody (1991) defines mentors and mentorship as a supportive relationship between adult and child developed to be facilitated to the child's education, social and personal group. The adolescent or child must believe that the person really cares and is there to help him and will treat him with respect. The mentor must have competence and knowledge which the mentee does not posses and must be willing to share the knowledge with the young person.

Some studies involving mentorship have evaluated programmes that lasted three months (Slicker and Palmer 1993) and six months (Roberts and Cotton 1994). These did not show improvement in school behaviour. Other studies are much more in-depth (Jackson 2002) requiring student mentors to spend between 15 and 20 hours a week with their mentees and the programme lasting for two years. Mentoring in such studies has been shown to be associated with low levels of drug and alcohol use while promoting prosocial behaviours like self-confidence, self-control and cooperative attitudes. Young people who have had mentoring relationships show more knowledge about how to handle drug situations and related skills (Lo-Scuito et al. 1996). Young people on mentoring programmes show marked improvement in attendance with few absences without leave. They also show a tendency to follow through to higher education. They show an increasingly more positive attitude to school which results in fewer dropouts. They also tend to indulge in less dangerous acts and negative behaviours, all of which are directly related to the development of conduct disorders in later life.

There are also examples of other approaches that have focused on particular themes. A programme designed to help children at risk of school failure through classroom interventions, teacher–pupil activities (to address their diverse needs) and home visits by teachers led to lower rates of antisocial behaviour even at a follow-up 13 years later (Weikart and Schweinhart 1992). A programme of classroom sessions to enhance social competence through self-control, stress management, responsible decision making, social problem solving and communication skills has been shown to reduce antisocial behaviour (Weissberg and Greenberg 1998). An intervention called Second Step consisting of social skills lessons to address anger management, impulse control and empathy demonstrated some reduction in aggressive behaviour (Grossman, Neckerman and Koepsell 1997). A nationwide intervention with impressive results in Norway aimed at decreasing aggressive behaviour or 'bullying' in schools by increasing awareness, designing and implementing appropriate school policies and creating an effective infrastructure of support (Olweus 1991). McCarthy and Carr (2002) reviewed four studies and concluded that whole-school bullying prevention programmes effectively reduce both reports of bullying and reports of being bullied in the short term, but external training, consultancy and support are essential to ensuring proper implementation of whole-school bullying prevention programmes.

The Life Skills Education Project promoted by the World Health Organization (1997) is also aimed at the development of psychosocial competence (please see Chapter 8 by Coley and Dwivedi in this volume for a detailed treatment of the subject). Group processes can be mobilised to ensure the requisite changes in knowledge, attitudes, behaviours and skills of the children (Dwivedi 1993, 2004; Dwivedi and Gupta 2000).

Monitoring and reinforcement of behavioural management can also be done in the form of games. For example, the Good Behaviour Game consists of dividing a classroom into teams and monitoring their non-disruptive behaviours to determine the winning team (Kellam et al. 1994). Similarly, there is a huge quantity and good quality of stories already available in the literature (such as Barker 1985; Bettelheim 1978; Dwivedi 1997b; Gardner 1993; Gersie and King 1990; Kale 1982); so that one can creatively use them for preventive and therapeutic purposes. For example, the book Therapeutic Use of Stories (Dwivedi 1997b) contains chapters relating to anger management (Dwivedi 1997c) and use of stories in school setting (Compton 1997).

Some pupils can also be trained in conflict mediation skills and assigned to act as peer-mediators on the school playground (Cunningham et al. 1998). The School Transitional Environmental Programme (STEP) was designed to facilitate the adaptation of pupils during the process of school transitions and was found to have a direct impact on conduct disorders as well (Felner and Adan 1988).

Community-based interventions

Such programmes use existing community resources such as recreational and other facilities through youth work to improve prosocial behaviours. In one such programme, adults from the local community were recruited and trained to conduct behavioural management through recreational activities with delinquent youths, obtaining good results (O'Donnell 1992). Another programme sought the help of college student volunteers to help delinquent youths using behavioural management approaches and community involvement leading to reduction in recidivism (Davidson *et al.* 1987).

Conclusion

There is, therefore, an enormous potential for the prevention of conduct disorders and promotion of prosocial behaviours in children and adolescents. It makes sense not only from the humanitarian point of view of reducing suffering, but also from the economic point of view of reducing the burden on a number of agencies, to focus resources on promoting the development of prosocial behaviour and the prevention of conduct disorders.

References

American Psychiatric Association (1968) *Diagnostic and Statistical Manual of Mental Disorders,* 2nd edn. Washington, DC: APA.

American Psychiatric Association (1994) *Diagnostic and Statistical Manual of Mental Disorders,* 4th edn. Washington, DC: APA.

Bailey, V. (1998) 'Conduct Disorders in Young Children.' In P. Graham (ed) *Cognitive Behaviour Therapy for Children and Families.* Cambridge: Cambridge University Press.

Barker, P. (1985) *Using Metaphors in Psychotherapy.* New York: Brunner/Mazel.

Barlow, J. (1999) *Systematic Review of the Effectiveness of Parent Training Programmes in Improving Behavioural Problems in Children Aged 3–10 Years.* Oxford: Health Services Research Unit, Department of Public Health.

Barnett, M. (1987) 'Empathy and Related Responses in Children.' In N. Eisenberg and J. Strayer (eds) *Empathy and its Development.* Cambridge: Cambridge University Press.

Bee, H.L., Barnard, K.E. and Eyres, S.J. (1982) 'Prediction of IQ and Language Skill from Peri-natal Status, Child Performance, Family Characteristics, and Mother–Infant Interaction.' *Child Development 53,* 1134–1156.

Behan, J. and Carr, A. (2000) 'Oppositional Defiant Disorder.' In A. Carr (ed) *What Works with Children and Adolescents: A Critical Review of Psychological Interventions with Children and Adolescents and their Families.* London: Routledge.

Bettelheim, B. (1978) *The Uses of Enchantment.* London: Penguin.

Brody, J. (1991) *New York State Mentoring Training Manual.* New York: New York State Education Department.

Brosnan, R. and Carr, A. (2000) 'Adolescent Conduct Problems.' In A. Carr (ed) *What Works with Children and Adolescents: A Critical Review of Psychological Interventions with Children and Adolescents and their Families.* London: Routledge.

Campbell, F.A. and Ramey, C.T. (1994) 'Effects of Early Intervention on Intellectual and Academic Achievement: A Follow-up Study of Children from Low-income Families.' *Child Development 65,* 684–698.

Capaldi, D.M. and Eddy, J.M. (2000) 'Improving Children's Long Term Well Being by Preventing Antisocial Behaviour.' In A. Buchanan and B. Hudson (eds) *Promoting Children's Emotional Well-Being.* Oxford: Oxford University Press.

Cloward, R. and Ohlin, L. (1960) *Delinquency and Opportunity.* Glencoe, IL: Free Press.

Comer, J.P. (1985) 'The Yale-New Haven Primary Prevention Project: A Follow-up Study.' *Journal of the American Academy of Child and Adolescent Psychiatry 24,* 154–160.

Compton, C. (1997) 'Stories Used Therapeutically with Children in Educational Settings.' In K.N. Dwivedi (ed) *Therapeutic Use of Stories.* London: Routledge.

Conduct Problems Prevention Research Group (1999a) 'Initial Impact of the Fast Track Prevention Trial for Conduct Problems, I: The High Risk Sample.' *Journal of Counselling and Clinical Psychology 67,* 631–647.

Conduct Problems Prevention Research Group (1999b) 'Initial Impact of the Fast Track Prevention Trial for Conduct Problems, II: Classroom Effects.' *Journal of Counselling and Clinical Psychology 67,* 648–657.

Cresses, P., Laudenback, V. and Morret, S. (2003) 'Mechanisms of Action of Tobacco Smoke on the Developing Brain.' *Journal of Gynecology Obstetrics and Biological Reproduction 32* (suppl. 1), 1330–1332.

Crick, N. and Dodge, K. (1994) 'A Review and Reformulation of Social Information Processing Mechanism in Children's Social Adjustment.' *Psychological Bulletin 115,* 74–101.

Cunningham, C.E., Cunningham, L.J., Marrorelli, V., Tran, A., Young, J. and Zacharias, R. (1998) 'The Effects of Primary Division, Student Mediated Conflict Resolution Programmes on Playground Aggression.' *Journal of Child Psychology and Psychiatry 39,* 653–662.

Davidson, W.S. II, Redner, R., Blakely, C.H., Mitchell, C.M. and Emsohoff, J.G. (1987) 'Diversion of Juvenile Offenders: An Experimental Comparison.' *Journal of Consulting and Clinical Psychology 55,* 68–75.

Dodge, K.A. (1986) 'Attributional Bias in Aggressive Children.' In P.C. Kendall (ed) *Advances in Cognitive Behavioural Research and Therapy*. San Diego, CA: Academic Press.

Dwivedi, K.N. (ed) (1993) *Group Work with Children and Adolescents*. London: Jessica Kingsley Publishers.

Dwivedi, K.N. (ed) (1997a) *Enhancing Parenting Skills*. Chichester: Wiley.

Dwivedi, K.N. (ed) (1997b) *Therapeutic Use of Stories*. London: Routledge.

Dwivedi, K.N. (1997c) 'Management of Anger and Some Eastern Stories.' In K.N. Dwivedi (ed) *Therapeutic Use of Stories*. London: Routledge.

Dwivedi, K.N. (ed) (2000) *Post-traumatic Stress Disorder in Children and Adolescents*. London: Whurr.

Dwivedi, K.N. (2002) 'Culture and Personality.' In K.N. Dwivedi (ed) *Meeting the Needs of Ethnic Minority Children*. London: Jessica Kingsley Publishers.

Dwivedi, K.N. (2004) 'Addressing Emotional and Behavioural Issues in Schools through Self-management Training: Theory and Practice.' In J. Wearmouth (ed) *Approaches to Understanding Student Behaviour*. Milton Keynes: Open University.

Dwivedi, K.N. and Gupta, A. (2000) 'Keeping Cool: Anger Management through Group Work.' *Support for Learning 15*, 2, 76–81.

Dwivedi, K.N. and Varma, V.P. (eds) (1997a) *Depression in Children and Adolescents*. London: Whurr.

Dwivedi, K.N. and Varma, V.P. (eds) (1997b) *A Handbook of Childhood Anxiety Management*. Aldershot: Arena.

Eisenberg, N. and Strayer, J. (eds) (1987) *Empathy and its Development*. Cambridge: Cambridge University Press.

Farrington, D.P. (1999) 'Conduct Disorder and Delinquency.' In H.C. Stien-Hanger and F.L. Verhulst (eds) *Risks and Outcomes in Developmental Psychopathology*. Oxford: Oxford University Press.

Felner, R.D. and Adan, A.M. (1988) 'The School Transitional Environment Project: An Ecological Intervention and Evaluation.' In R.H. Price, E.L. Cowen, R.P. Lorion and J. Ramos-McKay (eds) *14 Ounces of Prevention: A Casebook for Practitioners*. Washington, DC: American Psychological Association.

Freedman, M. (1988) *Partners in Growth: Elder Mentors and at Risk Youth*. Philadelphia, PA: Public/Private Ventures.

Galboda-Liyanage, K.C., Prince, M.J. and Scott, S. (2003) 'Mother–child Joint Activity and Behaviour Problems of Preschool Children.' *Journal of Child Psychology and Psychiatry 44*, 7, 1037–1048.

Gardner, R.A. (1993) *Storytelling in Psychotherapy with Children*. Northvale, NJ: Jason Aronson.

Gersie, A. and King, N. (1990) *Story Making in Education and Therapy*. London: Jessica Kingsley Publishers.

Gottfredson, D. (1986) 'An Empirical Test of School-based Environmental and Individual Interventions to Reduce the Risk of Delinquent Behaviour.' *Criminology 24*, 705–731.

Grossman, D.C., Neckerman, H.J. and Koepsell, T.D. (1997) 'Effectiveness of a Violence Prevention Curriculum among Children in Elementary School.' *Journal of the American Medical Association 277*, 1605–1611.

Hawkins, J.D., Catalano, R.F., Kosterman, R., Abbot, R. and Hill, K.G. (1999) 'Preventing Adolescent Health-risk Behaviours by Strengthening Protection during Childhood.' *Archives of Pediatric and Adolescent Medicine 153*, 226–234.

Hinshaw, S.P. (1992) 'Externalising Behaviour Problems and Academic Underachievement in Childhood and Adolescence: Causal Relationships and Underlying Mechanisms.' *Psychological Bulletin 111*, 127–155.

Hurley, L.P and Lustbacker, L.L. (1997) 'Project Support: Engaging Children and Families in the Educational Process.' *Adolescence 32*, 523–531.

Jackson, Y. (2002) 'Mentoring for Delinquent Children: An Outcome Study with Young Adolescent Children.' *Journal of Youth and Adolescence 31*, 115–123.

Johnson, D.L. (1988) 'Primary Prevention of Behaviour Problems in Young Children.' In R.H. Price, E.L. Cowen, R.P. Lorion and J. Ramos-McKay (eds) *14 Ounces of Prevention: A Casebook for Practitioners*. Washington, DC: American Psychological Association.

Kale, M.R. (1982) *Pancatantra of Vishnusharman*. Delhi: Motilal Banarasi Das.

Kazdin, A.E. (1993) 'Treatment of Conduct Disorder: Progress and Directions in Psychotherapy Research.' *Development and Psychopathology 5*, 277–310.

Kellam, S.G., Rebok, G.W., Ialongo, N. and Mayer, L.S. (1994) 'The Course and Malleability of Aggressive Behaviour from Early First Grade into Middle School: Results of a Developmental Epidemiologically Based Preventive Trial.' *Journal of Child Psychology and Psychiatry 35*, 259–281.

Kochanska, G. (1993) 'Toward a Synthesis of Parental Socialisation and Child Temperament in Early Development of Conscience.' *Child Development 64*, 325–347.

Lally, R., Mangione, P.L. and Honig, A.S. (1988) 'The Syracuse University Family Development Research Program: Long Range Impact on an Early Intervention with Low Income Children and their Families.' In D. Powell (ed) *Parent Education as Early Childhood Intervention: Emerging Directions in Theory, Research and Practice*. Norwood, NJ: Ablex.

Lochman, J.E. (1987) 'Self and Peer Perceptions and Attributional Biases of Aggressive and Non-aggressive Boys in Dyadic Interactions.' *Journal of Counselling and Clinical Psychology 55*, 404–410.

Lo-Scuito, L., Rajah, A., Townsend, T.N. and Taylor, A.S. (1996) 'An Outcome Evaluation across Ages: An Inter-generalised Mentoring Approach to Drugs Prevention.' *Journal of Adolescence Research*, special issue, *Preventing Adolescent Substance Abuse 2*, 1, 116–129.

McBurnett, K., Lahey, B.B. and Rathauz, P.J. (2000) 'Low Salivary Cortisol and Persistent Aggression in Boys Referred for Disruptive Behaviour.' *Archives of General Psychiatry 57*, 38–43.

McCarthy, O. and Carr, A. (2002) 'Prevention of Bullying.' In A. Carr (ed) *Prevention: What Works with Children and Adolescents.* Hove: BrunnerRoutledge.

Meltzer, H., Gatward, R., Goodman, R. *et al.* (2000) *Development and Wellbeing of Children and Adolescents in Great Britain.* London: Stationery Office.

Moffit, T. (1993a) 'Adolescence-limited and Life-course-persistent Antisocial Behaviour: A Developmental Taxonomy.' *Psychological Review 100*, 674–701.

Moffit, T. (1993b) 'The Neuropsychology of Conduct Disorder.' *Development and Psychopathology 5*, 135–151.

Moore, K., Moretti, M.M. and Holland, R. (1998) 'A New Perspective on Youth Care Programs: Using Attachment Theory to Guide Interventions for Troubled Youth.' *Residential Treatment of Children and Youth 15*, 1–24.

Morrell, J. and Murray, L.B. (2003) "Parenting and the Development of Conduct Disorder and Hyperactivity in Childhood: A Prospective Longitudinal Study from 2 Months to 8 Years.' *Journal of Child Psychology and Psychiatry 44*, 4, 489–508.

Nelson-Jones, R. (1983) *Practical Counselling Skills.* London: Holt, Rinehart and Winston.

Nelson-Jones, R. (1989) *The Theory and Practice of Counselling Psychology.* London: Cassell.

O'Donnell, C.R. (1992) 'The Interplay of Theory and Practice in Delinquency Prevention: From Behavior Modification to Activity Settings.' In J. McCord and R.E. Tremblay (eds) *Preventing Antisocial Behavior.* New York: Guilford.

Olds, D.L., Henderson, C.R. Jr and Cole, R. (1998a) 'Long-term Effects of Nurse Home Visitation on Children's Criminal and Antisocial Behavior: 15-year Follow-up of a Randomized Trial.' *Journal of the American Medical Association 280*, 1238–1244.

Olds, D.L., Henderson, C.R. and Kitzman, H. (1998b) 'Prenatal and Infancy Home Visitation by Nurses: A Program of Research.' In C. Rovee-Collier, P. Lipsitt and H. Hayne (eds) *Advances in Infancy Research.* Stamford, CT: Ablex.

Olweus, D. (1991) 'Bully–Victim Problems among School Children: Basic Facts and Effects of a School Intervention Program.' In D.J. Pepler and K.H. Rubin (eds) *The Development and Treatment of Childhood Aggression.* Hillsdale, NJ: Erlbaum.

Patterson, G.R. (1982) *Coercive Family Process.* Eugene, OR: Castalia.

Provence, S. and Naylor, A. (1983) *Working with Disadvantaged Parents and Children: Scientific Issues and Practice.* New Haven, CT: Yale University Press.

Raine, A., Brennan, P. and Mednick, S.A. (1994) 'Birth Complications Combined with Early Maternal Rejection at Age 1 Year Predispose to Violent Crime at Age 18 Years.' *Archives of General Psychiatry 51*, 984–988.

Raine, A., Brennan, P. and Mednick, S.A. (1997a) 'Interaction between Birth Complications and Early Maternal Rejection in Predisposing Individuals to

Adult Violence: Specifying to Serious, Early Onset Violence.' *American Journal of Psychiatry 154*, 9, 1265–1271.

Raine, A., Venables, P.H. and Mednick, S.A. (1997b) 'Low Resting Heart Rate at 3 Years Predisposes to Aggression at 11 Years: Evidence from the Mauritius Child Health Project.' *Journal of the American Academy of Child and Adolescent Psychiatry 36*, 1457–1464.

Ramey, C.T. and Ramey, S.L. (1998) 'Early Intervention and Early Experience.' *American Psychologist 53*, 109–120.

Reid, J.B., Eddy, J.M., Fetrow, R.A. and Stoolmiller, M. (1999) 'Description and Immediate Impacts of a Preventative Intervention for Conduct Problems.' *American Journal of Counselling Psychology 24*, 483–517.

Richardson, J. and Joughin, C. (2002) *Parent-training Programmes for the Management of Young Children with Conduct Disorders.* London: Gaskell.

Roberts, A. and Cotton, L. (1994) 'Note on Assessing a Mentor Programme.' *Psychology Report 75*, 1369–1370.

Robins, L.N. (1991) 'Conduct Disorder.' *Journal of Child Psychology and Psychiatry 32*, 193–212.

Robins, L.N. (1999) 'A 70-year History of Conduct Disorder: Variations in Definition, Prevalence, and Correlates.' In P. Cohen (ed) *Historical and Geographical Influences on Psychopathology.* Mahwah, NJ: Erlbaum.

Rogers, A.M and Taylor, A.S. (1997) 'Inter-generational Mentoring: A Viable Strategy for Meeting the Needs of Vulnerable Young.' *Journal of Gerontological Social Work 28*, 523–531.

Rutter, M., Tizard, J. and Whitmore, K. (1970) *Education, Health and Behaviour.* London: Longmans.

Schweinhart, L.J. and Weikert, D.P. (1988) 'The High/Scope Perry Preschool Program.' In R.H. Price, R.P. Cowen, R.P. Lorion and J. Ramos-McKay (eds) *14 Ounces of Prevention: A Casebook for Practitioners.* Washington, DC: American Psychological Association.

Schweinhart, L.J. and Weikert, D.P. (1989) 'The High/Scope Perry Preschool Study: Implications for Early Childhood Care and Education.' *Prevention in Human Services 7*, 109–132.

Scott, A., Shaw, M. and Joughin, C. (2001) *Finding the Evidence: A Gateway to the Literature in Child and Adolescent Mental Health.* London: Gaskell.

Scott, S., Knapp, M., Henderson, J. and Maugham, B. (2001) 'Financial Cost of Social Exclusion: Follow-up Study of Antisocial Children into Adulthood.' *British Medical Journal 323*, 191–194.

Shapiro, S. and Hynd, G. (1995) 'The Psychobiological Basis for Conduct Disorder.' *School Psychology Review 22*, 386–402.

Slicker, E.K. and Palmer, D.J. (1993) 'Mentoring at Risk High School Students: Evaluation of a School Bases Programme.' *School Counsellor 40*, 327–334.

Spivack, G. and Shure, M. (1982) 'The Cognition of Social Adjustment: Interpersonal Cognitive Problem-solving Thinking.' In B. Lahey and A. Kazdin (eds) *Advances in Clinical Child Psychology*, vol. 5. New York: Plenum.

Sullivan, H.S. (1953) *The Interpersonal Theory of Psychiatry*. New York: Norton.

Walley, M. (1987) 'Buddhism and Mental Health Care.' In G. Claxton (ed) *Beyond Therapy*. London: Wisdom.

Walley, M. (1990) 'Tibetan Buddhist Mind-Training.' In J. Crook and D. Fontana (eds) *Space in Mind*. Shaftesbury: Element.

Walley, M. (1993) 'Empathy and Prosocial Development.' In K.N. Dwivedi (ed) *Group Work with Children and Adolescents*. London: Jessica Kingsley Publishers.

Webster-Stratton, C. (1993) 'Strategies for Helping Early School Aged Children with Oppositional Defiant and Conduct Disorders: The Importance of Home–School Partnerships.' *School Psychology Review 22*, 437–457.

Webster-Stratton, C. (1998) 'Preventing Conduct Problems in Head Start Children.' *Journal of Counselling and Clinical Psychology 66*, 715–730.

Weikart, D.P. and Schweinhart, L.J. (1992) 'High/Scope Preschool Program Outcomes.' In J. McCord and R.E. Tremblay (eds) *Preventing Antisocial Behavior*. New York: Guilford.

Weissberg, R.P. and Greenberg, M.T. (1998) 'School and Community Competence Enhancement and Prevention Programs.' In I.E. Sigel and K.A. Renninger (eds) *Handbook of Child Psychology*, vol. 4, *Child Psychology in Practice*, 5th edn. New York: Wiley.

Welwood, J. (1979) *Meeting of the Ways*. New York: Schocken.

West, D.J. and Farrington, D.P. (1973) *Who becomes Delinquent?* London: Heinemann.

World Health Organization (1992) *The ICD-10 Classification of Mental and Behavioural Disorders*. Geneva: WHO.

World Health Organization (1997) *Life Skills Education for Children and Adolescents in Schools*. WHO/MNH/PSF/93.7A.Rev.2. Geneva: WHO.

Chapter 12

Prevention of Mental Health Problems in Socially Excluded Children and Young People

A model for mental health service provision

Jane Callaghan and Panos Vostanis

Issues relating to risk and resiliency

Young people looked-after, homeless youth and young offenders are exposed to many risk factors. These include social exclusion (Bailey 1999), homelessness, exposure to the care system and the criminal justice system (Zamble and Porporino 1990), histories of abuse, neglect, abandonment and poor parenting practice, and exposure to and involvement in criminal activity and violence (Dimond, Misch and Goldberg 2001; Farrington 1995, 1996; Haapsalo and Hamalainen 1996; Ireland 2000; Smith and Thornbury 1995). The marginalised status of these young people also places them at risk for intensifying periods of placement in care, reoffending behaviour (Rutter, Giller and Hagell 1998) and further social exclusion (Bailey 1999; Craig *et al.* 1996; Wrate and Blair 1999).

Exposure to institutional structures provided for the care of vulnerable youth is a particular issue in the development and maintenance of mental health difficulties. For example, the high levels of mental health need among young people in care have been related to their experiences both before and during their period in care. While histories of neglect and abuse might precipitate moves into care, placement instability and experiences in residential care can be very stressful to young people, contributing further to elevated levels of mental health difficulty (Lawder *et al.* 1986). Working closely with care providers within these institutional structures might be one way to work preventively and to promote mental health in young people in these kinds of institutions. Homeless children and families are a heterogeneous population, with multiple and interrelated needs. The episode of homelessness is rarely a one-off event. Most families have histories of previous chronic adversities, which constitute risk factors for both children and parents. Such events include family conflict, violence and breakdown; limited or absent family and social support networks; recurrent moves; poverty and unemployment. Mothers are more likely to have suffered abuse in their own childhood and adult life, and children have increased rates of placements on the Child Protection Register, because of neglect, physical and/or sexual abuse (Bassuk *et al.* 1996; Brooks, Ferguson and Webb 1998; Connelly and Crown 1994; Webb *et al.* 2001). These result in loss of protective factors, for example, social support networks, peer relationships and school attainment, which result in a cycle of further adversities and negative life experiences (Power, Whitty and Youdell 1995; Walters and East 2001).

Mental health need

The high levels of mental health need of young offenders, children looked-after by local authorities, and homeless young people have been well established. For example, young offenders (particularly in secure units and other institutions) have been demonstrated to have higher levels of mental health problems, educational and social needs (Bullock *et al.* 1990; Lengua, Handy and Dhariwal 1997; Nicol *et al.* 2000; Reiss, Grubin and Meux 1996). The few studies conducted in community samples of young offenders also indicate elevated mental health need (Anderson, Vostanis and Spencer, in press; Stallard, Thomason and Churchyard 2003). Similarly elevated levels of mental health need have been found among looked-after children and young people, where higher rates of emotional and behavioural problems and psychiatric disorders have been documented (Dimigen *et al.* 1999; McCann *et al.* 1996; Minnis and Devine 2001). For both these groups, levels of mental health difficulty are likely to be higher among young people exposed to institutional settings (for example, Dimigen *et al.* 1999).

A number of US and UK studies have found high rates of developmental, behavioural and emotional problems among homeless children and their parents (Vostanis 2002). In preschool and primary school age children, behavioural problems include sleep disturbance, feeding problems, aggression and hyperactivity. These are often comorbid with emotional or developmental disorders. Anxiety and post-traumatic stress disorders are often precipitated by life events such as witnessing domestic violence. About one-third of children admitted to hostels in a UK city were reported to have mental health problems, which required clinical assessment and treatment (Vostanis et al. 1997). Mothers' histories of abuse and presence of mental illness were the strongest predictors of child psychopathology. Child mental health problems remained one year later, in the absence of any intervention (Vostanis, Grattan and Cumella 1998).

Homeless adolescents and street youth are likely to present with depression and suicide attempts, alcohol and drug misuse, and vulnerability to sexually transmitted diseases, including Aids. Two major studies in London (Craig et al. 1996) and Edinburgh (Wrate and Blair 1999) found significant histories of residential care, family breakdown, poor educational attainment and instability of accommodation. These were associated with sexual risk behaviours, substance misuse and comorbid psychiatric disorders, particularly depression.

Lack of models of mental health provision for vulnerable groups

The absence of mental health services models for vulnerable children and young people has been noted by several studies. Service deficits are related to a number of factors, particularly the mobility of vulnerable children, and their lack of family and social stability, which result in poor access to and engagement with generic child and adolescent mental health services (CAMHS). Service deficits are further related to the conflicting and increasing pressures on stretched CAMHS resources.

Typically mental health provision has involved young people being referred either to the general child and adolescent mental health services, or to a single practitioner devoting a proportion of his or her time to homeless, looked-after or offending young people. This means that young people do not often receive a service that is appropriate to their needs, and there is very little space for practitioners to develop mental health promotion programmes, or primary or early level mental health interventions.

Kataoka *et al.* (2001) found that young offenders in the community received patchy mental health provision, subject to regional variation. In a focus group study with staff involved with looked-after children, participants noted that mental health service provision for young people in care was so variable as to be anecdotal (Callaghan *et al.* in press b), a contention that is supported by the research literature (Minnis and Del Priore 2001). There is considerable concern that the mental health needs of these vulnerable young people remain largely unmet (Kurtz 1996; Payne and Butler 1998; Richardson and Lelliott 2003). There are, however, promising trends, as recent inter-agency partnerships and funding have enabled the development of new services, particularly for looked-after children (Kelly *et al.* 2003; Street and Davies 2002).

Homeless families are a client group with particular difficulty in accessing mainstream services (Vostanis and Cumella 1999; Cumella, Grattan and Vostanis 1998). As most families will have changed address frequently or urgently, they are less likely than the rest of the population to be registered with a general practitioner or, in the best of situations, they are registered as temporary patients with a GP covering the hostel residents. This reduces their access to primary and secondary medical care, including immunisations and other preventive health procedures. Homeless families therefore tend to rely on accident and emergency departments for medical treatment, and have high rates of hospital admission (Lissauer *et al.* 1993). The same applies to social services (access teams, family teams, family support units) and other community agencies. In addition, homeless children are more likely to be out of school, as the family could be traced by a violent ex-partner, or because of the distance from the hostel (particularly in large cities). Parents may wait until they know where they will be rehoused before registering the children with a new nursery or school. Nurseries and primary schools in the proximity of the hostel usually have a high pupil turnover with resulting high costs, and there are often limited vacancies for short periods (Power *et al.* 1995).

The problems with services can be conceptualised in terms of accessibility, responsiveness and appropriateness for vulnerable children, young people and their families. These are discussed below.

Difficulties of accessing services

Many general CAMHS use strict referral criteria to determine the appropriateness of referrals, and will accept only young people who meet those criteria. This often makes it difficult for vulnerable young people to access services they might need. For example, young people with features of conduct disorders might not be seen because many CAMHS suggest that behavioural problems are best dealt with by social services, who in turn may claim that these are health problems. In reality, conduct disorders constitute a mixture of problems, which require the involvement of more than one agency (Vostanis *et al.* 2004). Many CAMHS will accept referrals only for young people in stable home environments, while residential mobility is an obvious feature of the lives of young people who are looked-after, young offenders and homeless youth.

A feature of the social exclusion of these vulnerable young people is that, for a range of reasons, they have difficulty accessing the health service generally, and consequently have particular difficulty accessing 'ordinary' child and adolescent mental health services, where waiting lists might be long. High levels of mobility, exclusion from structures like school, which typically feed into the health system, and underdeveloped strategies for accessing health services, result in many young people simply not being able to obtain the health and mental health services they need (e.g. Dolan *et al.* 1999). This is a strong argument for the development of designated services for vulnerable young people.

Waiting lists further complicate issues of access for vulnerable young people, and are an obvious way in which general CAMHS are unresponsive to the needs of vulnerable young people. Typically young people are referred at a time of crisis. Although it is not necessarily appropriate for CAMHS to be entirely crisis responsive, it is nonetheless incredibly important for vulnerable young people to receive assistance at the point when they try to engage the system. Alienated young people who are told to wait are unlikely to try to engage the system again, and when they are offered a service their life circumstances may have changed considerably.

Professionals and carers who work with vulnerable young people (tier one agencies) may also have difficulty identifying mental health needs and making appropriate referrals (Minnis and Del Priore 2001; Phillips 1997). This may be because potential referrers may have become so accustomed to working with disturbed young people that they normalise all but the most extreme and overt presentations of psychological distress. Consequently, many young people with less extreme presentation are being overlooked.

Appropriateness

It seems that, even when young people get through the gate and access CAMHS, the treatment they get is often not suited to their needs. It has been suggested that general CAMHS staff are not sufficiently specialised to recognise the particular mental health needs of vulnerable youth and their families, and need to use creative and engaging techniques of assessment and intervention for young people who are difficult to engage (Minnis and Del Priore 2001).

All psychotherapies (psychodynamic, family, cognitive) are essential for treatment and prevention, but need to be adapted to the needs and characteristics of different client groups. Also, elements of these modalities are important in the training of tier one staff (social workers, residential and hostel staff, youth offending teams' officers), who can then develop preventive strategies (e.g. in preventing further aggressive outbursts), while recognising that this is a different level of intervention from the provision of a specialist service. Overall, vulnerable and socially excluded young people often have complex social and emotional needs, which require a more responsive and better tailored service than that which can be offered within the remit of generic specialist CAMHS.

Overlapping populations and needs

This brief overview of mental health needs and services for vulnerable young people clearly illustrates that, in terms of issues of psychological well-being, looked-after children, homeless youth and young offenders have similar mental health needs. Further, a proportion of vulnerable youth will at one time or another fit into more than one of these categories; for example, they are likely to be both homeless and offending, or both offending and looked-after, at any given time. Consequently an integrated team, providing seamless services to these groups and supportive interaction between team members, is an effective way of meeting their mental health needs. Otherwise, there is fragmentation of limited resources, non-cost-effective service provision and lack of continuity of care, resulting in further disengagement of young people and their carers.

Why is there a need for a special team for vulnerable young people?

Young Person's Team: roles and functions

Leicester, Leicestershire and Rutland has a general population of 900,000, living in multiethnic inner-city, semi-urban and rural areas. One-quarter of the population, i.e. about 225,000 individuals, are under 18 years. A joint child and adolescent mental health strategy involves partnership between one health authority, three local authorities and the voluntary sector. There are two Youth Offending Teams (YOTs), one for the city with approximately 2000 annual referrals, and one for the county (semi-urban and rural) with 1000 annual referrals. Between 800 and 1000 children are looked-after by the three local authorities each year, while a similar number are statutorily classified as homeless at some point during the same period. The child and adolescent mental health service, in partnership with social services, the YOTs, and the Housing Department, has developed an innovative mental health service for young people. In this chapter, we describe the reasoning behind the development of this designated team and its structure. To complement this book's focus on the prevention of mental health difficulties, we concentrate on the team's role in primary level mental health intervention and mental health promotion. For this reason, there will be limited reference to specialist interventions with children and young people.

The Young Person's Team is structured according to the guidelines suggested by the Health Advisory Service (1995), using the four-tier model of service provision. The tiers of the model represent layers providing increasingly intensive forms of service, for clients with increasingly severe levels of need. Tier one represents primary care professionals, typically external to CAMHS (for example, social workers, residential and hostel staff, foster carers' link workers and youth offending team officers). The primary mental health worker (PMHW: tier two) works at the interface between primary care professionals (tier one) and specialist outpatient (tier three) CAMHS (see Figure 12.1). Within the Young Person's Team, the family support worker (who works with homeless children and their parents) is conceptualised as occupying a position at this interface too. This model increases accessibility to the service (through the role of the PMHW / family support worker) and ensures that a service is provided for young people with a wide range of mental health difficulties, ranging from fairly simple behavioural problems or emotional difficulties, to complex mental health difficulties and psychiatric disorders.

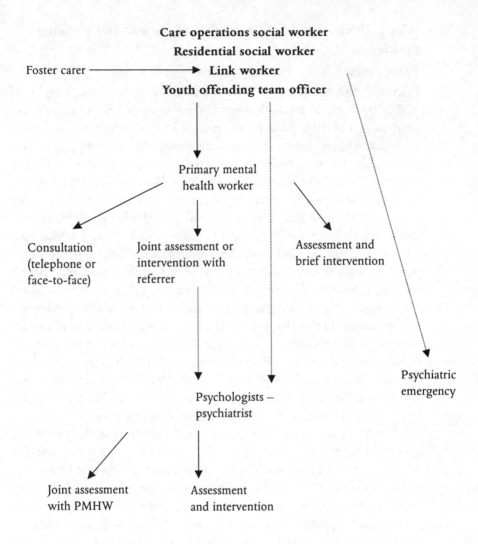

Figure 12.1 Levels of mental health service input and process of referrals

Primary mental health workers and family support workers provide consultation and training to carers and to tier one professionals, and focused interventions with young people and their carers. In the Young Person's Team, there are six primary mental health workers (two for looked-after children and four for the youth offending teams) and five family support workers for homeless children. A community psychiatric nurse works therapeutically with refugee or asylum-seeking children, their families, and agencies involved. Tier three input is provided by two clinical psychologists and one child psychiatrist, who work across all client groups. The posts have been established through a range of health and local authority funding streams, according to the joint child mental health strategy, which is overseen by a multi-agency steering group.

Within the children looked-after service, each residential unit has an allocated PMHW who regularly visits the home, and provides consultation and training to staff teams. In fostering, PMHWs work with fostering link workers, social workers and adoption workers, providing face-to-face and telephone advice and consultation, joint working, and input into social services training programmes for carers (Callaghan et al. 2004).

Within the YOTs, the role of the PMHWs involves a combination of direct mental health work with young people (assessment and a range of cognitive, behavioural, psychotherapy and family therapy interventions), and consultation, liaison, training and joint working with YOT professionals to develop their skills in the recognition of young offenders with common mental health problems, and in the cognitive and behavioural management of young offenders (Callaghan et al. 2003a). The PMHWs are full-time health professionals, located within the YOTs, but attend the weekly CAMHS team meetings and are supervised and line managed by a senior PMHW.

The family support workers for homeless children and their parents are also largely involved in preventive work. They coordinate services before and after rehousing, conduct individual and group parenting skills training, support the hostel staff, and provide resettlement work to the most needy families after they have been rehoused in the community. Their role is to identify a broad range of needs (such as child protection, possible mental health problems, substance misuse, or school problems); provide different levels of support to the majority of families; organise activities at the hostel for toddlers, older children and parents; ensure children's school placement and attendance; and maximise the involvement of specialist (social services, health visitor, child or adult mental health service, educational welfare, Sure Start) or non-statutory agencies (such as domestic violence or resettlement services). The family support workers are based at the main hostel for homeless families.

Training tier one agencies to develop preventive strategies
The PMHWs and family support workers provide an ongoing training programme open to childcare operations social workers, link social

workers, residential social workers, foster carers and pre-adoption carers, staff from the Youth Offending Team, and housing staff working with homeless families. The first level of training aims at developing mental health awareness, and clarifies with staff members and carers the role of the team, the way in which referrals to it might be made, and ways in which staff and carers might themselves contribute to the promotion of mental health in the young people they work with.

In this way, they empower frontline staff and carers with basic skills that help them to improve their identification of young people at risk, and to help them build resilience in vulnerable young people. The preventive objectives of the training programme were explicitly set out from the beginning, as the team recognised the broad definition of mental health and emotional well-being, and the crucial contribution of carers and all agencies. A second level of training has recently been initiated to provide a framework for the understanding of the impact of trauma and attachment difficulties on children's behaviour (Golding 2003).

This training is complemented by the consultative role of the PMHWs and family support workers. They aim to form good working relationships with the agencies that work with vulnerable young people, and to maximise their availability to staff and carers who wish to discuss concerns about young people. In this way, they serve as a valuable preventive and mental health promotion service, which ultimately avoids a range of unnecessary referrals.

Evaluation findings

Ongoing evaluation is essential for all preventive interventions and services, particularly in the light of the limited evidence available. There are different levels of evaluation, defined outcomes (client or referrer satisfaction, response time, symptomatic improvement, cost-effectiveness), designs (retrospective, cross-sectional, longitudinal) and measures (preferably both quantitative and qualitative). Several studies have been completed on the previously described service components, which are constantly fed back into the development of the team.

We initially conducted 13 focus groups with various stakeholders working with looked-after children – social services staff, foster carers and residential social workers – to inform the development of the mental health team (Callaghan *et al.* 2003c). The 13 focus groups comprised 58 participants in total, and all sessions were audiotaped and transcribed. Analysis of data using the constant comparative method revealed several emergent themes: difficulties accessing mental health services, the importance of developing a working partnership between CAMHS, social services and foster carers, the need for consultation, and the importance of developing a service that is appropriate to the specific needs of looked-after children. The direct work with the first 45 looked-after children and their carers was evaluated through interviews and psychosocial measures completed before and after the intervention (Callaghan *et al.* 2003c). Carers perceived the interventions as targeting different aspects of the child's functioning, but wished they were more involved in decision-making. Carers and children were generally positive about their clinical contact, and there was significant improvement in children's behavioural and emotional problems.

A similar design was applied for the mental health input to the Youth Offending Teams. Qualitative data from YOT professionals' focus groups indicated that the accessibility and responsiveness of PMHWs, as well as their clinical assessment and therapeutic interventions skills, were consistently valued (Callaghan *et al.* 2003a). There was mixed response on the evolution of roles within the team, and the nature of consultation and training. The mental health characteristics of 60 young people consecutively referred to these PMHWs, the assessment outcome and interventions offered, were also described (Callaghan *et al.* 2003b). In addition to the anticipated concerns about oppositional/aggressive behaviour, young people were referred for a range of mental health problems. There were high levels of emotional problems, self-harm, peer and family relationship difficulties, and school non-attendance. PMHWs offered a range of direct interventions, as well as consultation to YOT staff.

Homeless families' needs are more difficult to address during their brief stay in hostel accommodation, for which reason the Family Support Team gradually expanded to work preventively after rehousing in the community. However, there is evidence that parenting interventions for homeless families, even of brief duration and at times of crisis, result in improved child behavioural outcomes, which can be sustained in the community (Tischler *et al.* 2003).

The future

Vulnerable children and young people should receive prompt and continuing treatment within a comprehensive child and adolescent mental health service. However, this may not be universally possible, until CAMHS are adequately resourced to respond to primary care referrals (i.e. from general practitioners, schools and community paediatrics), which often take precedence in service referral pathways. For this reason, services have developed alternative and more accessible models for vulnerable and mobile groups of young people and their families, i.e. through designated sessions to local authority agencies from specialist CAMHS staff, development of jointly commissioned posts, or designated teams (Vostanis 2003). Designated posts integrated within generic specialist CAMHS may be appropriate for smaller districts and rural or semi-urban areas, while designated teams may be more effective in inner-city areas. Mental health services for vulnerable and socially excluded young people need to be developed within an integrated CAMHS model. Their planning, commissioning and implementation require ongoing inter-agency partnerships between health and local authority agencies.

Primary and secondary prevention has, inevitably, not been a priority for CAMHS during their transition from child guidance to a comprehensive tiered and inter-agency provision. This should clearly change and be applied at all levels, by an increasingly skilled workforce, across the local authority, community care and specialist settings.

References

Anderson, L., Vostanis, P. and Spencer, N. (in press) 'Health Needs of Young Offenders.' *Journal of Child Health Care.*

Bailey, S. (1999) 'The Interface between Mental Health, Criminal Justice and Forensic Mental Health Services for Children and Adolescents.' *Current Opinion in Psychiatry 12,* 425–432.

Bassuk, E., Weinreb, L., Buckner, J., Browne, A., Salomon, A. and Bassuk, S. (1996) 'The Characteristics and Needs of Sheltered Homeless and Low-income Housed Mothers.' *JAMA (Journal of the American Medical Association) 276,* 640–646.

Brooks, R., Ferguson, T. and Webb, E. (1998) 'Health Services to Children Resident in Domestic Violence Shelters.' *Ambulatory Child Health 4,* 369–374.

Bullock, R., Hosie, K., Little, M. and Millham, S. (1990) 'Secure Accommodation for Very Difficult Adolescents: Some Recent Research Findings.' *Journal of Adolescence 13,* 205–216.

Callaghan, J., Pace, F., Young, B. and Vostanis, P. (2003a) 'The Role of the Primary Mental Health Worker within Youth Offending Teams.' *Journal of Adolescence 26,* 185–199.

Callaghan, J., Young, B., Pace, F. and Vostanis, P. (2003b) 'Mental Health Support for Youth Offending Teams: A Qualitative Study.' *Health and Social Care in the Community 11,* 55–63.

Callaghan, J., Young, B., Richards, M. and Vostanis, P. (2003c) 'Developing New Mental Health Services for looked-after Children: A Focus Group Study.' *Adoption and Fostering 27*, 4, 185–199.

Callaghan, J., Young, B., Pace, F. and Vostanis, P. (2004) 'Evaluation of a New Mental Health Service for looked-after Children.' *Clinical Child Psychology and Psychiatry 9*, 1, 130–148.

Connelly, J. and Crown, J. (eds) (1994) *Homelessness and Ill Health: Report of a Working Party of the Royal College of Physicians.* London: Royal College of Physicians.

Craig, T., Hodson, S., Woodward, S. and Richardson, S. (1996) *Off to a Bad Start: A Longitudinal Study of Homeless Young People in London.* London: Mental Health Foundation.

Cumella, S., Grattan, E. and Vostanis, P. (1998) 'The Mental Health of Children in Homeless Families and their Contact with Health, Education and Social Services.' *Health and Social Care in the Community 6*, 331–342.

Dimigen, G., Del Priore, C. Butler, S. Evans, S., Ferguson, L. and Swan, M. (1999) 'Psychiatric Disorder among Children at Time of Entering Local Authority Care: Questionnaire Survey.' *British Medical Journal 319*, 675.

Dimond, C., Misch, P. and Goldberg, D. (2001) 'On Being in a Young Offender Institution: What Boys on Remand Told a Child Psychiatrist.' *Psychiatric Bulletin 25*, 342–345.

Dolan, M., Holloway, J., Bailey, S. and Smith, C. (1999) 'Health Status in Juvenile Offenders: A Survey of Young Offenders Appearing before the Juvenile Courts.' *Journal of Adolescence 22*, 137–144.

Farrington, D. (1995) 'The Development of Offending and Antisocial Behaviour from Childhood.' *Journal of Child Psychology and Psychiatry 36*, 929–964.

Farrington, D. (1996) *Understanding and Preventing Youth Crime.* York: Joseph Rowntree Foundation.

Golding, K. (2003) 'Helping Foster Carers, Helping Children: Using Attachment Theory to Guide Practice.' *Adoption and Fostering 27*, 64–73.

Haapsalo, J. and Hamalainen, T. (1996) 'Childhood Family Problems and Current Psychiatric Problems among Young Violent and Property Offenders.' *Journal of the American Academy of Child and Adolescent Psychiatry 35*, 1394–1401.

Health Advisory Service (1995) *Child and Adolescent Mental Health Services: Together We Stand.* HMSO.

Ireland, J.L. (2000) 'Bullying among Prisoners: A Review of Research.' *Aggression and Violent Behavior 5*, 201–215.

Kataoka, S., Zima, B., Dupre, D., Moreno, K., Yang, X. and McCracken, J. (2001) 'Mental Health Problems and Service Use among Female Juvenile Offenders: Their Relationship to Criminal History.' *Journal of the American Academy of Child and Adolescent Psychiatry 40*, 549–555.

Kelly, C., Allan, S., Roscoe, P. and Herrick, E. (2003) 'The Mental Health Needs of looked-after Children: An Integrated Multi-agency Model of Care.' *Clinical Child Psychology and Psychiatry 8*, 323–335.

Lawder, E., Pulin, J. and Andrews, R. (1986) 'A Study of 185 Foster-children 5 Years After Placement.' *Child Welfare 65*, 241–251.

Kurtz, Z. (1996) *Treating Children Well.* Mental Health Foundation.

Lengua, C., Handy, S. and Dhariwal, S. (1997) 'Survey of Young Offenders in a Regional Secure Unit.' *Psychiatric Bulletin 21*, 535–537.

Lissauer, T., Richman, S., Tempia, M., Jenkins, S. and Taylor, B. (1993) 'Influence of Homelessness on Acute Admissions to Hospital.' *Archives of Disease in Childhood 69*, 423–429.

McCann, J.B., James, A., Wilson, S. and Dunn, G. (1996) 'Prevalence of Psychiatric Disorders in Young People in the Care System.' *British Medical Journal 313*, 1529–1530.

Minnis, H. and Del Priore, C. (2001) 'Mental Health Services for looked-after Children: Implications from Two Studies.' *Adoption and Fostering 25*, 27–38.

Minnis, H. and Devine, C. (2001) 'The Effect of Foster Carer Training on the Emotional and Behavioural Functioning of looked-after Children.' *Adoption and Fostering 25*, 44–54.

Nicol, R., Stretch, D., Whitney, I., Jones, K., Garfield, P., Turner, K. and Stanion, B. (2000) 'Mental Health Needs and Services for Severely Troubled and Troubling Young People, Including Young Offenders, in an NHS Region.' *Journal of Adolescence 23*, 243–261.

Payne, H. and Butler, I. (1998) 'Improving the Health Care Process and Determining Health Outcomes for Children looked-after by the Local Authority.' *Ambulatory Child Health 4*, 165–172.

Phillips, J. (1997) 'Meeting the Psychiatric Needs of Children in Foster Care.' *Psychiatric Bulletin 21*, 609–611.

Power, S., Whitty, G. and Youdell, D. (1995) *No Place to Learn: Homelessness and Education.* London: Shelter.

Reiss, D., Grubin, D. and Meux, C. (1996) 'Young "Psychopaths" in Special Hospital: Treatment and Outcome.' *British Journal of Psychiatry 168*, 99–104.

Richardson, J. and Lelliott, P. (2003) 'Mental Health of looked-after Children.' *Advances in Psychiatric Treatment 9*, 249–251.

Rutter, M., Giller, H. and Hagell, A. (1998) *Antisocial Behaviour by Young People.* Cambridge: Cambridge University Press.

Smith, C. and Thornbury, T.P. (1995) 'The Relationship between Childhood Maltreatment and Adolescent Involvement in Delinquency.' *Criminology 33*, 451–481.

Stallard P., Thomason, J. and Churchyard, S. (2003) 'The Mental Health of Young People Attending a Young Offending Team: A Descriptive Study.' *Journal of Adolescence 26*, 33–43.

Street, E. and Davies, M. (2002) 'Constructing Mental Health Services for looked-after Children.' *Adoption and Fostering 26*, 65–75.

Tischler, V., Vostanis, P., Bellerby, T. and Cumella, S. (2003) 'Evaluation of a Mental Health Outreach Service for Homeless Families.' *Archives of Disease in Childhood 86*, 158–163.

Vostanis, P. (2002) 'Mental Health of Homeless Children and their Families.' *Advances in Psychiatric Treatment 8*, 463–469.

Vostanis, P. (2003) 'Invited Commentary on "Mental Health of looked-after Children".' *Advances in Psychiatric Treatment 9*, 256–257.

Vostanis, P. and Cumella, S. (eds) (1999) *Homeless Children: Problems and Needs.* London: Jessica Kingsley Publishers.

Vostanis, P., Grattan, E., Cumella, S. and Winchester, C. (1997) 'Psychosocial Functioning of Homeless Children.' *Journal of the American Academy of Child and Adolescent Psychiatry 36*, 881–889.

Vostanis, P., Grattan, E. and Cumella, S. (1998) 'Mental Health Problems of Homeless Children and Families: A Longitudinal Study.' *British Medical Journal 316*, 899–902.

Vostanis, P., Meltzer, H., Goodman, R. and Ford, T. (2004) 'Service Utilization by Children with Conduct Disorders: Findings from the GB National Study.' *European Child and Adolescent Psychiatry 12*, 231–238.

Walters, S. and East, L. (2001) 'The Cycle of Homelessness in the Lives of Young Mothers: The Diagnostic Phase of an Action Research Project.' *Journal of Clinical Nursing 10*, 171–179.

Webb, E., Shankleman, J., Evans, M. and Brooks, R. (2001) 'The Health of Children in Refuges for Women Victims of Domestic Violence.' *British Medical Journal 323*, 210–213.

Wrate, R. and Blair, C. (1999) 'Homeless Adolescents.' In P. Vostanis and S. Cumella (eds) *Homeless Children: Problems and Needs.* London: Jessica Kingsley Publishers.

Zamble, E. and Porporino, F. (1990) 'Coping, Imprisonment, and Rehabilitation.' *Criminal Justice and Behavior 17*, 53–70.

Chapter 13

Developing Culturally Sensitive Services to meet the Mental Health Needs of Ethnic Minority Children

Peter Brinley Harper and Radha Dwivedi

Introduction

Twenty-first-century British society encompasses a rich and diverse tapestry of cultural values, attitudes and behaviours. Services have long been challenged to become culturally (and linguistically) sensitive in their responses to the needs of ethnic minority groups, and (more recently) to the mental health needs of ethnic minority children. The social policy agendas of equality and inclusion, the recognition of institutional racism in key organisations and the need for partnership working across agencies have all increased awareness of the need to consider anew the response of services to the needs of people from ethnic minorities. Historically a lack of adequate resources has inhibited the development of generic mental health services and providers have been expected to address the challenges of service development from within existing resources. Small wonder then that mental health services, including prevention, for ethnic minority children are poorly developed. It is encouraging to note that more recent government imperatives have been accompanied by some funding being made available to hard pressed services and that some services have employed outreach workers for ethnic minority children and their families. Nonetheless, as Williams (2002, p.9) comments, 'It is not just how much resource we put in, but how we do so.'.

Meeting the mental health needs of ethnic minority children at every level of service delivery challenges us all to consider the culture and style of our service organisations. If we are to succeed in developing culturally sensitive services we need to be willing to make some fundamental personal, professional and organisational changes. There is an urgent need to make service provision go beyond the level of rhetoric that has so far characterised the field.

In addition to raising some of the core issues associated with the development of culturally sensitive services to meet the mental health needs of ethnic minority children, this chapter outlines the crucial role of the community outreach worker and describes some of the service development considerations, experiences and a case example from a preventive service in Northampton, UK. It is followed by Philip Messent's Chapter 14 in this volume outlining further examples of preventive services that 'reach out' proactively and provide easy access rather than responding to crises in the way that has characterised many child mental health services to date.

Problems in service provision

A report by the US Surgeon General acknowledges that the US 'mental health system is not well equipped to meet the needs of racial and ethnic minority populations' (US Department of Health and Human Services 1999). This could equally be said of the UK. The uptake of child and adolescent mental health services by people from ethnic minorities is notoriously poor. People from ethnic minority groups are under-served, they encounter numerous barriers to treatment and face considerable difficulty accessing services. Those services that they do manage to access are often experienced as inappropriate or alienating 'because of a variety of factors such as the clash of cultural values, lack of awareness of the role of professionals or lack of faith in such services' (Dwivedi 2002, p.31). The culture of many service organisations is strongly influenced by Eurocentrism, white middle-class values and the associated conditioning of many professionals; little account is taken of the strengths and resources implicit in other cultures. Many cultures have an extensive body of therapeutic knowledge and a range of practices to manage relationships, feelings and mental health. Assuming that Western psychotherapeutic approaches are superior is implicitly racist.

In June 1997 a joint policy on race and mental health was issued by five leading mental health charities in the UK. This statement highlighted the fact that:

- mental health problems reflect a diversity of cultural and socio-economic experiences and will vary between ethnic groups
- lack of sensitivity to these differences leads to a failure of mainstream services to meet the mental health needs of black and ethnic minority communities
- language and culture are primary obstacles to the quality of care received by black and ethnic minority people
- service deficiencies often reflect lack of user and community involvement in service planning and delivery
- racism and disadvantage is experienced by people from ethnic minority communities in the range of areas (employment, housing, education, etc.) that directly affect mental health.

Underutilisation of CAMHS

The uptake of CAMH services by people from ethnic minority groups is very low. A number of within-group reasons have traditionally been considered to underlie this situation. Such reasons include a lack of knowledge of what constitutes mental health, the stigma attached to mental health problems, and the associated perception that use of mental health services could result in loss of status and rejection by family and neighbours. The non-recognition and low awareness of mental health problems, combined with a lack of understanding of services that are available and how to access them, are additional reasons purported to underlie the low uptake of child and adolescent mental health services. Preventive work with ethnic minority families is unlikely to succeed unless these factors are addressed in the organisation and delivery of services.

Underutilisation of child and adolescent mental health facilities by ethnic minority families and their children, particularly the Asian population, is recognised, and commented upon by Stern, Cottrell and Holmes (1990). Possible explanations for underutilisation include:

- parents not recognising certain types of behaviour as problems
- Asian children may have lower rates of disturbance generally
- cultural norms are different and hence prevent help seeking

- a lack of fluency and an inability to communicate with professionals working in clinics.

Dwivedi (1996) provides a helpful summary of the stresses that are associated with the need for and use of services by young people from ethnic minority groups. These are:

- the risks and stresses common to any child, irrespective of ethnicity, e.g. family relationships, life events and conflict

- the all-permeating impact of racism and discrimination and the resultant undermining of culture, identity and self-image which leaves children and families feeling hopeless

- dislocation from family background leading to a fragmentation of support and vulnerability to the loss of cultural strengths.

Using data from the most recent ONS survey of child and adolescent mental health in the UK, Banhatti and Bhate (2002, p.75) comment that higher prevalence rates of mental health difficulties are more closely associated with 'factors relating to age (older children), sex (boys), number of children in the household (four or five), unemployment and lower social class' than with ethnicity. They acknowledge that utilisation of psychiatric services is strongly influenced by ethnocultural factors, including stigma, language barriers and discrepancies between the cultural beliefs of professionals and clients. Pertinently, Banhatti and Bhate (2002) also note that

> Byrne has described how people from ethnic minorities have to overcome 'double discrimination' (a co-incidence of mental illness and minority status) when they seek help for treatment of mental illness for themselves or their children. It is no wonder that their underuse of services is an almost universal reality. (Banhatti and Bhate 2002, p.82)

Barriers to receipt of treatment
Help-seeking behaviour
Among adults the evidence is considerable that people from minority backgrounds are less likely than whites to seek outpatient treatment in the specialty mental health sector. This makes it even less likely that parents of ethnic minority children will seek support for the mental health needs of their children.

Mistrust

This issue has been best studied among African Americans. People from these groups are more likely than whites to attribute fear (of hospitalisation and of treatment) and a lack of time as their reasons for not seeking professional help in the face of depression. However, the mistrust of services may arise more specifically from experiences of segregation, racism, and discrimination resulting in the perception of the 'host culture' as being hostile and untrustworthy.

In the development of a local outreach service one of the authors (RD) identified evidence of fear, disillusionment, mistrust and animosity towards professionals (including GPs and the police). Her role therefore had to be sufficiently flexible to allow her to address a number of 'off issue' expectations (e.g. housing and benefit problems) to establish her credibility and to gain the trust of the community before she was allowed to attend to child mental health issues more directly.

Lau (2002) has written eloquently about minority issues, cautioning us to consider carefully the impact of the markers of professional identity and status on our capacity to encourage people to engage with services. These markers include the use of jargon, patterns of speech and other communication methods that we traditionally use – letters, appointment systems, the ritual of professional meetings and the white coats of the past.

Services often conclude that clients are not motivated when they cancel appointments (often at the last minute, but usually because of family or other cultural obligations). The tensions arising from these essentially simple situations become very significant in whether or not service users are engaged. If people from ethnic minority communities are to increase their use of child mental health services, it is crucial that those working in the field are responsive to issues of cultural and behavioural style, the hierarchies and roles operating in different cultures, and the customs associated with aspects of daily living and important life events such as marriage, birth and death.

Stigma

The role of stigma in preventing use of mental health services has already been raised. In this context the use of denial, and emphasising self-reliance and determination as characteristics crucial to overcome mental health problems all contribute to the non-recognition and stigmatisation of mental health needs. Cultural factors may tend to encourage the use of family, traditional healers and informal sources of care rather than to encourage treatment-seeking behaviour. However, Patel *et al.* (2000) conclude that the assumption that mental health difficulties are more stigmatised in ethnic minority groups than in the general population is not upheld in the evidence. Generalisations should therefore be avoided and clinicians are encouraged to develop their understanding of individuals and their cultural context rather than resorting to stereotypical conclusions which can have a profound impact on service delivery, the uptake of services and in the promotion of mental health.

Clinician and therapist bias

The cultural bias of clinicians has a significant impact on the outcomes of work undertaken with children and families from ethnic minority groups. White Western clinicians value independent thinking, and where children do not express independent views, concerns are often raised and professionals intervene with the assumption that the youngster's family may have been repressive and over-restrictive, thus preventing 'self-expression'. As Dwivedi (1996) points out, many professionals may therefore feel passionate about 'rescuing' such children, resulting in the child being alienated either from their parents or from the professional – both unsatisfactory outcomes.

In the mental health field, diagnosis relies heavily on behavioural signs and the reporting of symptoms rather than on tests providing unequivocal results. The judgements exercised by clinicians are therefore particularly susceptible to bias that may lead to over- or under-diagnosis. Judgements about the behaviours associated with parenting styles promoting secure or insecure attachments are not universally applicable. In one cultural context behaviours considered to be indicative of obedience and respect may in another context be suggestive of poor self-esteem and unhealthy parental dominance. Generalisations (e.g. people from certain groups have extensive family support) and myths held by those from the dominant culture will frequently discount the existence of difficulties among people from ethnic minority cultures. White therapists have a particular challenge in terms of bias, because their interpretations of material in the therapeutic hour are often undertaken from their own embedded cultural heritage.

Many people from ethnic minorities experience caring professionals as being 'emotionally unavailable'. Caring professionals may fail to respond empathically because they cannot understand the cultural ways of the families, or alternatively they may use 'culturalistic pseudo-insight' (Deveraux 1953) in which they look for a quick cultural explanation or confuse psychopathology with cultural differences. Such actions are an insult and an assault on the identity of the child from an ethnic minority (Dwivedi 1996).

At times of distress youngsters may need to turn to peers and professionals. Professionals need to be very sensitive to the way in which help is sought and to be cautious about colluding unhelpfully with youngsters against the family and cultural systems when the presentation of difficulties is couched in the context of cultural practices and styles, e.g. 'fear of arranged marriage' or 'restrictive parents'.

> It then becomes important that professionals dealing with the child are able to look through the smokescreen (their own and the child's) to identify pathological or maladaptive patterns of behaviour or symptoms. (Banhatti and Bhate 2002, p.69)

Language and the use of interpreters

Access to services is frequently inhibited, particularly in migrant families, where service users lack fluency in English. The resulting frustration and dread of using services (both primary care and secondary CAMHS) is a particular barrier to service uptake. Many services have attempted to address this issue by using interpreters, though the use of interpreters needs to be carefully considered. The ethic of confidentiality, the impact of the interpreter (and their background, etc.) on the process of the clinical contact, and the skill of the interpreter all have the potential of significantly influencing the delivery of services. Further, particularly in the mental health arena, it is crucial that in addition to sharing a common understanding of content of language, there should be 'shared meaning'. Developing such shared meaning is often very time-consuming and developing a familiarity with nuance and the meaning of idiom in different cultures is a particular challenge in our multicultural society.

Mental health and ecological factors

Lower socio-economic status – housing employment, education, income, etc. – has been strongly linked to mental illness, and many ethnic minority people may have limited financial resources. Poverty disproportionately affects minority women and their children (Miranda and Green 1999) and we know that poor women experience more frequent, life-threatening and uncontrollable life events than do members of the population at large (Belle 1990). Those with an awareness of systemic issues will no doubt already have made the connection with the impact of poverty on the lives of children from ethnic minority communities: the psychological development of children is significantly affected by poverty and poor housing conditions, parental absence resulting from long working hours or working night shifts, and the stresses associated with living under such life conditions. In this light Banhatti and Bhate (2002) suggest that change at the level of the general population can be more effectively undertaken when the focus of intervention is on social and psychological variables. Developing services to promote child mental health services for ethnic minority children and their families should therefore incorporate such a focus from the outset.

Cultural diversity and coping styles

Idioms of distress often reflect the values and themes found in the societies from which people from ethnic minorities originate. Somatisation (the expression of mental distress in terms of physical suffering) occurs widely and has been thought to be particularly apparent in South Asian communities. However, the evidence base for this assumption is now being challenged (Patel et al. 2000). The non-recognition of mental distress is perhaps more attributable to the professional lacking experience of the cultural background and language of the client.

In some traditional societies, mental health issues are viewed as spiritual concerns and occasions to renew one's commitment to a religious or spiritual system of belief, and to engage in prescribed religious or spiritual forms of practice.

In all cases it is important to consider the yardstick being applied to make judgements, and reference has already been made to the problems associated with adopting an approach based exclusively on western standards.

Family and community as resources

Families play an important role in providing support to individuals with mental health problems. However, a lack of understanding of the way in which children express their internal distress may mean that the child is not entirely understood. Where the extended family system is not emotionally supportive and the 'institutional' network of support is either alienating, fragmented or absent, young people from ethnic minority communities face a considerable dilemma: 'What do I need to say or do in order to access support?' In such situations children and young people face excruciating pressures arising from their bicultural identity and there is a considerable danger of problems being escalated and distorted in their attempts to ensure that they are heard and responded to.

What are culturally sensitive services?

In the USA, the Bureau of Primary Health Care's (2001) Cultural Competency Program has at its core the mission 'to demonstrate that culturally and linguistically competent practices increase access to services and reduce disparities in the health status of ethnic, racial and cultural populations' (US Department of Health and Human Services, HRSA, Bureau of Primary Health Care 2001). The range of activities involved in the development of culturally competent services should be embedded in meaningful, appropriate policy frameworks. From the policy springboard, the activities include appropriate data collection and research, active community involvement at both individual and organisational levels, staff education and training, the provision of supportive and sensitive administrative structures and clinical practices which take account of cultural identity and its associated norms, nuances and behaviours (Malek and Joughin 2004).

In the UK there is a preference to refer to the need for services to be 'culturally sensitive' and to respect all cultures and traditions. It is only when services respect the cultural uniqueness of each individual and understand their histories and traditions and take account of the health-related beliefs, attitudes and practices in different cultures (Stephenson 1999) that the barriers preventing access to services will begin to be removed. Breaking down cultural and linguistic barriers and directly encouraging community participation will begin the process of closing the gaps in access to mental health services. It is important that service commissioners and clinicians step out of their often linear, Western perspectives which assume that differences in rates of the incidence of mental health problems can be simplistically explained away in terms of 'culture'. This is a complex area in which the theoretical underpinnings (linked to methodology, the process of diagnosis and the link between disorders in children and their cultural context) are beginning to be challenged (Maitra 2004).

The nature of child mental health issues

Working in situations of cultural diversity provides a particular challenge for the mental health professional. Entrenched community beliefs, exacerbated by concerns about discriminatory practice in mental health settings means that work undertaken, particularly with children and families is slow and painstaking. Where it is not undertaken the cost to children in terms of exclusion and educational failure is enormous. This is most frequently to be seen in the escalating numbers of children and young people with antisocial behaviours and can be observed in the suffering of the increasing numbers of children with emotional problems.

Although not quantified at the demographic level, one of the authors (RD) undertook a needs assessment while developing a mental health outreach service for ethnic minority groups in Northampton, UK. This undertaking highlighted the fact that although all families are entitled to universal services, such as access to general practitioners and health visitors, there was a pervasive cultural resistance to acknowledging mental health issues in the population. Various primary care initiatives had been undertaken in an attempt to engage people from ethnic minorities, but these appeared not to have met with success. On further exploration with local families it was apparent that a considerable level of need existed. The issues identified from the data collected included the following.

Social and systemic issues

- There was a pervasive cultural taboo regarding mental health and an associated fear that contact with mental health service would result in the removal of children.

- There were ongoing concerns about racial violence, domestic violence, marital anxieties pertinent to specific cultural issues, and issues of loss resulting from divorce or parental separation and their sequelae (including rejection by the community or relatives).

- Poverty and overcrowding impacted on family functioning and the social and emotional development of children.

- Social isolation was exacerbated when parents were afraid to let their children socialise outside of the home. This frequently resulted in children feeling restricted, bored, frustrated and angry. The absence of a parental network and the resultant social isolation was clearly seen between parents and their children. Parents under stress were noted to be coercive, with a high incidence of shouting.

- Particular difficulties were associated with instances where parents had identified mental illness, where one parent was in prison or when faced with the stresses of growing up in families in which one sibling had a learning disability.

- Specific cultural customs were noted to compound the stress experienced by girls where customs invited social restrictions inside and outside the home.

- Many parents had limited education and therefore had difficulty comprehending the nature of services provided. This also left them feeling excluded from participating in the educational development of their children.

Individual or child issues

- Children reported a high incidence of being bullied at school and in the community.

- There was a high incidence of hyperactivity, stealing, lying, self-neglect, temper tantrums and boredom among children, with parents struggling to manage their children's behaviour.

- The incidence of self-harming behaviours was often masked as young people from ethnic minority communities tended not to access traditional services following such an incident.

- A high incidence of symptoms of emotional disorder was identified in children and young people. These symptoms included tearfulness, reports of depressive feelings, anxiety and eating disorders.

- Low self-esteem was clearly evident in many children.

- A significant number of children were bedwetting or soiling.

- Some clear instances of young people with significant psychiatric disorder were identified. These included young people with obsessive compulsive disorder and psychosis which was being managed by families at great social and emotional cost to those involved.

Service development and the role of the outreach worker

The developing national service framework for children provides a number of important and helpful principles that it is believed should underpin all policies and services for children (Department of Health 2003). These centre on the key issues such as equitability and non-discrimination, inclusivity, the coherence and integration of services, respect, and empowerment. These are important principles in the development of any service for children and young people, but are perhaps even more important when considering the need to develop culturally sensitive services for people from ethnic minority communities. Translating this laudable policy into services which are used and valued by ethnic minority communities

> requires setting up of community outreach work, interpreter and translation services and culturally sensitive family and other work and also giving voice to subjugated narratives. Also professional development needs to incorporate the perspective of difference and diversity aiming not only to raise cultural awareness by gaining knowledge but also cultural sensitivity through experiences that challenge one's respective cultural identities and their influence on understanding and acceptance of others. (Dwivedi 1996, p.6)

In summary, fundamental change to the way in which services have traditionally been delivered is required.

Community outreach work

Community outreach work is a complex and time-consuming undertaking. The level of skill and flexibility required to engage community leaders, community development workers and people from ethnic minority communities is considerable, particularly when promoting child mental health services. It requires patience, a high level of commitment, persistence, skills in systemic work, the flexibility to undertake many off-issue activities and considerable acumen in blending community work skills with clinical or therapeutic skills.

The process of engaging with communities is often slow, requiring enormous skill and dedication. Establishing credibility is a prerequisite, and to succeed, outreach workers need to spend considerable energy 'tracking' (Minuchin 1974) communities and families, undertaking what often seem irrelevant (in terms of developing mental health services) activities e.g. liaising with the housing or pension authorities. The community grapevine is a very powerful source of communication and once established, news of the acceptability of the outreach worker and their willingness to help will develop an increasing momentum.

In the same way that families should be entitled to clear communication about what support to expect from services, outreach workers too should be given clear information about the nature and level of support to expect in their challenge to develop services. Developing such services cannot be undertaken in a vacuum, and clarity of policy directives (including the articulation of the expectations of stakeholders) appropriate supervision, and the provision of informed and supportive administrative and clerical support will all contribute to success or failure when developing appropriate mental health services for ethnic minority children, young people and their families.

The way in which services appoint and induct colleagues undertaking community outreach work is likely to parallel service and organisation views on engaging and providing for the needs of children from ethnic minority communities. All too frequently, in busy services, time is not taken to attend to, or provide information (e.g. on service configuration, how people access the service, the biographies and interests of staff providing services, maps, lists of key agencies, professionals and staff, etc.) that is crucial to developing a familiarity with service structures and provision. Negotiating one's way through professional networks and internal politics can be a nightmare for the professional. For the service user, systemic obstacles such as these serve only to increase alienation, mistrust and the non-use of services.

Local experience has also highlighted the importance of personal introductions, and engaging service users has been promoted by having an outreach worker first brief the mental health professional about the family's concerns and cultural style, before introducing him or her to the family on their own territory. This requires flexibility of mental health professionals and a willingness to leave behind their markers of identity and status as highlighted by Lau (2002). Outreach workers may help to bridge the gap between core services and the community, but it is also important for professionals in core CAMHS to be actively engaged in the provision so that they are willing to offer their expertise when it is needed. Unless CAMHS professionals are actively involved in the outreach service, there is a danger that they may adopt a position in which they believe the ethnic minority client is 'someone else's responsibility'.

Networking and engaging local resources

Networking is a primary activity of the outreach worker. There is an inordinate number of professionals working in the field, and it is a very time-consuming undertaking to engage the professional network on both an individual and a group basis. The dividends accruing from building a successful network provide opportunities for liaison about specific clients, an opportunity to increase the profile of mental health both generally and specifically as it pertains to ethnic minority communities, and the opportunity to provide consultation and training.

Development of more direct services will depend on the skills of the individual. However, by involving other members of the professional community in delivering services (either collaboratively or using the apprentice model), the preventive impact can be widened. In Northampton we were able to provide services that included individual community-based therapeutic work, a drop-in opportunity for children and/or parents, a range of groups (for girls across the age range, and for boys who had a history of trauma), parenting groups for the mothers of young children, filial play therapy sessions involving parents and their children supported by a local play therapist, access to family therapy within the local CAMHS, and residential weeks for children and young people. The provision of this range of services ensured that it was much more possible to access psychiatric input in a seamless way when it was specifically indicated.

Attention to issues of process and content is critical to success in the delivery of many mental health services. In developing services for ethnic minority groups, it is important that the activities undertaken have face validity and that they are culturally relevant. The use of activities such as cooking, henna painting, music, drama, dance, aromatherapy, day trips and celebration of religious festivals all provided a vehicle through which children, young people and their parents were able to engage in the service and begin openly to discuss their feelings and concerns. These activities enabled more direct therapeutic interventions to then be undertaken in a more culturally sensitive way.

Outcomes and resources

The development of meaningful outcome measures in outreach work is notoriously difficult, and this is particularly so in the case of developing outreach services to ethnic minority communities. It is unrealistic to use quantifiable data such as 'number of clinical contacts' as an exclusive measure of the success of outreach work in child mental health. The complex and multiple activities involved are simply not accounted for in traditional 'counting exercises'.

It is often expected that outreach work as a precursor to engaging children, young people and their families in the core CAMHS is conducted on a shoestring. In addition to meeting appropriate staffing and accommodation costs, clear account should be taken of the need for the provision of additional resources, which may include transport, the provision of food and refreshments (because food is such an integral part of social customs in ethnic minority populations), decorative items, displays of arts and crafts, and posters (so that services are not seen as exclusively Eurocentric) and the provision of opportunities to promote family, group and day activities as part of addressing the mental health issues of children and young people.

The development of information packs which address many of the obstacles to service use mentioned in this chapter, and which give information about the nature of the services offered and how to access them, translated into appropriate languages, is one important step in the development of a culturally sensitive service. This may include

- the development of a leaflet for parents to increase their awareness of emotional problems in children and to familiarise the parents with psychological language

- the provision of literature and leaflets to schools and teachers to increase their awareness of the 'shame' encountered by many ethnic minority families when they encounter 'mental health issues'

- translation of the Royal College of Psychiatrists' leaflets on common childhood difficulties into the appropriate languages to make them accessible to parents

- using local radio services to publicise issues concerned with mental health and the role of the outreach worker

- providing information on customs and various cultural taboos to members of core CAMHS

- developing posters and information for use at workshops.

Staff training

The service model promulgated in Northampton acknowledged from the outset the need for training professionals (at all levels of service delivery) in issues of diversity and cultural difference, and for encouraging them to consider the implications of developing a culturally sensitive service with congruent interventions.

The process of staff training was addressed both explicitly and implicitly, and included the following:

- providing workshops for CAMHS professionals, run by acknowledged national experts
- developing a range of written resources on different cultural practices
- attending to the decoration in the service so that it included culturally diverse symbols
- celebrating different cultural festivals in the service
- offering workshops and conferences to colleagues working within primary care
- persuading CAMHS professionals to present at workshops for primary care professionals and for clients
- encouraging CAMH professionals to join the outreach worker on home visits as a way of encouraging the ongoing involvement of the professional
- providing formal and informal consultation opportunities on cultural issues where professionals were already offering a clinical service to an ethnic minority family.

These activities were helpful in increasing the knowledge and awareness of diversity issues among the professional community, with cultural sensitivity being concomitantly addressed by highlighting the 'dynamics of difference' at every possible opportunity. Clinicians who were willing to explore their own cultural identity and issues formed an important informal nucleus in which practice issues could be more fully discussed.

Supervision and management arrangements

The development of an outreach service requires specific attention to the issues of supervision and management. The 'systemic positioning' of the service will often determine the success or failure of the initiative. Without the clear commitment of commissioners, managers and professional colleagues the work of even the most skilled and dedicated outreach worker will be doomed. Herein lies the formidable task of challenging the establishment to commit itself to the development of culturally sensitive and relevant services. This commitment needs to be embedded in the daily activity and concerns of all involved in the chain of service provision.

Supervision arrangements are particularly challenging. The task being asked of the outreach worker is an almost impossible one – 'be a community worker without being a clinician, but be sure to bring expert mental health knowledge and therapeutic acumen to bear in all your activities!' Sensitivity to personal, cultural and professional differences is a prerequisite to success in supervision. In the same way that outreach workers are expected to be flexible, so too should their supervision be flexible. This may require providing access to consultation and supervision from sources beyond the immediate service – an undertaking that managers and internal supervisors may experience as a challenging one.

Case Example: Salim

This typical, though complex, case example illustrates the nature of work undertaken in Northampton by one of the authors (RD) in her role as outreach worker.

Salim, an 8-year-old boy, was referred by a school nurse following a year's unsuccessful treatment for secondary enuresis. The child had also been seen by his GP and prescribed medication for his enuresis and for the headaches of which he complained. A preliminary home visit by the outreach worker highlighted significant systemic issues. There was concern that the children in this large family (there were five siblings) were being physically and emotionally rejected. Although issues of child protection were considered, they did not meet the threshold criteria for referral to social services. Initial parental reluctance to allow the outreach worker to meet the children was addressed by engaging the parents both individually and as a subsystem, always assuming that they loved and cared about their children. It soon emerged that the father was seldom home and the absence of nurturing relationships in his history was mirrored in his neglect of his wife and his punitive style towards his children. In turn his wife appeared depressed and was socially isolated. She would not allow the children to play outside because she was concerned about the dangers of the neighbourhood. The family were also in considerable financial difficulty. This latter issue had a significant impact on communication in the family. In an attempt to mask the family's financial plight the mother met any request from her children with harsh rejecting retorts. Shortly before the outreach worker's visit, an older brother of the referred child had 'stolen' money from his parents. They were about to evict him and to involve the police in an attempt to manage the issue.

Engaging the father in this family was critical, and after positively reframing the importance of his role in the family it was possible to confront some of his behaviours and then to promote the role he could play as change agent. This was followed by parental agreement that a child psychiatrist and clinical psychologist from the local CAMHS visit the family at home. This key intervention had multiple implicit purposes: to engage the family on their own territory before inviting them to the central clinic; to allow a preliminary assessment of the mental health of the parents to be undertaken; to provide a practical training opportunity for the professionals seeing people in their own home environments; to dispel the family's fantasies about mental health professionals; to allow the family to judge for themselves the 'trustworthiness' of the psychologist who co-facilitated the group for children from ethnic minorities to which the children were later to be referred. At this visit the family also agreed to visit the clinic for family therapy.

In the interim the outreach worker was allowed to meet the children. The 8-year-old soon disclosed that he was frequently punished by his parents; that he had frequent thoughts about either running away or harming himself; and that he was struggling academically at school. An older brother reported symptoms of anxiety and a high incidence of sibling conflict. Finally the child accused of 'stealing' was able to voice his distress at not being allowed to play with children in the neighbourhood and his wish to have shoes like the peers he met at school.

The boys later attended the group and enjoyed a residential workshop run for children from ethnic minority communities. The referred child did not wet his bed while on the residential trip and at follow-up has remained essentially dry.

Communication in the family was addressed in family therapy and the structure of relationships was strengthened as a result. The father's increasing involvement in the family and his wife's decreasing social isolation (after she agreed to join a local community women's group) contributed to their ability to learn and implement an increasingly nurturing child-rearing style, resulting in a significant decrease in sibling conflict and the difficult behaviours about which the mother had initially complained.

Without the sensitivity of the outreach worker in engaging the family and associated helping resources, the prognosis for each family member can only be considered to have been poor. The resultant resource cost to service agencies would have been considerable without this multifaceted preventive intervention.

Regrettably, in Northampton this service was discontinued after commissioners decided that funding a dedicated CAMH outreach service for ethnic minorities was not warranted and that other service priorities should take precedence.

Conclusion

Mental health is increasingly being acknowledged as 'everyone's business'. In developing child mental health services that are culturally sensitive and relevant for people from ethnic minority communities it is important not only that mental health professionals increase their awareness of the barriers faced by people from ethnic minorities but also that they are actively committed and willing to implement substantial change in the way they deliver services. It is only in this context that access to services will become truly open and user oriented and services will be willing to incorporate the numerous strengths of ethnic minority cultures in preventive and therapeutic endeavours.

References

Banhatti, R. and Bhate, S. (2002) 'Mental Health Needs of Ethnic Minority Children.' In K.N. Dwivedi (ed) *Meeting the Needs of Ethnic Minority Children*, 2nd edn. London: Jessica Kingsley Publishers.

Belle, D. (1990) 'Poverty and Women's Mental Health.' *American Psychologist 45*, 3, 385–389.

Department of Health (2003) *Getting the Right Start: National Service Framework for Children Emerging Findings*. London: Stationery Office.

Deveraux, G. (1953) 'Cultural Factors in Psychoanalytic Therapy.' *Journal of American Psychoanalytic Association 1*, 629–655.

Dwivedi, K.N. (1996) 'Services to Meet the Mental Health Needs of Children.' *Child Psychiatry On–Line* www.priory.com/psych/chneeds.htm

Dwivedi, K.N. (2002) 'Culture and Personality.' In K.N. Dwivedi (ed) *Meeting the Needs of Ethnic Minority Children*, 2nd edn. London: Jessica Kingsley Publishers.

Health Advisory Service (1995) *Child and Adolescent Mental Health Services – Together We Stand*. London: HMSO.

Lau, A. (2002) 'Family Therapy and Ethnic Minorities.' In K.N. Dwivedi (ed) *Meeting the Needs of Ethnic Minority Children*, 2nd edn. London: Jessica Kingsley Publishers.

Maitra, B. (2004) 'The Cultural Relevance of the Mental Health Disciplines.' In M. Malek and C. Joughin (eds) *Mental Health Services for Minority Ethnic Children and Adolescents*. London: Jessica Kingsley Publishers.

Malek, M. and Joughin, C. (eds) (2004) *Mental Health Services for Minority Ethnic Children and Adolescents*. London. Jessica Kingsley Publishers.

Mental Health Foundation (1997) 'Joint Policy Statement on Race and Mental Health'. *MHF Briefing* no. 8 www.mentalhealth.org.uk

Minuchin, S. (1974) *Families and Family Therapy*. Cambridge, MA: Harvard University Press.

Miranda, J. and Green, B.L. (1999) 'The Need for Mental Health Services Research Focusing on Poor Young Women.' *Journal of Mental Health Policy and Economics 2*, 73–89.

Patel, N., Bennett, E., Dennis, M. *et al.* (2000) *Clinical Psychology, 'Race' and Culture: A Training Manual*. London: BPS Blackwell.

Stephenson, J. (1999) 'Cultural Barriers to Care.' *Journal of the American Medical Association 282*, 23, 2201.

Stern, G., Cottrell, D. and Holmes, J. (1990) 'Patterns of Attendance of Child Psychiatric Out-patients with Special Reference to Asian Families.' *British Journal of Psychiatry 156*, 384–387.

Sue, D.W. and Sue, D. (1990) *Counselling the Culturally Different*. New York: Citadel.

US Department of Health and Human Services (1999) *Mental Health: A Report of the Surgeon General*.
www.mentalhealth.samhsa.gov/features/surgeongeneralreport/home.asp

US Department of Health and Human Services, Health Resources and Services Administration, Bureau of Primary Health Care (2001) 'Some facts about BPHC: Cultural Competency' (Inventory code PC518). http://www.ask.hrsa.gov/detail.cfm?id=PC518.

Williams, R. (2002) 'Foreword.' In K.N. Dwivedi (ed) *Meeting the Needs of Ethnic Minority Children*, 2nd edn. London: Jessica Kingsley Publishers.

Chapter 14

Ethnic Minority Children and Families and Mental Health

Preventive approaches

Philip Messent

Ethnic minority children and families tend to be under-represented among referrals to child and adolescent mental health services (Hillier *et al.* 1994; Stern, Cottrell and Holmes 1990). It could be argued that this is a measure of a lack of such problems among such communities, and there is a certain amount of evidence that some particular minorities are indeed more psychologically healthy. Meltzer *et al.* (2000) found that Indian children have a lower prevalence rate of mental disorder than any other group. However, there is also evidence to suggest that the reasons why such families are not referred or when they are referred do not attend such agencies is more to do with a lack of knowledge about such services among some migrant communities (e.g. Messent and Murrell 2003), and a belief among ethnic minority communities that statutory mental health services are stigmatising, and are largely run by the white majority community, following Western norms about how children should be understood and families should be organised (Fatimilehin and Coleman 1998). Referrers meanwhile may not see some minority communities as benefiting from the sort of psychological help on offer. Bal and Cochrane in an unpublished study in Birmingham in the 1980s describe how more Asian than white UK patients came to GPs there with somatic complaints, but the doctors were more likely to refer their white UK patients for psychological help. Some communities may receive help only when they reach a level of seriousness that necessitates the most 'heavy end' of interventions – medication and inpatient care (Messent and Murrell 2003).

Elsewhere (Messent and Murrell 2003) the author has argued that if services are to avoid allegations of institutional racism, there is a need for them to examine the take-up of help by different ethnic minority communities, and explore ways of offering services to ensure that they can be accessed by such communities. The National Service Framework emerging findings document (Department of Health 2003) urges services to ensure that they are equally accessible to all children and young people.

One way in which services can make themselves more accessible to members of ethnic minority communities who are not accessing services is to develop outreach and preventive ways of delivering services. Rather than waiting for problems to develop to such an extent that such children have to receive help only in a crisis, services could be offered to young people who are at a less serious stage of difficulty in ordinary settings such as schools that they are routinely attending.

The emerging findings of the Children's National Service Framework for Child and Adolescent Mental Health (Department of Health 2003) require services to be contributing to both universal child health programmes and preventive services aimed at particularly vulnerable groups. This chapter will focus in some detail on some particular initiatives in the London Borough of Tower Hamlets, a particularly ethnically diverse area familiar to the author. These are described not as a model to be followed indiscriminately elsewhere (the whole point of such initiatives is that they should be designed to meet the circumstances of particular ethnic communities), but as examples of the kind of preventive approach which can reach out more proactively to ethnic minority communities.

The Multi-Agency Preventative (MAP) Project

In Tower Hamlets the Bangladeshi community has been growing such that by 1997 they represented a majority (54%) of the school-age population (London Borough of Tower Hamlets 1999). However, as a proportion of the children and young people referred to clinics they represented only 19 per cent (Messent and Murrell 2003). In a multi-agency review of local child and adolescent mental health services carried out in 1997, many local schools requested that services should be offered within schools. They saw many Bangladeshi young people, boys in particular, as at risk of becoming alienated and losing interest in their education, but felt that they were not going to be able to persuade the parents of such boys of the relevance of the sort of child and adolescent mental health services being offered in outpatient clinics.

Funding was obtained using this finding to argue for the need to develop a preventive service aimed at this particular group of young people in three local secondary schools. A multidisciplinary team of youth workers, child clinical psychologists and social workers was formed, which developed over the course of two years a model of work which included as important elements:

- initial individual support offered to boys referred within school
- developing relationships with the boys' families through home visits to ensure that they understood and supported the sort of help being offered and to undertake an assessment of family needs
- group work with young people in schools, run on brief solution focused therapy (De Shazer 1988; George, Iveson and Ratner 1990) lines, encouraging a sense of competency and increasing the boys' self-confidence
- courses, outings, residential weekends and events offered outside of school hours to increase a sense of group cohesion and connection with workers
- psychologists in the team seeing young people with the more severe difficulties and facilitating a referral where appropriate to mainstream outpatient services
- group work with mothers
- a video on the project's work being developed and used for community education.

During its first two and a half years the project has worked with a total of 108 young people, aged between 11 and 15, offering the sorts of interventions described above. The outcome of the work has been independently assessed by a team from the Royal Holloway College (Barn, Lee and Loewenthal 2001) and has been found to be well received by young people, families and teachers, and to have had an impact on attendance levels at school and boys' self-esteem. Professionals have found themselves working in new and unusual settings, which have in turn helped them to develop new ways of working, for example using brief solution focused therapy ideas to develop a style of running short-term groups in schools that is sustainable and effective in raising self-esteem, resulting in significantly increased scores on a self-image profile (Barn *et al.* 2001) Youth workers have commented on how their involvement in the project has led to their being able to provide mental health advice in other work settings; a psychologist has spoken about the very different kind of relationship it is possible to develop with a young person of Bangladeshi origin with whom you have been out canoeing, as opposed to the more usual forms of professional contact. A number of Bangladeshi social workers and youth workers have been recruited who have developed an expertise in the area of child mental health. This project is mentioned in the green paper *Every Child Matters* (Department for Education and Skills 2003) as an exemplar of how a multi-agency team can offer effective early intervention.

Case Example: The boy who hated dirt

Jamal, a 14-year-old Bangladeshi boy, was referred to the MAP project due to concerns about his increasing rebelliousness and worsening attendance. He lived at home with his mother, older brother (aged 19) and two younger siblings. His brother had met with the head of year and agreed to a referral to MAP; he complained about Jamal's behaviour at home – refusing to get up, being aggressive and showing a lack of interest in his religion.

After two unsuccessful attempts to meet Jamal in school, the clinical psychologist was introduced to Jamal by the school 'link worker' in an empty classroom. Jamal had his cap on, his hood up and was slumped on his desk. When alone, the psychologist gave an explanation of the project, who she was and his right to choose whether to meet. She acknowledged some of the differences (for example in gender and ethnicity) between her and Jamal and raised some of the possible affordances or constraints of these in building a relationship. Using ideas from narrative therapy (White 1989) she led the discussion on to his interests and plans for the future rather than focusing on 'problem-saturated' stories. By the end of the session Jamal was making eye contact and his hood was down. Further meetings took place in school and a relationship of trust began to form as Jamal responded to externalising questions (White 1989) about what was getting in the way of him fulfilling his life plans (which included succeeding in his GCSEs). Jamal described wanting to have friends and not to be seen as a 'boffin', wanting to develop his own relationship to Islam, and finding school a dirty, unpleasant place.

It was agreed between them that in order to help him to achieve these life plans, he would need to instruct school staff in how they could best help him. Two meetings were held in school which included a learning mentor, Jamal's head of year and his big brother, in which a solution-focused (De Shazer 1988) approach was used, focusing on the times when Jamal was in school and what helped him to learn best. These meetings had the effect of reducing mutual blame between home and school, and increasing the level of practical support offered to Jamal, and the head of year spoke appreciatively about the accessibility of the MAP project.

Jamal had spoken about how at home he felt his point of view was heard only when he was angry and agreed with some reluctance for the psychologist to visit with a Bengali-speaking social worker from the project. These visits allowed discussions with Jamal's mother about dilemmas she faced in raising her son in an unfamiliar cultural and social environment and her difficulties in knowing who to turn to. The social worker introduced her to some local community resources, which she reported helped her to feel she was being a more effective parent. Discussions with her and her eldest son about their hopes and expectations of Jamal, and how he could have his ideas heard while respecting cultural beliefs about showing respect to his elders, seemed to allow them to feel their good intentions were appreciated and to consider what they could do differently to help Jamal to achieve his potential.

During school holidays Jamal was invited to attend a four-day residential trip, where project youth workers observed Jamal having difficulties in making relationships with other young people and participating in some of the activities. In a later individual session, the psychologist raised these observations, which allowed

Jamal to open up about intrusive, obsessive thoughts about dirt which were making it difficult for him to attend school. A detailed exploration of 'exceptions' followed, times when Jamal got the better of these thoughts, and over time Jamal built a resource folder including a list of 'ideas for overcoming intrusive thoughts' and helpful music.

Seeing Jamal in school initially allowed for the development of a relationship of trust between him and the psychologist. This opened the door to the social worker becoming involved who could connect with the family, helping them towards a new perspective, and identifying resources in the community available to them. It also allowed Jamal to be involved in activity programmes where youth workers were able to encourage Jamal to find more examples of success in new activities, reinforcing his stories of success. Feedback from Jamal and his family revealed that individual family members felt that the MAP project had provided an accessible service for all involved, and an appreciation of the different contributions of the team.

The African Families Project

Anane-Agyei, Lobatto and Messent (2001) describe the African Families Project, another local initiative aimed at a particularly vulnerable community. African families represent 3.36 per cent (2001 census) of the local population in the London Borough of Tower Hamlets, the area the project serves. While children and young people referred to formal CAMHS from this community are not under-represented, there is some evidence to suggest that they tend to come to the service only in an acutely ill condition, such that the service they receive is skewed towards relatively heavy end interventions, seeing psychiatrists as opposed to other members of the multidisciplinary team, being seen over a more extended period of time, and more likely to receive medication and/or periods of in-service treatment. (Messent and Murrell 2003). Goodman and Richards (1995) also found a high rate of more serious diagnoses (autism and schizophrenia) among children of African Caribbean origin attending child psychiatric clinics. One possible hypothesis about the sequence of interaction here is that African families do not approach psychiatric services until they are forced by circumstances to do so because they fear stigmatisation, a lack of understanding and being trapped into their children receiving the sort of heavy end interventions described above. But by avoiding having any such contact until problems have become acute and severe, they render the sort of response from services that they fear rather more likely to occur. Or from another point of view, largely white services are more likely to understand the problems presented by African children and young people as warranting a certain style of intervention, and this tendency is reinforced and exaggerated by the way in which such families tend to find their way to such services, out of a fear that they are going to be seen in such a light.

In order that such an endlessly reinforcing negative cycle can be interrupted, there is a need for the development of services which are more user-friendly to members of this community. Anane-Agyei *et al.* (2002) describe attempts to develop such a service including the following key elements:

1. Workers of African origin from services working in the community – tiers one and two, in terms of the model of service development described in *Together We Stand* (Department of Health 1995) – co-working with white workers from within mainstream CAMHS to help to ensure that service users have the feeling that their perspective is being understood.

2. Services being offered in a way that honours African parents' sense of themselves as having authority to decide about interventions offered to their children and families, meeting with them for example first to obtain their permission before engaging in work with their children.

3. Services being sensitive to issues arising from the disruption in many African families' lives arising out of the process of migration.

4. Services making use of 'Afrocentric' tools and ways of understanding, for example using 'ecomaps' (Department of Health 1988) rather than family trees as an initial tool for understanding webs of important relationships which may go well beyond the nuclear family.

5. Services needing to confront and challenge African parents about using forms of punishment which are not acceptable in the UK, but doing this from a position of respect for

parents' good intentions for their children, and without taking away their sense of empowerment to remain in a position of authority and responsibility in their families.

6.   Services needing to address negative views towards African families of other agencies, intervening in negative cycles of interaction which maintain problems in children and young people.

Case Example: The boy who loved his grandmother's dog

An 11-year-old Nigerian boy, Anthony, was referred to the Social Services Department for a child protection investigation as he had told teachers at school that he was being locked in the toilet for extended periods at home when he was naughty. He had a history of having been reunited with his birth parents in the UK two years previously after being raised until that time in Nigeria with extended family members. He presented with behavioural problems in school such that he was always in trouble there, although his parents felt that he was no more difficult than other pupils and that he was 'picked on' by teachers because of his reputation. He had been wetting his bed and was seen by teachers (though not his parents) as needing 'counselling'.

An African social worker commenced an investigation, working as a part of an African Families Project partnership with a white CAMHS social worker in order to ensure that Anthony's mental health needs were addressed. In the course of her investigation she got Anthony to draw an ecomap of the people or things that he felt closest to, and was struck by his positioning of his grandmother's dog, his neighbour's dog and his Sega Megadrive game as most important to him. The importance of the dogs seemed to stem from a previous close relationship with the dog of informal foster carers who had looked after Anthony when he had first arrived in the UK.

Sharing this finding with his parents acted as a powerful intervention in itself, helping them to begin to think differently about Anthony's need for more of a sense of relationship with them. When the parents came with their African social worker to meet with the white CAMHS worker they were already speaking more positively about Anthony, seeing him as communicating more with them and now having stopped bedwetting. When Anthony did his ecomap again it was noticeable that now it was his immediate family members who featured as his most important relationship. Problems remained at school, however, where he was continuing to get into trouble with teachers.

The two African Families Project workers undertook a visit to Anthony's school, meeting with his teacher and his headmistress, and finding Anthony in trouble again, sitting outside the headmistress's office. The school had made strenuous efforts to better meet Anthony's needs, to the extent of recruiting a black male teacher for his class; however, the headmistress felt that this had had little effect. In fact when the black teacher was interviewed separately, he felt that Anthony had made some improvements but these hadn't been noticed by the headmistress or anyone else in a position of real power in the school, despite his efforts to draw their attention to these changes. The workers suggested to the headmistress that she institute a new system whereby instead of Anthony coming to her only when he was in trouble, he should be sent by his teacher to see her on a regular daily basis to report on things that had gone well for him. This intervention was based on narrative ideas (White 1995) about the need to mark and call attention to change among significant audiences in order that these changes should become consolidated and long-lasting.

Anthony's daily visits to his headmistress with his messages of hope and success seemed to have the desired effect in altering her and other teachers' views about him, which in turn improved their relationship with his parents, enabling more of a sense of partnership and working together between home and school. This will have in turn contributed to Anthony feeling more contained by the sense of parents and teachers working together and in accord, and established a positive cycle of interaction in which change leads to more change.

Parents reported in feedback interviews a sense of being heard and understood, particularly by their African social worker, and that their love and good intentions for their children were being appreciated in a way that had not been the case in their previous dealings with white workers.

Building links with the community

Messent and Murrell (2003) asked groups of the Bangladeshi parents of service users about what sense they made of the comparatively low level of referrals to the local CAMHS of families from their community (30% as against 55% among the school-age population in 1997), and in particular the fact that there were practically no self-referrals by parents or families. This was not, they felt, due to any sense of stigma about attending such services, but was due to a lack of knowledge about such services among the community. They recommended that the service should be more proactive about advertising its service on posters, in newspapers and on local radio.

Since then service representatives have held meetings with representatives of the largest of the local mosques, building a sense of a shared understanding of problems and towards a collaboration in the form of a shared conference on fate and disability. This idea followed upon a successful conference organised by the local Social Services Department on the subject of forced marriages, attended by 85 imams and out of which a shared agreement had been reached about how this problem should be addressed both in the mosques and by the local authority. In the course of such discussions many mutual prejudices can be checked out and dissolved, making the prospect of CAMHS professionals working alongside imams and mosque officials in preventive initiatives a practical possibility.

Similarly following the Victoria Climbié inquiry (Department of Health and Home Office 2003) there is an onus on statutory services such as social services and CAMHS to establish connections and working relationships with African and African Caribbean churches. As a first step towards establishing such links the local authority sent out a letter to churches they had found operating within the borough, inviting representatives to attend a meeting. This attempt at making connections was not successful, so a worker was employed from one of the churches to go out and visit as many of the church groups as she could manage to contact, talking with church leaders and representatives about why, following the Climbié inquiry, it was in everyone's interest for the churches and the local authority to find a common understanding regarding child abuse and ways of communicating and working together on cases that present themselves.

For CAMHS to participate in preventive approaches to the problems of ethnic minority young people it is going to be necessary for services to develop similarly proactive ways of establishing connections with different communities, and a willingness to offer services in innovative ways in a variety of locations – schools, community centres, youth clubs and doctors' surgeries. Dwivedi (2002) has written about developing such links in Northampton, networking with local Pakistani, Bangladeshi, Sikh, African and Gujarati groups, stressing that such efforts need to be undertaken with continued mainstream funding rather than relying on temporary initiatives. Other requirements laid out in the National Service Framework emerging findings (Department of Health 2003) to contribute towards preventive services, to map need, to ensure that the needs of particularly vulnerable groups such as ethnic minority groups are met sensitively, and to offer outreach services in a variety of settings all provide opportunities for service planners to increase mainstream initiatives in this area of work.

Child and adolescent mental health services will also need to find ways of recruiting ethnic minority staff. Hillier *et al.* (1994) found that Bangladeshi service users in Tower Hamlets wanted most of all a CAMHS in which they were receiving help from Bangladeshi professionals. While some Bangladeshi social workers have been recruited to the service (and ethnic minorities in general are comparatively well represented among social workers and nurses) the training of Bangladeshi and other ethnic minorities for the other main CAMHS professional groups (psychiatry, psychology, family therapy and child psychotherapy) has lagged behind. As proactive ways to encourage such recruitment, services can arrange to visit schools and colleges to speak about opportunities in such professions (Mahtani and Marks 1994), give preference to ethnic minority students seeking placements, and create entry-level training posts for members of local communities such as the bilingual co-worker posts developed in the London Borough of Newham CAMHS in recent years and emulated in 2003 in Tower Hamlets.

Acknowledgements

I wish to thank Nicola Webb, clinical psychologist, for contributing the case example of Jamal.

References

Anane-Agyei, A., Lobatto, W. and Messent, P. (2002) 'The African Families Project: A Black and White Issue.' In B. Mason and A. Sawyyer (eds) *Exploring the Unsaid: Creativity, Risks and Dilemmas in Working Cross-culturally.* London: Karnac.

Bal, S.S. and Cochrane, R. 'Asian Patients, Somatisation and Psychological Distress.' Unpublished paper.

Barn, R., Lee, M. and Loewenthal, K. (2001) *Tower Hamlets Multi-Agency Preventative Project Evaluation Study.* London: Royal Holloway, University of London.

Department for Education and Skills (2003) *Every Child Matters.* London: Stationery Office.

Department of Health (1988) *Protecting Children: A Guide for Social Workers Undertaking a Comprehensive Assessment.* London: HMSO.

Department of Health (1995) *Together We Stand: A Thematic Review of the Commissioning, Role and Management of Child and Adolescent Mental Health Services.* London: HMSO.

Department of Health (2003) *Getting the Right Start: National Service Framework for Children Emerging Findings.* London: Stationery Office.

Department of Health and Home Office (2003) *The Victoria Climbié Inquiry: Report of an Inquiry by Lord Laming.* London: Stationery Office.

De Shazer, S. (1988) *Clues: Investigating Solutions in Brief Therapy.* New York: Norton.

Dwivedi, R. (2002) 'The Mental Health Outreach Work for the Ethnic Minority Children in Northampton.' Unpublished paper.

Fatimilehin, I. and Coleman, P. (1998) 'Appropriate Services for African-Caribbean Families: Views from One Community.' *Clinical Psychology Forum 111,* 6–11.

George, E., Iveson, C. and Ratner, H. (1990) *Problem to Solution: Brief Therapy with Individuals and Families.* London: Brief Therapy Press.

Goodman, R. and Richards, H. (1995) 'Child and Adolescent Psychiatric Presentations of Second Generation Afro-Caribbeans in Britain.' *British Journal of Psychiatry 167,* 362–369.

Hillier, S., Loshak, R., Rahman, S. and Marks, F. (1994) 'An Evaluation of Child Psychiatric Services for Bangladeshi Parents.' *Journal of Mental Health 3,* 327–337.

London Borough of Tower Hamlets (1999) *Fact Sheet No. 4* Corporate Equalities. London.

Mahtani, A. and Marks, L. (1994) 'Developing a Primary Care Psychology Service that is Racially and Culturally Appropriate.' *Clinical Psychology Forum 65,* 27–31.

Meltzer, H., Gatward, R., Goodman, R. and Ford, T. (2000) *Mental Health of Children and Adolescents in Great Britain.* London: Stationery Office.

Messent, P. and Murrell, M. (2003) 'Research Leading to Action: A Study of Accessibility of a CAMH Service to Ethnic Minority Families.' *Child and Adolescent Mental Health 8,* 3, 118–124.

Stern, G., Cottrell, D. and Holmes, J. (1990) 'Patterns of Attendance at Child Psychiatry Outpatient with Special Reference to Asian Families.' *British Journal of Psychiatry 156,* 384–387.

White, M. (1989) 'The Externalising of the Problem and the Re-authoring of Lives and Relationships.' In M. White, *Selected Papers.* Adelaide: Dulwich Centre Publications.

White, M. (1995) 'Reflecting Teamwork as Definitional Ceremony.' In M. White, *Re-Authoring Lives: Interviews and Essays.* Adelaide: Dulwich Centre Publications.

Chapter 15

The Mental Health Europe Projects and the Greek Perspective

G. Kolaitis and John Tsiantis

Introduction

Mental health promotion and prevention of mental disorders in early life has increasingly been of immense interest among professionals, researchers and also policy makers. Mental health problems in young children and adolescents are common, ranging from 7 per cent for children to 22 per cent for teenagers (European Commission 2003). They affect the functioning of the young person and are frequently associated with school failure, impaired peer relationships, work and interpersonal difficulties and may also lead to increased involvement with police, legal, mental health and social services in adulthood (Angold and Costello 1995; Robins and Rutter 1990; Rutter and Smith 1995). They are often accompanied by emotional pain and suffering, increased physical problems, mortality, poor quality of life, social stigma and discrimination with subsequent social, financial and political consequences (Lavikainen, Lahtinen and Lehtinen 2000; World Health Organization 2002b).

Moreover, it has been estimated that only 10–15 per cent of children with mental health problems reach the existing child mental health services (Cox 1993; Offord 1987) and of the childhood mental disorders which spontaneously remit, approximately 50 per cent still persist later in life (Cohen, Cohen and Brook 1993). It has also been estimated that approximately two-thirds of 3-year-olds with emotional disorders have mental health problems when followed-up as 8–12-year-olds (Campbell 1995).

It is also worrying that, as estimated, by the year 2020, mental ill health will account for 15 per cent of the burden of disease worldwide with depression becoming the second leading cause for disease burden (Murray and Lopez 1996; WHO 2002a). Among academics, clinical staff and policy makers there has been increasing attention directed to both the prevention of mental disorders and the promotion of mental health among young people.

The latter involves 'promoting the value for mental health and improving the coping capacities of individuals rather than amelioration of symptoms and deficits' (WHO 2002b). Promotion and prevention are considered overlapping and complementary activities; the combination of such programmes in mental health within overall public health strategies 'reduces stigma, increases cost-effectiveness, and provides multiple positive outcomes' (WHO 2002b).

Three categories of primary prevention have been identified:

- *universal*: targeting the general public or a whole population group
- *selective*: targeting individuals or subgroups being at higher risk than that of the rest of the population of developing a mental disorder
- *indicated*: targeting persons at high risk for mental disorders.

There have been evidence-based interventions and programmes in mental health prevention and promotion for mothers during pregnancy and perinatal period, and for children, adolescents and young people. We know, for example, that visits by nurses, health visitors and other primary care workers can prevent poor childcare and abuse, improve child–parent attachment, mothers' emotional well-being and parenting skills (e.g. Papadopoulou *et al.* 2002). It is also possible to improve children's self-esteem through school-based curricula while teachers can be trained effectively to detect mental health problems and facilitate appropriate interventions.

The projects

Between 1997 and 2001, Mental Health Europe, a non-governmental organisation committed to the promotion of mental health and prevention of mental disorders, carried out two action projects financed by the EC in the framework of the EU Community Action Plan for Health Promotion, Information, Education and Training. The projects were part of a wider programme designed to seek out, disseminate and promote best practices for children and adolescents (in mental health promotion and the prevention of mental disorders) throughout the European Community. For each project, experienced practitioners from member countries were invited to participate. Partners were selected on the basis of their personal expertise and the expertise of the organisation they represented. Both projects were intended to include representatives from each of the member countries. The Association for the Psychosocial Health of Children and Adolescents (APHCA), a non-governmental, scientific, non-profit organisation, which was founded in 1991 and is linked to our university department, was selected to act as the representative for Greece in the following projects:

1. Mental Health Promotion for Children up to 6 Years. The project started in September 1997 and ended in December 1999 with the publication of a directory of projects in the European Union.

2. Mental Health Promotion of Adolescents and Young People. The project began in March 2000 and was completed in September 2001. A directory containing a wide range of initiatives collected by the national partners was published in January 2000.

Representatives from Greece also participated in a more recent project called Mental Health Promotion and Prevention Strategies for Coping with Anxiety and Depression (APHCA was represented at the youngest age group, i.e. children, adolescents and young people).

Objectives

The specified objectives of the projects were to

- identify best practices, as defined by the group of expert advisers, in each of the member states
- publish directories with best practice from each of the member states
- organise the exchange of information, knowledge and experiences encountered
- raise awareness about mental health promotion and the prevention of mental disorders in the general population, in public, services and in government

- develop a European strategy in the field of mental health prevention and promotion.

Criteria for selection of best practices

A group of expert advisers was appointed for each of the projects and undertook the task of setting criteria for selection and subsequently reviewing the nominated projects prior to final selection of projects that constituted best practice.

The major criteria for selection of best practices were that the project

- was evaluated by randomised control trials (RCTs) or utilised a control or comparison group or by pre- and post-assessment
- established both short-term and long-term goals and was of sufficient duration and intensity to achieve the targeted goals and aims
- had a multi-component character, e.g. had been designed and implemented by multi-professional teams and used multi-methods and approaches
- was applied on a large scale and has been in place for some time
- was sustainable and based on a needs assessment
- had low complexity and credibility regarding staffing and financial costs
- could be easily transferred to different sociocultural contexts (feasibility for replication).

Process and methods: search and identification of projects on a national level

In accordance with the criteria established by Mental Health Europe, the Greek partners reviewed a range of programmes submitted by mental health services (for children, adolescents and young people), university departments, non-governmental organisations, designated persons in the Ministries of Health and Education and key personnel from a wide range of institutions, from all over Greece. In addition to disseminating relevant information and a questionnaire, the partners also contacted the selected agencies by telephone to ensure that the fax/post/email had been received but just as importantly to remind the agencies about the aims and objectives of the project and to encourage the agency personnel to complete the questionnaire and thereby participate in the project.

The task of the Greek partners was to identify specific programmes, within Greece, that came within the terms of reference as defined by the criteria established by Mental Health Europe. Contacts between the partners and the agencies submitting programmes helped the partners to identify some very interesting projects on mental health promotion and prevention that hitherto were not known within the wider professional community. Furthermore, the need to exchange information, develop cooperative links and promote networks became apparent to those engaged on the Mental Health Europe projects.

Results: selected Greek projects

From the initial Mental Health Europe programme, Mental Health Promotion for Children up to 6 Years, 3 projects were selected as models of good practice from a total of 27 submitted from Greece. The total number of projects submitted from all the national partners to Mental Health Europe for assessment, was 195. The selected programmes from Greece were the following ones.

1. Infancy in Crete (starting year: 1994). This programme was developed by the Department of Psychology, University of Crete. The primary target group was infants from prenatal until 24 months of age and the intermediate target group was parents, primary care nurses and grandmothers. The objective was to explore and understand basic aspects of cognitive, emotional, perceptual, communicative and behavioural co-development of infants with their parents and their grandmothers. Methods used were systematic, longitudinal investigation of the free interaction between infants and their parents and grandmothers in a natural setting, and systematic, longitudinal and cross-sectional study of perceptual, communicative abilities of infants in the laboratory setting. For the intermediate target group, individual and group education was provided, while there were presentations and discussions on specific issues concerning the infants' psychological development.

2. Birth and Future – Training of Trainers for a
    Medico-Psychological Approach of Perinatal Age (starting
    year: 1996, ending year: 1998). This programme was the
    product of Greek–French collaboration: the Greek Research
    Institution for the Child with partners the Athens P. and A.
    Kyriakou Children's Hospital, the Mitera (Mother) Infant
    Centre and the French non-governmental organisation
    AFREE (Association de Formation et de Recherche sur
    l'Enfant et son Environment). The primary target group
    consisted of children of unmarried mothers and children
    born at medical risk (e.g. premature or others with
    congenital problems) aged prenatal to 30 months; the
    intermediate target group consisted of parents, primary
    health care nurses, paediatricians and midwives. The
    objectives for the primary target group were to prevent
    situations that led to social marginalisation and to promote
    the mother–infant bond in high-risk groups. The objectives
    for the intermediate target group were to reinforce coping
    mechanisms of vulnerable mothers, to provide social support
    to vulnerable families, and to train and sensitise professionals
    working with parents and children to enable them to
    actively support vulnerable parents or parents with
    vulnerable children. Methods used were self-help groups of
    parents and education to increase awareness of professionals
    working with parents and infants (Cahier de l'Afrée).
    Professionals who participated in the programme became
    the key persons who continued interventions in two of the
    largest neonatal units of Athens.

3. Prevention of Psychosocial Dysfunction in High-Need
    Children and Families through Primary Health Care
    Services (starting year: 1997, still ongoing). This was a
    EU/WHO multi-centre, multicultural programme which
    included participants from UK, Greece, Finland, former
    Yugoslavia and Cyprus. The objectives (primary target
    group) were to prevent psychosocial dysfunction, and to
    promote healthy psychosocial development as well as
    (intermediate target group) to develop specific methods of
    inquiry and to train primary health care workers (PHCWs)
    as to how best to identify risk factors that pose a threat to

the psychosocial development of children. Furthermore the programme was designed to assist parents to be sensitive and appreciate those issues that may adversely affect a child's psychosocial development. The approach to the initiative was to utilise a series of approaches including formal training sessions, supervision of target primary health care professionals, the assessment of the training efficacy by pre- and post-training measures, assessment of family level of need at 4–14 weeks (by the application of a range of measures/tests designed by specially trained professionals) and follow-up assessment at 18–24 months. There were three components of the evaluation process: evaluation of the PHCWs' training programme, evaluation of the impact of training on practice by semistructured interviewing and evaluation of the outcome of the programme in terms of its impact, for example, on maternal well-being, infant language development, etc. (Tsiantis *et al.* 2000).

During the second Mental Health Europe programme, Mental Health Promotion of Adolescents and Young People, there were again three Greek projects among those finally selected as models of good practice and included in the directory of projects (Mental Health Europe 2000).

1. Health Education Programme to Prevent the Use of Psychotropic Substances (Tobacco, Alcohol, Drugs) in High School Students (starting year: 1995, still ongoing). This initiative has been developed by the Counselling Centre for Combating Drug Abuse of the Prefecture of Ioannina. Its main target group consists of high-school students living in a big city (Ioannina). It takes place within regular school hours and is based upon the use of experiential, behavioural and cognitive skill techniques within groups. In addition, as a secondary target group, the programme approaches teachers and parents of students. The objectives are to prevent students from experimenting with substances and to motivate users to seriously consider to stop; to decrease the self-reported intention for future use of substances; to enhance students' social skills with particular emphasis on the 'say no' skills in order to deal with peer pressure for substance use. The programme has been evaluated in its methodology, process and outcome (pre- and post-test), the

basic evaluation being the percentages of tobacco/alcohol/drug consumption, the percentages of the self-reported intention for future use and the percentages of coping skills during peer pressure for use.

2. Counselling Centre in the Juvenile Court of Athens (first phase: October 1998 to December 2000). The objective of this programme was the assessment and provision of support and psychoeducational interventions to young offenders (13–20 years old) with substance-abusing problems who are engaged in the justice system The programme is part of 'Strofi' (Greek for 'Turn') which belongs to KETHEA, the greater Greek therapeutic organisation for drug users. The programme has started to collaborate with Greek police (especially the section for children and adolescents) and probation officer services from various Greek cities. The counselling centre participates in the Greek Network for Support to Young People at Risk.

3. Experiential Sensitization Seminars on Mental Health and Psychosocial Development of Children and Adolescents for Teachers of Primary and Secondary Education (first implementation: January–December 1999). The project was developed and implemented by the Association for the Psychosocial Health of Children and Adolescents. The objective of this programme was to develop, implement and evaluate six experiential sensitisation seminars on mental health and psychosocial development for elementary and high-school teachers in order to increase their awareness and capacity for timely recognition and appropriate response to psychosocial difficulties in young people. The seminars were conducted in small groups of 10–15 teachers. There brief lectures and the use of experiential role-plays and group discussions drawn from case studies were designed appropriately to reflect real-life student situations. The working of the groups was coordinated by two experienced mental health professionals. The evaluation of the seminars was conducted with two evaluation instruments, i.e. Quantitative Evaluation Questionnaire of Teachers' Satisfaction with the Seminar and the Qualitative Evaluation Vignettes of Seminars' Effectiveness. The programme was

re-implemented in 2001 following the positive comments of those who participated.

Conclusions and recommendations

The overall impression gained by the authors, acting as representatives for Greece in the Mental Health Europe project, is that although mental health professionals and services in Greece engage in the assessment and treatment of mental health disorders in children and adolescents, their role in the field of prevention and promotion is relatively very limited. There are prevention interventions, mainly within schools, but these initiatives are rather sporadic, not well organised, generally in limited scale and not evaluated (in general, only about 50% of the projects selected during the second programme had been subjected to any evaluation: Mental Health Europe 2000). Such interventions are normally undertaken by mental health professionals, working in cooperation with school directors and teachers, sensitive to promotion/prevention issues, are usually limited to seminars in schools, are lacking in innovation, and certainly not focused on sensitive and difficult-to-address matters like mental disorder and death. Other methods or combination of methods, e.g. creation and distribution of resource packs, tutoring and coaching by peers, school contests, are not often used.

Most of the promotive or preventive initiatives in mental health in Greece have more general goals in this area, e.g. enhancing self-esteem, self-efficacy, independence, increasing the ability to say no to substances by pupils. A number of these programmes are implemented by the Ministry of Education in cooperation with institutions of high standing and repute in Greece, e.g. the University Mental Health Research Institute.

The conclusions to be drawn indicate that there is no clear government strategy in the field of mental health promotion and the prevention of mental disorders in Greece, a situation similar to other European countries which lack clearly defined mental health policies. In the case of Greece, this is perhaps to be expected as it is only since the late 1980s that the Greek government has, with the help of the European Community, provided significant funds devoted to the development of mental health services in the community to reduce the population of psychiatric hospitals, the long-term objective being the closing of such institutions. An example of one such programme is Health-Welfare 2002–2006, which is directed mainly at deinstitutionalisation, the development of new community services and the training of professionals. However, in

2001 there was a call for proposals in the field of mental health promotion and prevention by the Greek Ministry of Health and Welfare under the name Health 2001.

There is now increasing awareness in Greece about the need for implementing prevention programmes in the field of mental health, but unless professionals in the field are supported and trained it is difficult to make much progress. One method to assist in this process is the development of systematic databases and the exchange of information on existing projects in mental health promotion and the prevention of mental disorders. This can be done on a national level, as with the Mental Health Europe project, with the results disseminated widely. Of course with the increased ease of communications and networking dissemination can be across borders and cultures. Consequently as with the project led by Mental Health Europe, examples of best practice can be disseminated and replicated on an international basis, the results being used to develop promotion and prevention strategies across countries and cultures. In two interesting articles from the USA, Rotheram-Borus and Duan (2003) and Jensen (2003) aim to identify barriers that impede broad dissemination and adoption of efficacious programmes into routine practice of community providers and to suggest strategies that could be used by prevention researchers to overcome these barriers.

This experience, in accordance with WHO (2002b) guidelines, shows that, since the burden of mental disorders is too heavy, more attention should be given to prevention and promotion in mental health of young people by professionals from different sectors, i.e. policy formulation and legislation, resource allocation and the overall health care system. Collaboration of all organisations and sectors with a responsibility for mental health, such as professional associations, governments, non-governmental organisations, health industry and donors, is required to help the successful implementation of the programmes. The Hippocratic 'Better to prevent than to cure' will always remain a necessity, and should be seriously considered by everyone, especially policy makers.

References

Angold, A. and Costello, E. (1995) 'Developmental epidemiology.' *Epidemiologic Reviews 17*, 74–82.

Campbell, S.B. (1995) 'Behavior Problems in Preschool Children: A Review of Recent Researchers.' *Journal of Child Psychology and Psychiatry 36*, 113–149.

Cahier de l'Afrée. Cahier 14: 'L'accès à la parentalité des familles vulnerables: facteur d'exclusion ou d'intégration?' Proceeding of the 4th European Forum 'Naissance et Avenir', December 1998.

Cohen, P., Cohen, J. and Brook, J. (1993) 'An Epidemiological Study of Disorders in Late Childhood and Adolescence: Persistence of Disorders.' *Journal of Child Psychology and Psychiatry 34*, 869–897.

Cox, A. (1993) 'Preventive Aspects of Child Psychiatry.' *Archives of Disease in Childhood 68*, 691–701.

European Commission (2003) *The Health Status of the European Union: Narrowing the Health Gap.* Luxemburg: European Communities.

Jensen, P. (2003) 'Commentary: The Next Generation is Overdue.' *Journal of the American Academy of Child and Adolescent Psychiatry 42*, 5, 527–530.

Lavikainen, J., Lahtinen, E. and Lehtinen, V. (eds) (2000) *Public Health Approach on Mental Health in Europe.* Tampere, Finland: National Research and Development Centre for Welfare and Health, STAKES Ministry of Social Affairs and Health.

Mental Health Europe (1999) *Mental Health Promotion for Children up to 6 Years.* Directory of Projects in the European Union. Brussels: Mental Health Europe.

Mental Health Europe (2000) *Mental Health Promotion of Adolescents and Young People.* Directory of Projects in Europe. Brussels: Mental Health Europe.

Murray, C. and Lopez, A. (1996) *The Global Burden of Disease.* Cambridge, MA: Harvard University Press.

Offord, D. (1987) 'Prevention of behavioral and emotional disorders in children.' *Journal of Child Psychology and Psychiatry 28*, 9–19.

Papadopoulou, K., Tsiantis, J., Dragonas, T. and Cox, A.D. (2002) 'Maternal Postnatal Emotional Well-Being and Perceived Parenting Hassles: Does Community Intervention with Normal Populations Make a Difference?' *International Journal of Mental Health Promotion 4*, 3, 13–24.

Robins, L. and Rutter, M. (1990) *Straight and Devious Pathways from Childhood to Adulthood.* Cambridge: Cambridge University Press.

Rotheram-Borus, M.J. and Duan, N. (2003) 'Next Generation of Preventive Interventions.' *Journal of the American Academy of Child and Adolescent Psychiatry 42*, 5, 518–526.

Rutter, M. and Smith, D.J. (eds) (1995) *Psychosocial Disorders in Young People: Time Trends and their Causes.* Chichester: Wiley.

Tsiantis, J., Smith, M., Dragonas, T. and Cox, A. (2000) 'Early Mental Health Promotion in Children through Primary Health Care Services: A Multi-Centre Implementation.' *International Journal of Mental Health Promotion 2*, 3, 9–17.

World Health Organization (2002a) *The World Health Report 2002: Reducing Risks, Promoting Healthy Styles.* Geneva: WHO.

World Health Organization (2002b) *Prevention and Promotion in Mental Health.* Geneva: WHO.

Health and Psychological Well-being module of the Children's National Service Framework (NSF) in 2002–3.

Sachin Sankar trained in Psychiatry at the Central Institute of Psychiatry in Ranchi, India. He subsequently worked in Ireland and Wales. At present he is Locum Consultant in Child and Adolescent Psychiatry in Northampton General Hospital. His special interest is in conduct disorders and how they are affected by attachment and pervasive developmental disorders.

Anne Stewart is a consultant child and adolescent psychiatrist at the Highfield Adolescent Unit, Oxford, and Honorary Senior Lecturer, Oxford University. She works with adolescents with a range of psychiatric problems, but has a particular interest in eating disorders. Her work involves providing specialist family and individual treatment for eating disorders, as well as promoting primary intervention and early intervention strategies. She has conducted a controlled evaluation of a school-based primary prevention programme for young adolescent girls.

John Tsiantis is Professor in Child Psychiatry, Director of the Department of Child Psychiatry, Athens University Medical School and Scientific Director of the Association of Psychosocial Health for Children and Adolescents (APHCA). He is chairman and founding member of the Hellenic Association of Child and Adolescent Psychoanalytic Psychotherapy. He is founding member of the European Federation of Psychoanalytic Psychotherapy, for which he served as vice-chairman and founder of the series and chief-editor of the EFPP monographs in Psychoanalytic Psychotherapy since 1996. He was also a vice-chairman of the European Society of Child and Adolescent Psychiatry (ESCAP) and representative of Greece to the Child Psychiatry Section of the European Union of Medical Specialties (UEMS). Current research interests include development of child mental health promotion programmes within primary health care services and evaluation of psychodynamic psychotherapy for children.

Panos Vostanis is Professor of Child and Adolescent Psychiatry at the University of Leicester. In his clinical capacity, he works with a designated mental health team for vulnerable children and young people (looked-after, homeless, refugee and young offenders). His research involves the evaluation of interventions and service models for these client groups.

Annie Waldsax is a senior Primary Mental Health Worker with the Child and Adolescent Mental Health Service in Northampton and is also a practising UKCP registered psychotherapist. Her role has been to develop a community-based mental health service jointly with her colleague Sue Buckland. The service aims to make mental health expertise accessible in order to support families and family-focused professionals. She has one daughter and two sons who focused her attention on the parent–child relationship, families and the community. Following parenthood she pursued a career with Social Services and NCH Action for Children as a group worker. During this period she concentrated on the psychological impact that parents and children have on each other's mental well-being and how to maximise the benefits of different parenting styles to enhance self-esteem.

Jillian Wragg completed her doctorate at the University of Birmingham in 1998. Since graduating she has worked for the Birmingham Children's Hospital NHS trust. Her work has covered the whole age range but mostly centred around adolescents with severe mental health problems, in an inpatient setting. She has also worked in a multi-disciplinary community team for children and young people with complex emotional and behavioural difficulties and with an early intervention initiative, providing a drop-in service to children and families in the community.

Subject Index

Note: page numbers in bold refer to diagrams.

Author Index